SOMME HARVEST

Memories of a P.B.I.
in the Summer of 1916

By

GILES E. M. EYRE
(Ex-Rifleman, R/9885)

LONDON STAMP EXCHANGE LTD.
1991

INTRODUCTION
TO THE 1991 EDITION

A LTHOUGH this account of a soldier's experiences in the Great War covers a period of no more than two months, in that brief time the author saw enough concentrated and violent action to satisfy any longer serving survivor of that awful conflict. The book is written as a continuous narrative describing, often in vivid detail, events as they occurred and with all the dialogue, banter and backchat between the men—as in Frank Richards's *'Old Soldiers Never Die'* or MacGill's book on Loos *'The Great Push.'* The sustained ferocity of the fighting and the appalling conditions of the war in the trenches have seldom been described with such intensity as that shown by the author when recounting his worm's eye view of the battles of Bazentin Ridge and Pozières Ridge in July 1916.

We are not provided with any introductory background to the author's military service, but it is possible to put something together from the odd remarks made here and there throughout the book. Rifleman Eyre evidently enlisted in August 1914, and after a few days with one of the two Special Reserve battalions (5th or 6th) at Sheerness he was posted to the newly formed 7th K.R.R.C. at Winchester, the first of that regiment's Kitchener battalions. The battalion was in 41st Brigade, 14th (Light) Division which went to France in May 1915. Its first major action was at Hooge in July, just over a month after its arrival, when the Germans first used flame-throwers. The date, 30th, was etched in Eyre's memory, not because of the flame-thrower but because of the machine gun fire 'beating a mad tattoo round me for hours on end.' On that day 7 K.R.R.C. suffered 302 casualties including nine officers killed and four wounded.

His first spell of active service came to an end in December 1915 when Eyre was either wounded or sick and invalided home. After some time in hospital and then on leave, he went to the reserve battalions at Sheerness to await drafting. When the story opens in late May 1916, Eyre has arrived back in France to join the 2nd Battalion K.R.R.C., one of the four regular battalions of the regiment, which had been in the original B.E.F. in 2nd Brigade, 1st Division, still was in the same brigade and division, and would remain in them for the rest of the war. The G.O.C. was Maj. Gen. E. P. Strickland and the Brigade Commander was Brig. Gen. A. B. Hubback. The other three battalions in the brigade were the 2nd Royal Sussex, 1st Loyal North Lancs. and 1st Northants., all regular battalions. At this time the division was part of I Corps, First Army (Gen. Monro) which was holding that part of the front stretching from Laventie to Vimy. The 1st Division was occupying the Loos sector.

The 2nd K.R.R.C. was resting out of the line at Mazingarbe-les-Brebis when Eyre's draft of sixty plus reported, and he was allotted to C Company. The O.C. Coy was T/Capt. R. F. Sherlock who had been gazetted to the regiment in October 1914, had been posted to the 2nd Battalion in early January 1915 and had been wounded in the following June. He had recently rejoined the battalion, some time between 11th and 17th May. The C.S.M. was McNicoll, who already knew Eyre and put him in 9 Platoon where he had friends in his section. Another member of the section was the battalion hero, Rifleman Mariner, V.C. (spelled 'Marriner' in the book) who had won the award a year earlier at Cambrin. Finally, the C.O. of the battalion was Lt. Col. H. F. W. Bircham D.S.O. ('Beecham'), who had been commissioned into the 4th K.R.R.C. in 1896 at the age of twenty-one. He commanded a company of Mounted Infantry in South Africa where he was severely wounded. When the Great War broke out he was serving in India with the 4th Battalion as adjutant. He returned home in October 1914 and went to the Western Front where he served with 4th Battalion till wounded near St. Eloi on 2nd March 1915. He returned to the 3rd Battalion in June and in September 1915 he took over command of the 2nd Battalion, where he was evidently a very popular C.O. He was killed on 23rd July 1916 just three days after his great friend, Major Billy Congreve, V.C., D.S.O., M.C., The Rifle Brigade. The two lie almost side by side in Corbie Communal Cemetery Extension.

Since the Battle of Loos in September/October 1915, fighting on this part of the line had died down somewhat and had reverted to routine trench warfare in highly unpleasant conditions, interspersed with raids, mining and assaults on enemy trenches. One of these was Eyre's first major action since joining the battalion—a battalion raid during the night 30 June/1 July on a position known as 'The Triangle,' located in front of the Double Crassier, one of the more malevolent landmarks of the dreary Loos battlefield. This operation was one of a number being carried out in support of Fourth Army's preparations for the Somme offensive, intended to keep the Germans on the hop. Large scale raids like these were also very much in favour with senior commanders, if not with the battalions themselves, for they were seen as evidence of the offensive spirit which commended itself (and the commander) to higher authority. In this particular case it achieved nothing, but cost 2nd K.R.R.C. 238 casualties including five officers killed and six wounded. Among the dead was Mariner, killed by a direct hit with a shell right in front of Eyre, who was splattered with fragments of Mariner's body. The whole affair is graphically described. Mariner's name is now one of the seventy three thousand and more engraved on the Thiepval Memorial.

Five days later, the division was relieved by the newly arrived 40th Division and began to move down to the Somme to Fourth Army (Gen. Rawlinson). Here it came under command of III Corps (Lt. Gen. Pulteney), taking over from 23rd Division which had just completed the capture of Contalmaison. 2 K.R.R.C., in reserve, bivouacked in Bécourt Wood, located between Albert and Fricourt at the head of Sausage Valley. From here Eyre and his friends took the opportunity to explore what had recently been the British and German front lines and beyond, and he paints a grim picture of the dreadful scenes of carnage that remained as the battle lines receded. Before long, Eyre was back in the thick of it. Selected along with his friends for a bombing group he found himself attached to 1st Loyals who in turn had been attached to 110th Brigade (6th, 7th, 8th and 9th Leicesters) of 21st Division for the forthcoming attack on Bazentin Wood. The bombing party's rôle was to go in with the leading Leicester battalions and Eyre devotes a chapter to a blow by blow account of the ferocious struggle that ensued after the assault had been launched at dawn on 14th July. His share of the fighting, which cost the life of one of his friends, ended that evening when he and the group of bombers rejoined their battalion in Bécourt Wood; but the Battle of Bazentin Ridge, as it is officially known, continued till the 17th July. Eyre's part in the war had now but a few days to run. The 2nd K.R.R.C. moved forward to Scots Redoubt, a one-time German strong point some 1500 yards SE of La Boisselle, from where, a couple of days later on 18th July, they went into the line in the ghastly shambles of Bazentin-le-Petit. The sights that met their eyes were appalling, likened by one of them to an an 'open cemetery leading to the kingdom of Hell!' After only two days the battalion was relieved and returned to Scots Redoubt, and on 22nd July they received orders they were to attack on the following morning the German 'Switch' line where it joined with Munster Alley just NE of Pozières. In what turned out to be his last battle, the Battle of Pozières Ridge, Eyre was company runner, not an occupation with long life expectancy. He saw his sergeant major, McNicoll, his company commander and his battalion commander killed; his platoon commander, 2Lt. Walker, was also among the dead. The attack failed and that evening the remnants of the battalion withdrew to Scots Redoubt. Since 30th June the battalion had suffered just under 600 casualties. Eyre was not with the battalion when it withdrew; losing his way in the course of the fighting, he ended up in the German front line and was taken prisoner—the sole survivor of the small group that had come together at Mazingarbe some two months earlier.

These final hours are recounted with all the descriptive powers that are such an outstanding feature of this book. The author manages to convey, with telling effect on the reader, not only the awful

INTRODUCTION

reality of the battlefield with its death and destruction, but also that spirit of comradeship and self sacrifice that prevailed despite all the stresses of life in the trenches.

TERRY CAVE

WORTHING,
APRIL 1991.

FOREWORD

By

MAJOR-GENERAL SIR HEREWARD WAKE, BART.,
C.B., C.M.G., D.S.O., late 60th Rifles

MANY books in many languages have been
written about the Great War, but comparatively few tell the story from the point
of view of the infantry soldier in the ranks. *Somme
Harvest* is one of the latter. The story only covers
some three months of 1916 in France and Belgium,
finishing in the middle of the Battle of the Somme,
when the author, with a few surviving comrades,
wandered during a night attack into a German
trench and was taken prisoner. The unit in which
the author served as a Rifleman was the 2nd Battalion 60th Rifles, 2nd Infantry Brigade, 1st Division.
It is a personal narrative and the people men-
tioned are given their actual names. The author
was beside his gallant C.O., Lieutenant-Colonel
Humphrey Bircham, D.S.O., when the latter met
his death, and was in the same Section as Rifleman
Marriner, V.C., who was also killed in action.

Of thrilling adventure the book is full, but it has
more in it than that. It makes one realize those
peculiar characteristics, not always on the surface
and easily unnoticed in ordinary times, which make
our nation so formidable when once roused to action
in defence of the things that really seem to us to
matter; but which make us so incomprehensible
abroad. Not that foreigners will ever understand us,
with the possible exception of the kindly French
folk who for four years housed our soldiers behind
the British front.

The reader will find indeed that the British
soldier is an odd mixture altogether. He will

hear him grousing and cursing, with pet names unprintable for spades and everything else. But behind all that he will discover a type of whimsical philosophy, a sort of cheerful pessimism, very hard to beat anywhere; a sturdy shrewd insight; a sympathy that even includes the enemy; a judgment not much disturbed by the curse of war-time propaganda. It will be noticed that he makes no claim to heroism or immunity from ordinary human failings. His lack of cunning and ingenuity is obvious; but, after all, that was characteristic of the High Command, too, and appears to be a national trait. As a nation we seem to prefer straightforward slogging, cost what it may, to finding a way round. Our one effort at originality was the tank, and the way it was employed spoilt its chances of decisive effect.

But the British soldier got along in the war without any blind faith in the wisdom of the higher authorities. His unshaken confidence in ultimate victory enabled him to advance again and again to the attack, to do his best and make the most of the opportunity. He is seen at his finest, in fact, when all is lost. And in the scenes of tragedy and horror which this book so frankly describes, you see the British soldier just as he was under Marlborough and Wellington, human and afraid, but still undaunted, with faith and loyalty unshaken, unmoved by losses, failure or defeat. In the end that and the naval blockade won us the war.

If the author's aim, in writing this book, was to show the spirit which animated our soldiers on entering the war and throughout it, he has, I think, achieved success. His story is vivid, but simple and direct, and it rings true in every line. For those who survived the battle it cannot fail to have an intense interest : for the rising generation it seems to teach a lesson that cannot be learnt too well, that there was a purpose in the war, that its heroism and sacrifices were well worth while.

It is nineteen years since the roar of battle ceased, but the clouds gather again, our task is never finished. Only by being ready can we avert another or even worse calamity. Who can doubt that the faith, courage and comradeship which sustained the Army and the Nation in its hour of trial will ever fail us, whether in peace or war ?

HEREWARD WAKE

COURTEENHALL,
NORTHAMPTON,
1938.

A MEMORIAL

Laughing faces, youthful splendour,
Manly hearts with courage high ;
All are fallen 'neath Thor's hammer,
Human harvest in July !

BUT
" Age shall not dim them, nor the years condemn ! "

SOMME HARVEST

CHAPTER ONE

I

"BULLE-E, biscuits—Tomm-e-ee!"
That shrill piping cry yelled by the horde of squawking, squalid and jostling children scrambling about on the station siding greeted me as I stepped out of the crowded *hommes et chevaux* truck and left the slow, dirty troop train with a sigh of utter relief.

This was Nœux-les-Mines railhead! A depressing, drab, overgrown village ringed round by slag heaps, mine works and tall chimneys, criss-crossed with narrow, dirty lanes teeming with a motley throng of troops, frowsy, loud-voiced Frenchwomen jabbering excitedly, and cowed-looking elderly Frenchmen in dingy blue jeans drifting about in seeming aimlessness. The station side is echoing with the clatter and babel of the troops pouring out from the train, laughing and joking, grabbing rifles, packs, accoutrements.

What a variegated mixture! Artillery, infantry, A.S.C., men returning from leave, drafts, details, officers and privates of all corps, sizes and types that the bugles of Britannia have mustered in from every corner of the Homeland and Empire.

I buckle my equipment and, shouldering the load the benighted infantryman must fain carry, I plunge into the crowd and make my way to where a raucous-voiced sergeant is bellowing for my draft, like a very bull of Bashan.

The indefinable atmosphere of the battle-front impregnates the scene. In an instant it seems as if the intervening months since last December, spent in hospital, on leave and in the uncongenial surroundings of the reserve battalion at Sheerness, with its boring training, endless fatigues, mud and dull routine, have been but a dream.

These last few days since leaving that centre of
red tape, nostalgic huts and endless activity, the
hurry and scurry of the Havre base camp, the " bull
ring " with its blood and fire sergeant-major
instructors, its bustle and hard tack, have been
crowded with interesting incidents. I am back
again in the familiar environs of the front line and
en route to our 2nd Battalion.

I fell in with the other sixty-odd men of the draft
under the command of a raw sub., humped my pack
and, at the word of command, we moved off towards
Mazingarbe-les-Brebis, the " resting " place of our
new battalion.

It felt fine to be alive in the sunshine and warm
spring air, free at last from the odours and cramped
quarters of the overcrowded trucks, able to stretch
one's limbs in complete comfort.

The detachment, with subdued chaff and laughter
rippling down its ranks, the new men looking at the
strange scenes around them with interest, swung
through the narrow lanes of Nœux, filled with the
pungent smell of onions, fried potatoes, coffee and
the odour of overcrowded humanity ; passed the
heaps of coal-dust and clutter and out on to the
open highway leading to our destination. Green
fields, cultivated patches, small cottages peeping
out here and there. Blue sky flecked with fleecy
clouds, tall smoke-grimed chimneys clustering
round buildings. A typical rural-cum-industrial
zone. Far different to the flat, depressing Belgian
landscape I had been familiar with the previous
year. Now and again a distant sullen rumble came
to our ears as we marched on our way. The growling
voice of the War God in all his might was greeting
its future fodder ! With occasional halts, swinging
by horse lines, artillery parks, dumps, R.E. depots
and making way for clattering carts and ambulances
which covered us with filmy dust, we trudged
on.

Heavy battery positions under camouflaged

screens, belts of rusty wire, speckled tents in all colours, assault courses and, farther up in a field on our left front, men tugging at ropes and levers as an observation balloon went up. All the thousand and one *minutiæ* of the immediate back areas, spread out in procession before us. At long last—a cluster of red roofs with a tall, brown brick church spire towering above them came into view—Mazingarbe had been reached.

Steadily we swing into the main square and halt before a house at one corner of the square with a divisional flag fluttering in the breeze from a ground floor window and a couple of Cameron Highlanders on sentry before its door.

We line up, form two deep and stand at ease. A peaceful calm reigns over this biggish-looking townlet. Very few people seem to be about, although it is well past ten o'clock in the morning. Our sub. speaks with a sergeant in the doorway, looks around and is on the point of moving off somewhere when without the slightest warning :

Whe-e-w! Whe-e-w! Whe-e-w! Screech! Bang! Three or four heavy-calibre shells smash out of the blue and burst with a crash plump into the square, sending up a cloud of acrid dun-coloured smoke full of reddish flashes. A desperate scurry, swirls of dust envelop us as a quivering house reels drunkenly. A crash of falling masonry! A hit! Shrill cries and curses rise, we scatter—blindly seeking cover somewhere, somehow. Brother Boche has prepared us a right warm welcome!

Pitiful moans fall on my ears as I peep round from the shelter of the D.O. door. Stretched out on the square lie several blood-soaked, still forms in pathetic abandon ; one or two other men are writhing and squirming in the dust groaning in agony.

Our draft, mostly composed of " Derby scheme " men, new to the game, peeping from odd corners, views the scene white-faced and trembling. They have received a grim and abrupt baptism of fire

and their blooding has been rude, sudden and
soul shattering.

We wait in anxious suspense behind cover,
nothing further happens. Cautiously we come out.
A quick rush in the Divisional office, stretcher-
bearers appear on the scene with stretchers and carry
off the casualties, other men wielding pick and
shovel hurry to clear the square and commence to
fill in the shell-holes. With shaken nerves and
frightened glances the draft gets together again,
bemused and silent.

" Hey, Jock," I query, turning to the Cameron
sentry near whom I had taken shelter, " does this
sort of thing happen often here ? "

" Och, mon ! " he replies. " Fritz must ha'e gone
fey ! Oop to a week ago, no shell had touched this
toon for months. But laist Sunday they dropped a
dose of gas and shells. Mon, 'twas awfu'. The
wummen and the puir wee bairns running aboot anyhow and greetin' and wailin' like a lot of daft folk.
People spittin' and coughin' and wrigglin' and
moanin'. And noo he keeps on chuckin' a few shells
over every mornin' ; the dirty baisterd ! " with a
deep heartfelt curse as he resumes his post.

After a few minutes' wait, a sergeant of ours suddenly appeared from nowhere, spoke to our sub.,
and we moved off again through some side streets
and so to our battalion headquarters.

Now that the shelling had subsided, the French
civilians began to crowd out into the open, jabbering
excitedly and cursing the " sale Boche." Women
especially were shrilly loquacious in expressing their
feelings in forcible French, heaping maledictions on
the enemy.

We halted in front of a house in a side street.
Battalion headquarters. A tall, fair-haired R.S.M.,
wearing the ribbon of the Croix de Guerre, came out
and looked at us as our officer disappeared into the
orderly room. Sundry members of the Battalion
eyed the draft from near by.

" Listen to your names and postings," cried the R.S.M., standing us at ease, " and fall in into four separate groups accordingly." He proceeded to read out names and divide the draft into the four companies, and I found that I had been allotted to " C." We shuffled into our new formations, as a tall, well-built and clean-shaven captain came out of the orderly room, followed by a slim, upright and soldierly-looking colonel, Lieutenant-Colonel Bircham, D.S.O., " one of the best " in the Regiment's estimation. The R.S.M. barked out, we sprang to attention. The C.O. looked us over with a keen quick glance, smiled and :

" Stand at ease, men ! Sorry you have had such an unfortunate welcome to the Battalion," he said in incisive kindly tones. " However, such events in the field are unavoidable at times. We are very proud of our regimental traditions here," he continued, " and we are a very happy crowd. Good soldierly qualities are essential, however, and I shall expect all of you to help keep our reputation up. If you do this you will have as easy a time as can be hoped for. You will now join your companies and get your dinners. Sergeant-Major, you can dismiss ! "

Guides came to lead us to our various destinations, and my little group of fifteen turned into another lane rejoicing in the name of " Rue Poincaré " and into a small square whose most prominent object was a huge 12-inch dud in one corner with a notice over it, in French, on a board : " Gardez-vous ! Obus non-éclâté ! "

In the other corner stood field kitchens from which appetizing, tempting odours greeted us, greasy and grimed cooks looking like satanic imps bustling about at their work. Crowds of cheerful men, canteens in hand, were thronging round eyeing the draft and passing pointed compliments. Quite a nice lot of tough, hard-bitten lads, I decided.

Once again we formed up. Our Company Commander with the C.S.M. and Q.M.S. looked us over this time. I was pleased to note that the C.S.M. was McNicoll, an old acquaintance of mine in the reserve battalion. The skipper looked a capable and pleasant sort of bloke.

"Hallo, so it's you, E—— ? " said old Mac, halting in front of me and smiling chaffingly. " I thought old Fritz would have done you in by now, but bad pennies always come back ! All right, you can go to No. 9 Platoon. There are some pals of yours there. Let's see, you are the bloke who speaks the Bhat ? "

" Yes, Major," I replied.

" Good, you will be useful at last ! " with a grin.

The skipper eyed us, spoke a few words and dismissed us to our platoons.

II

I have been jolly lucky to get into " C " Company, and in No. 9 Platoon. I am amongst fellows after my own heart, hardened war veterans with a high morale. My Section is a fine one—there's Marriner, tough, brown-faced, reckless, fond of a drop—an old regular of the Kipling type—and the Battalion hero —he won the V.C. last year at Cambrin in a daring one-man stunt.

O'Donnell and Rodwell, both sporting the D.C.M. ribbon now, had been old chums of mine as recruits at the beginning of the war. The first, a fiery-haired blue-eyed Irishman about twenty-two, a black-and-white artist and a bit of a poet, impulsive and quick-tempered. Rodwell, tall, dark, nervy, sardonic, a law student of about the same age.

Oldham, our " lance jack "—a shrewd, whimsical Lancashire cotton hand from Preston, grey-eyed, darkish, squat and short—a dependent sort of cove. The others, three Cockneys, sharp as needles, Rabelaisian in speech, cheerful and chirpy, and a solid young Norfolk yokel, straw-coloured, slow, obstinate, but terribly earnest. I soon found myself at home in the loft that served as our billet. Dinner and introductions were soon over and I settled down. Late in the afternoon, O'Donnell, Rodwell, Oldham, Marriner and self, I being the only one " flush, " adjourned to the " estam." to sample the vintage of France and its thin watery beer. Place crammed to capacity. Tobacco smoke eddying up, laughter, songs, chatter. In one corner " Tiny " Rodway from No. 10, another " tough " proposition, presiding over his Crown and Anchor board, rattling his dice-cup and inviting the lads to patronize him, his seductive harangue punctuated with jovial asides and only ceasing momentarily while he quaffs from a frothing jug of beer at his elbow. A " housie-housie " game in full swing in the other corner, the patrons mostly Jocks, and *Madame la patronne* pushing through the jostling, jovial crowd, serving drinks and raking in the shekels cheerfully. The whole a scene Hogarth would have loved to portray with all its picturesque detail.

For a brief spell the grimness of war had been forgotten and carefree young manhood was relaxing and enjoying itself to the full. Eat, drink and be merry, for to-morrow you may die—the philosophy of the fighting man, a jolly sound one, for who dare say it is wrong ? Life, after all, consists of this, to make the most of one's fleeting moments.

A cognac and a couple Malagas soon got O'Donnell argumentative, and he began to declaim some interminable ode about quiet sunlit seas and dusky southern maids.

Rodwell kept banging on the table with his glass, keeping time to the tune of " Here's to the good old Beer," ringing out from a lusty-throated group of jolly fellows. Oldham, silent, drank sparingly and spoke but seldom. Marriner, true to the old soldiers' motto, put away as much as possible, making most of the opportunity. As for myself, I was content to sip my wine and enjoy the scene. Suddenly our talk veered on the war—Rodwell is a pronounced pessimist as far as this is concerned. In his view, it will go on and on until the arms manufacturers have swelled their bank balances to the limit and the manhood of Europe has disappeared in the furnace of Moloch.

"Rats, me bhoy," counters O'Donnell, "you wait until the Russians have another proper bang at Fritz, and all our new Army comes into action. We'll be back in Blighty and the Kaiser finished off before this Christmas—ye can't go on killing men for ever like this!"

"Eh, you'd like to think so!" retorted Rodwell sarcastically, "but, then, you are a poet and live up in the clouds! As far as I can see, this bloody business will go on and on until all of our unfortunate generation are dead and rotting. Look how things are even in Blighty! It makes one sick to go on leave. Thousands scrambling for cushy jobs, talkers and politicians egging people on to go out and fight to save our glorious civilization! And all the while they are grabbing money in handfuls! Curse them!" he cried, fiercely banging his glass on the table, "it's money soaked with blood! Our blood they are drinking, the bastards! And the same thing is happening in France. Look how they even make money from the very water we drink. And in Germany I expect the same game goes on. While we bloody fools kill people we have never met, decent lads like ourselves, the old men behind grow fat. The financiers make the money while youth, enthusiasm, patriotism, call it what you will, dies on the wire and pays the price. All the old folk at home are fire-eaters, they stick pins in their war maps every day, and collect the newspaper war reports. And when it is all over, these dirty skunks will come out of their funk-holes and claim all the credit. Those of us who manage to live through it all will get a big kick in the pants, and will be laughed at for having been such bloody fools! I am not a Socialist or rebel, but it makes my very heart boil

when I think of it all ! I can see, of course, that all
this humbug called civilization was getting top-
heavy. Those who had misgoverned for so long saw
the glaring mess they had made, they grew afraid of
what we, the young generation, would say when we
found them out. They knew we would have given
them short shrift. So they struck first and are getting
rid of us in this 'Holy War !' And the murder will go
on and on, killing and getting slain, enemies who are
just like us, who think much as we do. And the red-
faced, fiery generals miles behind the line, who
would have a fit if their morning tea got cold, the
civvy strategists, all that nasty gang of politicians,
propagandists, agitators, conscientious objectors,
war manufacturers, financiers making money out
of war loans, the bishops preaching sermons of
hate; in short, pelf, Church and power will collect
the laurels and wax fat on the heaps of our
decomposing bodies littering the battle-fields of
Europe. Think of the millions of young men of all
nations, creators, workers, writers, poets. What
wealth of human power is being squandered here !
And they'll talk of sacrifice and the righteousness of
our cause, and blame the Kaiser for it all. The lousy
hypocrites ! "

"Blimey," chimed in Marriner, lost in wonder
and admiration at Rodwell's tirade, "you do lay it
on thick and heavy. I, meself, am quite satisfied.
Give me plenty of booze, a woman now and again, a
bit of excitement and a chance of making a bit of
'tin ' over the side, and Bob's yer uncle ! This is
a sight better than all the spit-and-polish life of
garrison towns in peace-time ! You lads should have
soldiered along with me in South Africa. That was
a bit of a good war all right ! I could tell you a thing
or two about scrounging around the Boer farms on
the Vaal ! "

"Well, me lads, all the grousing in the world
won't alter nothing," put in Oldham ; "just carry
on and enjoy life, that's the ticket. As for those

Roosians you was talkin' about, O'Donnell, I
reckon it's us who'll have to do all the dirty work.
The Frogs and the others will swing it on us all
right, you mark me words ! "

"Come along, fill 'em up, boys, and let's have a
song ! " I chimed in.

We drank, struck up a song and pushed carping
care away.

"Down she goes on the old Sergeant-Major ! "
roared out Rodway in stentorian tones. "Come
along, me lucky lads ! Faint heart never won fair
lady ! " And rattle, rattle, rattle, echoed his dice-
cup. The crowd of players pressed close to his
table, eager to lay out their stakes on the lap of
elusive Fortune and—Rodway.

Darkness fell quickly. Lights flared up, intensify-
ing the dark corners. The eddying smoke hung
heavy in the air. The fumes and smells of wine,
beer, tobacco and coffee blanketed the atmosphere.
Songs, laughter, clatter. Din engulfed us. And so
the speeding minutes passed until at length a sharp
order from the doorway and the Battalion orderly
sergeant appeared.

"Come along, the Rifles ! Fall in, in your
Company lines ! Fighting order ! " he yelled.

We downed our drinks hurriedly, rose and scur-
ried off to our billets to get ready for the night's
work.

III

Our platoon mustered in the semi-darkness.
After the usual shuffles and curt orders, we moved off,
led by our 2nd Lieutenant. Round the corner we
swung into another road lined with horse-stalls and
displaying a big board with " To Maroc " and a
large arrow pointing the direction. In a few minutes
the houses were behind us, and the Company
marched on. Darkness deepened and the column
tramped onward, with subdued talk rippling down
its ranks and fags alight. O'Donnell, Rodwell

and I, in the same fours, carried on a desultory conversation, busily arguing over the philosophy of cause and effect. For some time we marched on along the *pavé*. Traffic rumbled by, ambulances hurtled on. Presently we were on the edge of a half-wrecked village—Bully Grenay—and we halted by a big dump on the edge of the road. In single file now we gathered picks and shovels and bundles of sand-bags, reformed and wended our way onwards. Guns were growling and drumming, Very lights appeared far off. Away on our left lay Loos, Maroc somewhere in front. The Field Artillery lines were left behind us, and we now swung into Maroc's main street with its demolished houses.

" Put those blasted Woodbines out ! " yells a voice in the darkness, in a mincing " Oxford " drawl.

A chuckle rips down the column.

" That's old Barty from ' B,' " sniggers Marriner behind me, " a blasted schoolmaster 'e is, and 'e thinks 'e owns creation."

Out go our gaspers as we enter a deep trench between two buildings.

Barty, a dumpy-looking captain wrapped up in a Burberry, steel-helmeted and grasping a thick stick, appears through the murk, standing on the trench lip. Fussily he urges the men on, peering down into the trench and hopping about like a broody hen gathering in her chicks. Apparently he is in charge of this fatigue party.

Slowly we make our way forward through the twists and turns of the communication trench. With sundry haltings, blocks and spurts, a few occasional blasphemies, through the reserve and support positions and on to the firing-line. A huge slag heap looms dark and mysterious on our left. The plonk ! plonk ! of occasional rifle shots, and the short, sharp chatter of a machine-gun burst comes to my ears. The front again ! We debouch into a deep, dry trench. It certainly is a vast improvement to the muddy shallow front trenches of my Ypres days last year. Dug into chalky soil and well sand-bagged. Funk-holes, dug below the parapets, are scattered at intervals.

The night is dry and fine and the front quiet. I catch the silhouettes of crouching sentries on the banquettes, as I move forward bay by bay. At length the line halts at the very foot of the slag heap. There is a bit of a clearing here, and we have to build up some sort of sand-bagged wall to cover the entrance to a tunnel. They are busy tunnelling into the bowels of the slag heap and occasionally the clink of spades can be faintly heard.

We begin our task of digging and filling sandbags.

" You mind how you go, E—— ! " whispers O'Donnell. " The Boches up on the slag heap enfilade this corner with machine-guns ! "

" All right, I'll keep my eyes open ! " I reply.

We work on. One digging, one holding the bags, one stacking. Now and again a shell whistles and crashes, and up go Very lights. The night wears on, a fresh breeze springs up. The trench barricade grows, and the men's efforts slacken.

I note that very little rifle firing is taking place on our frontage. Oldham, from whom I enquire, explains :

" Our trenches and Fritz's are below the slope on both sides here," he says. " There are saps running out in front. It's pretty hot for trench-mortars and grenades up there, but rifle firing is out ! "

Trench-mortar shells in fact thud down somewhere behind me, and a sharp machine-gun burst sends me to cover.

" I wonder how much longer it's going to last," mutters Marriner, resting on his spade, " about time we packed up. It's about one o'clock ! "

" Make way there ! " comes a voice. I look round and see some chalk-covered figures crawling out of the tunnel mouth. Grimed, sweaty and tired they straighten out and tramp into the trench.

" It's bloody close down there, I guess ! " growls a big husky Canadian miner, " the Huns are counter-mining somewhere too. I'll be glad of a flop down ! " And they disappear down the trench, without further ado.

We continue our task, working spasmodically. At last our subaltern comes along and speaks to the sergeant.

" Come along, boys, finish up the sand-bags, we are nearly through," yells this latter. We work furiously. Everything is very quiet. The machine-guns are silent, but heavy thunderous rumbles farther south inform us that Mars is busy on Vimy Ridge to-night.

In the comparative quiet the rattle of Boche limbers behind the German trench lines comes to our ears. They are at their nightly task of bringing rations up. Somewhere a telephone buzzer gets to work—a few moments and then a whizzing rush of shells overhead followed by distant crashes. Our gunners are shelling the roads behind the Boche trenches. In my mind's eye I can picture the scene. I have witnessed many such on the Menin road on dark nights. The limbers going up, ration parties waiting to unload them, men crowding by the carts, all is feverish activity. Then, without warning, death like an avalanche falls from the sky, and in a moment horror and death assume control. Screaming frenzied horses falling in heaps, kicking and strug-gling, limbers overturning and smashing. Dust, stones and debris flying about. Men being killed, mangled and destroyed, by shell, fear-maddened horse and limber wheel ! Confusion, a helter-skelter rush for cover. Acrid smoke billowing round and the darkness fitfully lighted up by the red and yellow flashes of exploding shells ! Men crouching in the roadside gutters, cursing and moaning. There is no romantic glamour in such scenes. Fate descends suddenly from nowhere, and its sweeping scythe brings death, agony and terror. There is nothing to hit back at, all man can do is to grit his teeth, wait in suspense and curse impotently !

At length the order to finish work reaches us. We pick up our tools, shake ourselves and begin our return journey speeded on by close bursts of trench-mortar fire. The enemy is retaliating for the shelling of his roads. Quickly we move along the front line, down the communication trench, past support and reserve positions and so out of the communication trench into the Maroc high street.

Old Barty was there to meet us. We had not seen anything of him the whole time the work had lasted, so very probably the sly blighter must have been taking it easy somewhere. He seemed very pleased with himself. A good night's work had been accomplished without any casualties.

" You may smoke now, men," he cried, taking the head of the line and moving off.

" Thanks for nothing, you big b——! " muttered Marriner, taking a fag-end from behind his ear and lighting up.

We marched quickly in the chilly air. Bully Grenay was soon left behind and with it the need for silence. Someone started singing. The sleepy, tired men livened up as if by magic, and without further ado the immortal adventures of Barnacle Bill, enriched with many a Regimental allusion, rang in the stilly night. Old Barty was kept running up and down the marching column, essaying to pick out offenders whenever pungent personal references entered into the theme of the ditty, but in the murk of night it was an impossibility and merely aided our gaiety.

Cheerily we swung into Mazingarbe, and in the early hours of dawn, after a swig of hot tea, we made for our billets and " so to bed " in the words of Pepys. But that Restoration worthy would have written some trite comments into the famous diary had his comfort-loving frame been compelled to use our couches—wooden flooring, a thin layer of straw and our overcoats. Fatigue, however, makes light of such trifles, and it soon wafted us into untroubled and deep sleep.

CHAPTER TWO

I

THE next was a busy day, getting supplied with odd necessaries, parading for draft inspection, finding my feet in the Company, etc. Captain Sherlock, our skipper, seems a nice efficient type of bloke, and Mr. Walker, my tall platoon officer, quite a good sort. Our sergeant, a regular of the old stamp, brown faced, sharp and a bit of a stickler for discipline. The majority of the N.C.O.s and men " Kitchener's Army," with a small leaven of regulars, these last great talkers and lead swingers. One can't blame them for this, though ; two years of war in the raw is quite enough for any man's stomach.

Towards late afternoon I paid a visit to " B " Company lines in Rue des Alliées, the next turning to ours. I wanted to see some fellows I had known in the 7th Battalion last year. I found them, Clarke and Higginson, billeted like us in a loft. In the house below dwelt the usual mining family to be found in these parts of France. Men over age, or unfit for military service, work on in the mines even when these are close to the firing-line—for coal is in great demand just now !

Madame here carried on the customary trade of the back areas, coffee, eggs, chips, etc., for the troops. That is the only consolation the thrifty French country-folk have. They are certainly filling their stockings well for " l'après guerre ! "

Her daughter, a sallow-looking creature, raven-haired and with big, dark and passionate eyes, served the guests. After a chat with my two former acquaintances, we adjourned below for some grub. I spoke to the wench in French and bandied a few idle compliments with her. After which I could not get rid of her, try as I might. At every pause in the service she was at my elbow jabbering away heartily.

" Looks as if you have clicked all right, E—— ! "

sniggered Clarke, enviously, " and yet she has been a sour bitch to us in this billet here. How the hell do you manage it ? "

" I understand the Latin temperament, that's all ! " I answered grinning, " and the best part of the joke is that I am not interested in the slightest, I only meant to be just polite and nothing else ! "

" Well, I wish you'd tell her that there are some of us here in the billet who are quite willing and able to oblige ! " suggested Higginson meaningly.

However, food and other badinage claimed our attention and the subject dropped. Presently we rose, chatted a bit and eventually parted, I made my way to the door, while Clarke and Higginson went up to their loft.

Madame was sitting by the stove busily stirring some appetising smelling mess which was bubbling away in a saucepan. The room was dark and empty, but for us. The girl strolled to the doorway just as I was on the point of turning away, intercepted me and broke into a flood of rapid French. I had to pause and answer her, while she began a tale of hardships and woes—brothers at the front, troops all over the place. Hardly any time to breathe or sleep decently, always up and on the move.

" Do you know, Monsieur," she added artlessly, " we have had to give up practically all the house to the English soldiers, and I have to sleep on a pallet in the same room as papa and mamma ? "

" This is very hard, I am sure, Mademoiselle," I replied gravely, " but que voulez-vous, c'est la guerre ! "

" Oui, c'est ça," she said sighing. " But do come and have a look before you go," she invited, with a wary glance at Madame at the stove, at the same time leading me towards a small doorway.

I hesitated, but then decided to let her have her way and followed her. A typical French peasant bedroom with a high double bed and sundry pieces of heavy furniture here and there met my gaze.

Hardly had we stepped into this chamber, when the girl without warning flung her arms around my neck, and commenced to whisper a torrent of endearing words, rubbing her cheek against mine, behaving like a perfect cat, eyes all-asparkle and with tense body against mine. The situation became very awkward. I was nonplussed for a moment. The more she pressed her attentions on me, the less grew my inclinations. I have always been an average healthy male with all the faults and failings of my species, but to be the hunted quarry of women has always been my pet aversion. I have always preferred to lead the hunt myself. Gently but firmly I removed her arms from round me and :

" Maintenant, ma cherie, c'est trop tard," I told her. " I must go. Perhaps when I come back from the next trench tour, we may arrange matters better."

Very reluctantly she regained her composure and let me walk out after having extracted my promise to return on some future occasion, telling me that she was a *fille très serieuse* and by no means at everyone's disposal.

I made a bee-line for my own billet quickly as the night was falling fast. There I found my two partners with Oldham and Marriner squatting on the floor-boards, a stump of candle stuck in a bottle in the middle, busy in a game of rummy.

Shouts of laughter and Rabelaisian ribaldry greeted the account of my adventure, and Marriner, after telling me forcibly that I was far too slow for the old army, added :

" Where is she, me lad ? Come and lead your old Uncle Bill to her, and I'll show you how a real swaddy will do a proper job of it."

" Can it, Marriner, you'd be out of luck, you old blighter, she wouldn't understand you, you can't manage the lingo ! " I replied laughing.

" Oh, wouldn't she just ! " he replied indignantly. " Look here, me young gamecock, I have had dealings with Indian girls, half-chats, niggers, Africanders and what-not, and I'll bet you what you like, there's no woman, least of all a Froggy, who wouldn't catch on to my meaning ! ''

'' All right then, you Don Juan,'' I countered, '' I'll tell you what I'll do. Which would you rather have. A souse of beer and *vin rouge* or the girl ? You makes yer choice, I pays ! ''

Faced with the problem of selecting either Bacchus or Venus, Marriner thought a bit, eventually choosing the former, for as he remarked :

'' I'm broke ; I can always pick up a bit of skirt when I fancy it for nixes, even in this bloody country where they charge you for the very air you breathe, and anyhow I have never said no to a free drink yet ! ''

We all got up laughing and clattered away to the '' estam.'' and stuck there in jolly amity until the M.P.s put the closure to the nightly session.

II

The following night our Company went into the support trenches for a four-days' tour in the sector to the left of Maroc, a very quiet spell, in good dry dug-outs. Weather perfectly summerish. Our days and nights busy with the customary carry, dig and general roustabout fatigues. During this tour I made a closer acquaintance with my pals and my Company Commander.

We were cleaning our rifles and furbishing up our equipment one morning, Marriner, O'Donnell, Rodwell and I sitting on the fire-steps working away, chaffing and arguing. O'Donnell and Rodwell as usual going it hammer and tongs. The former flourishing a copy of *John Bull* with its war-slogan '' Watch Russia '' in bold type, was quoting from one of Bottomley's flamboyant, optimistic and don't-care-a-damn articles. '' There you are,

Rodwell, me lad," he was saying with a sparkle in his eyes, " Horatio is dead right. He knows what he is about too ! Pity we have no more like him to waken the people up ! And I tell you the ' steam roller ' will be moving along soon ! "

" Aye," sarcastically from Rodwell. " ' Watch Russia,' says Bottomley. ' Heads I win, tails you lose.' Clever fellow that ! Sitting snug and cosy in London and writing trash at ten bob a line. And whatever happens, he'll turn round and say smugly : ' I told you so ! ' What a silly game it all is ! And what mugs the people must be. While Horatio is busy gathering the money in and having a damn good time, praying all the while for the war to go on, *ad lib*, the boys have to put up with filth, muck and death ! Hey ! " in a loud alarmed voice, " Look out ! "

We flattened ourselves against the parapet as the familiar whee ! whoosh ! crash ! rang in our ears and a shell burst somewhere around.

Marriner resumed his place with a wry grin.

" Blimey ! Every time you two ruddy blighters argue the point you bring old Fritz round our hides like a bloody hungry midden-hawk looking for tasty gobs of meat to snap up ! " We retrieved our belongings and continued with our work. The sun was shining and the morning was warm and fine. Grass was sprouting out on the parapet-top, with a wild flower here and there. Nature had awakened. A stillness reigned over everything, to be broken at rare intervals by isolated thuds and dull plops when some misguided gunner or other on both sides had to mar the brooding quiet by flinging an occasional shell over.

Presently Captain Sherlock, accompanied by the Sergeant-Major, debouched round the bay on a morning inspection tour. We sprang up.

" All right, sit down and carry on, men ! " he said as he stopped and turned to Marriner. " Well, how do you find things to-day ? " he queried.

"All nice and cushy and A1, sir!" was the cheerful reply.

"Good, I am glad to hear it," and the Skipper opened his cigarette case and offered us a smoke all round.

"Not them Turkish, sir!" ejaculated Marriner in mock horror, "they fair poison me. I like me old Woodbines best, sir!"

We others accepted with thanks and lit up.

"And how's your poetry getting on, O'Donnell? Are you going to set London on fire with your stuff?"

"I cannot manage much at present, I am afraid, sir! What with one thing or another and Rodwell here, with his pro-German pessimism, keep on putting me right off," he replied, making a comical gesture of despair.

We all laughed.

"That's right, men; keep your peckers up and your eyes open," remarked the Skipper.

The Sergeant-Major chipped in: "This is the new man I was telling you about, sir," pointing in my direction. "As he had been with these men before at home I got him in this Section. This way I can keep my eyes on all the biggest scroungers and sea lawyers in the Company!" he added jocularly.

The Skipper smiled: "I hear this Section has a peculiar reputation. I am glad to see so many leading spirits and useful men. Mind you fellows don't indulge in silly heroics, but just carry on as all of us must do. Well, E——, I hear you are somewhat of a linguist as well as a bombing specialist, so I expect I shall find an occasional odd job in your line. Have you men had your breakfast?"

We assured him on this point, and after a few other kindly remarks he moved on.

"Decent bloke the Skipper," said Marriner, "he treats us like men, not like some of the blighters I have served with, who looked upon the likes of us as if we were dirt. I hope he'll see the whole bloody

schemozzle through with us. There ain't so many
of his kind knocking about spare now ! "

Our reserve tour ended uneventfully, and on a
blustering wet miserable night we moved into the
firing-line. There was nothing I hated worse than
going into a new position on a dirty night, crawling
through mucky pits, with water trickling down one's
neck, getting into one's boots, stumbling into dank,
unfamiliar holes, with rats squeaking and scuttering
away in the gloom. The prospect of standing, cold,
wet and miserable, on fire-steps, with no possibility
of a hot mug of something to look forward to, was
something I loathed more than anything else in the
whole ghastly business. The only consolation was
that with the dawn one would get a mouthful of
rum.

The rum ration was one of the few inspired
measures a high command, generally devoid of
imagination, managed to hit upon. It undoubtedly
prevented thousands of men from breaking down
through sheer hopelessness, and instilled new
warmth and courage in chilled, disconsolate bodies.
Yet there were cranks, mostly at Home of course,
who deplored the issue of liquor to the Army, and
were constantly bawling for its abolition ; fortunately for all of us they did not succeed. Cranks
are a curious genus. Very possibly, when they
reach their particular heaven or Hades in their after-
life, they will protest that the tunes played on the
heavenly harps are unseemly, or that Lucifer has the
wrong shape in gridirons and his fires waste fuel !

Our party was rather lucky. We were able to
ecure a snug, well-boarded dug-out running under
he parapet. Oldham, Marriner, Rodwell, myself
and O'Donnell crowded in and took possession.
Off came our packs, but alas, we had hardly made
ourselves comfortable when Rodwell and I had to
go out on sentry ! With waterproof sheets over our
heads we crouched on the fire-steps, peering out at
the scene of wet desolation in front, Very lights were

going up fitfully, throwing into momentary relief the barbed wire glistening in the rain, the scarred, pitted ground, full of mud-holes, dank lush grass, and God knows what other debris, and many huddled bundles of mystery here and there. Half-way out in no-man's-land a mass of wrecked farm buildings stood silhouetted as a darker mass in the surrounding gloom, and a couple of hundred yards beyond, on the crest of a slight slope, the Hun trenches, their barbed wire shining now and again as the Very lights dropped near it.

Its occupants, no doubt just as miserable as ourselves, were cursing the fates and the weather as heartily as we were. In trench warfare there is nothing to compare with a good bout of rain and a cold night to wash away all the martial ardour from the most bloodthirsty fire-eater breathing.

III

Dawn stole in wet and pallid as our duty spell ended. Oldham and all the rest of the Section came out into the bay for the customary stand-to. Sergeant Wilson came along presently with the rum jar and a spoon, doling out the precious liquid much in the spirit of an old school marm dosing her class with brimstone and treacle ; but in our case, however, there were no tearful scenes of stubborn refusals !

After the stand-to the rain ceased and the rising sun chased the clouds and glumness away. Marriner managed to scrounge a little coke from some mysterious source, and soon we had a fire going inside an old bucket and our canteens bubbling up. The appetizing smell of frying bacon rose here and there, our clothes got dry and our outlook became more cheerful. This sector was a nasty one for trench-mortars and snipers ; therefore, as soon as morning advanced, under cover was the rule, and except for occasional sentries on the fire-steps the front line was empty. The livelong morning the crack! plonk! of isolated rifle-shots resounded, and presently the daily dose of trench-mortars came crashing over. Further to our right, for reasons unknown, the Hun plastered " A " Company's sector for about twenty minutes with an assortment of shells, wrecked their parapets and accounted for some casualties.

The day dragged on—dozing, cooking, looking for lice, taking our turn on sentry and so on until night closed in and all became busy once again.

Ration parties coming up, wiring and working parties, officers buzzing about. We front-line troops continued our normal routine, glad that for once somebody else would be busy with the chores.

Presently our platoon sergeant, like a bird of ill-omen, appeared at our funk-hole entrance.

" Corporal Oldham, get hold of four men of your Section and report to Company headquarters at once. Captain Sherlock wants a patrol out while the wiring is being done. The rest of your Section will join the Platoon and form a covering party."

" Well, lads," queried Oldham, getting ready as Sergeant Wilson disappeared and looking at us, " what about it ? Are you coming with me, or shall I get the others for the patrol ? "

" Might as well go on patrol, rather than freeze in the mud with the covering party," growled Marriner. " You can count me in ! "

We all assented, picked up our hipes and followed Oldham to Company headquarters. Captain Sherlock was there when we arrived.

" Ah, Corporal Oldham, I see you have your men ready. What I want you to do is to get out in front of the covering party and patrol along the line of the Boche wire for a hundred yards or so. Keep your eyes open, and if you find that things are normal get back to the ' Red House ' and keep in touch with the covering party. Remain by the ' Red House ' for a couple of hours, then have another good prowl round and get back to the covering party. If you spot any Huns you are not to use fire-arms. Take a couple of bombs with you, trench-sticks and your side-arms. Only use the bombs in the last extremity. I need add nothing further. All you men are experienced and know how to act."

"Very good, sir!" answered Oldham. We saluted, went back to our funk-hole and dumped our rifles. O'Donnell and Marriner had German automatics, so that in any emergency we would prove a tough handful to handle.

We waited a while; when we learned that the covering party were already out and the wirers had begun their night's task we slipped quietly over the parapet and, led by Oldham, we crept through our wire gaps and into the open beyond. The earth was still very wet and soggy, shell-holes full of mud and water, derelict objects scattered on all sides. Rats scuttled away squeaking as we inched forward, their red eyes gleaming in the dark—Very lights rising and falling. Occasional rifle-shots and short bursts of machine-gun fire. We reached the covering party, Oldham whispered a few words to the sergeant, and then we slowly forged ahead into the unknown. I had always had a penchant for patrol work. It held a spice of welcome adventure, breaking the dull monotony of trench warfare. One felt that here it was individuality that counted, and the matching of one's wits against the other fellow's; it held a peculiar attraction for me because it became a sporting proposition in which a careless slip or the inability to best the opponent entailed the loss of the stake—life!

Halting whenever the flares soared up we advanced slowly in a " V " formation. Oldham at the spear-head, Rodwell and O'Donnell on one side, Marriner and I on the other. We reached the ruins of the Red House without mishap, everything was calm and still; cautiously we circled round, trench-sticks in hand—nothing! The Hun wire loomed dark ahead—we crawled to it and crept along quietly. No sound, no movement from their trenches. Only once the cough of a sentry brought us to a dead stop. A bit further, sounds of low talk in the Hun trench, but not the weeniest sign of activity. We continued our crawl, and having reached the limit of our patrol we made our way back to the Red House and crouched behind the broken walls, while Rodwell sped back to the covering party to report all well. The night was cloudy and rather chilly. We started chatting in cautious tones, with our watchful eyes boring into the darkness. A slight noise, a dark creeping form, and Rodwell rejoined us. The dull thuds of the wiring party driving in stakes came to us fitfully. A Boche machine-gun broke out into its tac-tac-tac, fired a few rounds and stopped. Time passed. Suddenly Marriner, having peered intently into the gloom, uttered a stifled ejaculation, nudged me violently and whispered fiercely : " Look over there ! " I jerked round ; scarce twenty yards away from the Red House some indistinct forms could be descried in the half light.

" The bloody Boche, by jingo ! " muttered O'Donnell. We became alert, grasped our sticks and gripped our grenades.

" Careful, boys ! " admonished Oldham, " creep round the house. You, Rodwell, get back to the covering party and warn them."

Rodwell slid away, and we four, keeping well apart in case of bombs being thrown at us, began to circle round the broken bricks, ready for any sudden move the enemy might make.

With infinite caution we moved round, until we were clear of the heaps of rubble and lay facing towards the Boche line in extended order. And there, lying a few yards in front of us, were the moon-faced members of a German patrol !

It was a tense moment—and we lay stark still. My first impulse was to sling a bomb at them—but I realised what its burst might entail. The Germans,

just as astounded, remained pat and made no move.
Both parties had come to the same conclusion—that
it was a case of Brer Rabbit—lay low and say
nothing! Scuffling sounds behind me—a dread
seizes me—has the enemy worked round and
surrounded us? I turn nervously, and sigh with
relief. It is Rodwell back from the covering party.

" The covering party is going in," he whispers,
" and we are to do a bunk back at once."

We look towards the Boches. They look at us
and seem to hesitate. Complete silence reigns.
We are wondering what the next move will be.
Suddenly, as if a common purpose animates us,
both groups jump to their feet, and, throwing caution
to the winds, leg it as fast as possible for their re-
spective trenches. We move quickly, as we know
very well that unless we get in first, the Huns will
rake us with machine-gun-fire. We scutter through
our wire somehow, with sundry tears and scratches,
and as we drop pell-mell into our trenches, a Lewis-
gun opens up a sweeping fire on to the Boche
parapets. A single wail of agony echoes across no-
man's-land—the German patrol must have been
slower than us, and one of them has paid the
penalty! Lights go up in bunches, then furious
rifle and machine-gun blasts strike our bags, parapets
and trenches, whizzing and pinging like myriads of
bees.

" Duck down, lads! The Huns have got their
dander up!" yells a voice, then phe-e-ep goes a
whistle, followed by the cry: " Trench mortar to the
right!" A heavy crash—a swirl of earth and dust,
and an indignant, blaspheming voice, consigning the
Kaiser to eternal perdition, rises from farther down.

" Blast the bloody Huns! There goes my blankety
fire and all me grub!" The shell from the German
mortar had burst on the edge of the parapet, blown
up some sandbags and showered their contents on
Price's coke fire over which a Maconochie stew had
been bubbling merrily!

We laughed strainedly when we saw Price come round covered all over in bits of potatoes and meat, and as savage as a lion deprived of his hunk of flesh. We dived into our funk-hole, leaving both sides to their waste of ammunition. The strafe continued for some time and then gradually died down. No further incident disturbed the night.

IV

Rain fell steadily during the remainder of our tour in the front line. Bleak, clouded skies, cold wind, muddy trenches, wet clothes, were our portion. Quite trying to carry on with the usual routine in such dismal settings. To make matters worse, we ran short of fuel. No coke, wood or anything else to cook on or warm ourselves with.

" This won't do at all, boys," growled Marriner, coming off sentry duty, soaked and miserable, into our damp funk-hole and finding no hot tea. " We'll have to scrounge something to ruddy well burn somehow. Come on, O'Donnell, we'll have a scout around."

While the two went off on their quest I also became active, and wended my way down to the Sergeant-Major's den. Old Mac had a soft spot for me, and I determined to wheedle some coke or charcoal out of him somehow. He was busy writing by the light of a candle-stump as I entered.

" What is it ? " he growled. " Can't you see I'm busy ? "

" How would you like a bottle of wine when we go out, Major ? "

He looked at me suspiciously: " It would be all right, but what's the game ? "

" Well, we know you use a spirit cooker, Major, so I thought you might have a bit of coke or wood lying about spare," I replied artlessly.

" I thought there was a catch somewhere. You fellows in that ruddy section of yours have got a cheek ! All right, E——, you can have half a sack of coke. But mind, no bottle of wine when we go out and I'll have the lot of you on the dirtiest jobs I can find ! "

" Thanks, S'nt-Major ! I knew you'd be a sport ! " I answered gratefully, and grabbing the half-sack of precious fuel I returned to our funk-hole in triumph. Rodwell and Oldham had also been on the scrounge. They had unearthed a tin of anti-frost-bite grease and Rodwell had annexed a little charcoal when the Skipper's batman wasn't looking. Soon a cheerful fire was going, and tea was on the way when O'Donoghue and Marriner returned carrying a few trench-board cross-sections.

" Couldn't find anything else," explained Marriner, " so we walked into ' A ' Company and pinched a few pieces of their trench-boards. There's a hole full of water we've left uncovered up there, and I bet someone will be fool enough to fall in it when it gets dark ! "

The old bucket fire, warm tea and cooked food cheered us up considerably. When dark began to fall we gathered round it by the funk-hole entrance, completely at ease. A few visitors from the adjoining traverses came to enjoy our fire, envying us our scrounging capabilities. Later a new figure loomed in sight, Lance-Corporal Gottschalk from No. 11 Platoon. A loud-voiced, ignorant, domineering and pseudo-smart old regular, full of his own importance, and looking on us with the supercilious contempt of the old sweat for mere " armed civilians."

" Ah, a nice fire you've got here," he said, patronisingly. " Looks quite snug. Reminds me of the time we were on manœuvres in '12. Them were the days for real soldiering, me lads ! "

" Oh, have a warm and put a sock in it," snapped Oldham. " Where are you off to, Gottschalk ? "

" I'm going up to Sergeant Johnson in ' A.' He wants me to transfer to his Company, when we go out. No regular N.C.O.s left there, only bloody

civvies in uniform ! I expect I'll get another stripe ! "
he added, importantly.

" I know the stripe I'd like to give him ! "
muttered Marriner to me. " Right across his ——
backside, the stuck-up jackass ! " And he added :
" I hope he falls down that bloody hole ! "

Gottschalk, having toasted his hands a bit, left us
and disappeared round the traverse.

Marriner's hopes were fulfilled. About an hour
later a miserable, squelching figure, caked with mud
and with water dripping from its garments, clumped
round the bay. It was Gottschalk, all the bounce
and starch completely washed out of him. With
sundry groans and shivers he approached our fire
again.

" Hello, Gottschalk, been bathing on a night like
this ? " asked Marriner, with the ghost of a grin on
his lips.

Gottschalk broke into a terrific stream of blasphemy. " By Christ—I am soaked through ! I was
coming back from ' A,' and when I went to step on a
trench-board, it wasn't there ! " he cried pathetically.
" Down I went into a blasted pool full of water and
muck ! " And working himself to fury : " Some dirty
son of an asterisk bitch had pinched the boards !
If I catch hold of him, I'll make him sweat, the
——! Ow ! I am all a-shiver, blast his dirty soul ! "

A howl of laughter from the funk-hole where
Rodwell, O'Donnell and I were chortling with
delight.

Gottschalk scowled, looked suspiciously at Marriner, but he needed our fire badly, so whatever he
may have guessed at he kept quiet, dried himself
as best as he could, and then drifted on to his own
platoon, leaving us to enjoy the joke.

v

Down into reserve again, a period of fatigues and
carrying parties. Again forward into the support

line for a further spell. Just dull routine work, digging and revetting trenches. The weather is steadily improving and the sun is getting quite hot. One can feel that summer is in the air. For unknown reasons the Boche broke out into sudden activity while we were on this tour. At about 10 a.m. one day a sudden, intensive bombardment fell on the whole sector like a deluge of fire and steel. Alarm gongs began beating; hurriedly we snatched up our hipes and ran to man the fire-steps. Trench-mortar, gun and howitzer shells burst in our positions. We sought what cover we could, hugging the trench side, heads down, while earth, pieces of chalk, sandbags, trench-boards, and nasty whizzing lumps of metal rained about us, as projectiles of all sizes banged, hissed, crashed and burst everywhere. The noise was appalling. The air throbbed and quivered, the ground undulated like a ship in a heavy sea. O'Donnell dived under a shrapnel shelter, and following his usual habit in such circumstances, brought out his note-book and, undeterred by rocking walls, crashes and all the discordant sounds that accompany an artillery strafe, he proceeded to feverishly jot down some verses. Truly the vagaries of a poet are wonderful, but when in addition he happens to be Irish, then they become incomprehensible to ordinary material men.

Smack! Crash! A shell bursts above us on the parapet top, dust eddies round like a dun-coloured whirlpool, blotting out the daylight for a moment. Plop, plop, sandbags fall with dull thuds, and the wailing cry of " Stretcher-bearers " echoes down the trench. The shelling abates, we peer round. Into the bay staggers " Suet," a member of our platoon, who suffered from nerves, and was reputed to be the windiest man in the battalion. He is crying out in quavering tones : " Stretcher-bearers, where are you ? I am hit. A Blighty at last ! "

We look. He is covered in mud and chalk dust. His face is a bloody mash with crimson streamlets

splashing down on his tunic. His eyes glare insanely
and his lips are drawn back into a frightened snarl.
He is quivering and shivering as if ague held him
in its grip.

" Is it bad, old son ? " cries Marriner sympathetically springing forward and grabbing him. " Come,
let's see what we can do."

" Hurry up for Christ's sake, I'm bleeding to
death ! " yowled Suet shakily. Marriner and I wipe
his face with a hastily soaked bandage. But as we
look for the expected wound we find nothing !
A piece of chalk bursting into fragments under the
impact of some shells has peppered his face and
inflicted scores of little gashes and cuts, all bleeding
profusely, just as if a shot-gun had been fired at him
at long range. A few dabs of iodine and the worst is
over. But poor Suet is inconsolable when he learns
that his " wounds " are mere surface scratches.
The shock, however, wrecked what little nerve he had
left, and he managed to get evacuated just the same.
And about time, too ! That man had been a danger
to himself and others for quite a long time !

Crumps continued to fall for some time, till at
length the strafe stopped as suddenly as it had begun.
The Company had suffered some casualties, mostly
wounded, and as the shelling ceased a few wounded
staggered past us on the way to the first-aid post
down in the communication-trench. Wilkinson of
our Platoon lurched by ; short, dark, rabbit-faced,
walking as if in a daze, his eyes staring into vacancy,
blood slowly trickling from his bare head and soaking
through a hasty bandage ; dirt-encrusted face,
seamed with sweat-streaks, left arm swinging use-
lessly and dripping red. Silent and moody, he passed
beyond our ken.

We emerged to view the damage. Huge hummocks
and mounds of earth and heaps of scattered bags
marked part of our trench, traverses had collapsed,
dug-outs had been blown in and blotted out. A
little farther up men were digging frantically in an

effort to reach four men and a corporal buried in the debris of a shelter. Alas, their attempts proved vain ! Mr. Walker came along, and under his energetic direction we spent most of that trying day repairing the damage, and when we finished at sun-down another night's toil in the front line was our reward ! The tour ended, back we moved into cellars at Maroc " Garden City " and our troglodytic life continued until the early part of June, when we entered the firing-line for another spell.

This time we lay close to the Double Crassier, and had to man the saps running up from the front line to the edge of the slope. The Huns had also saps running well out, and in this part of the line warfare was mainly confined to trench-mortar bombard-ments, bombing strafes between the opposing sap heads and occasional sniping. On our second day in our Section did twenty-four hours' duty in the sap, and we took over at midnight. Snewin, Maddocks and George, the three Cockneys, and Unwin, the Norfolk lad, made up one relief, and our four selves the other, with Oldham in charge of the whole.

The night was quiet, and the ensuing dawn brought out a perfect summer day. In the early morning, while we were warily coaxing a small fire to burn without smoke, patiently slicing our wood to the thickness of match-sticks, a voice, with a marked Yankee twang, hailed us from the Hun sap.

" Hey there, you guys, are you the Royal Rifles ? "

" Yes, and who the 'ell are you, Squarehead ? " yowled back Marriner.

" We are from Holstein, here," answered the German, " but the Bavarians will be relieving us to-night. I guess you yobs have some corned beef, biscuits and jam to spare there, ' hein ' ? "

" We might," answered Marriner. " What will you give us for them ? "

" Some cigars, Schnapps, and Johann here will play you tunes on his violin. If you take it easy

to-day, we do the same. You don't bomb, we don't
bomb, that right, eh ? "

" All right, Yank, chuck us over your cigars and
the Schnapps, whatever it is, and over comes some
bully and jam," replied our negotiator, and then,
aside to me : " What the 'ell is Schnapps, anyway.
D'ye eat it or what ? "

" No, old scrounger, you heave it down your
throat. It's a kind of whisky-like liquor ! "

" Now, that's the ticket ! Who would think old
Fritz is keen to give it away, eh ? " Marriner mused,
pleasurably.

We looked up as three or four bundles came sailing
over and fell in and on the sap edge.

" Duck your nuts, boys," urged Oldham cautiously. " Old Fritz may have something up his
sleeve."

However, nothing untoward happened. We retrieved the bundles. Fat cigars, and a couple of
soda-water bottles, filled with yellowish spirit.

" All right, you guys, there ? " queried the voice
from the enemy sap.

" All A 1, old cock," replied Marriner cheerfully.
" Here comes our whack," and over we slung sundry
tins of jam, bully, Maconochie and packets of Army
biscuits.

Quiet reigned over all.

" Now this is what I call a bit of all right," purred
Marriner contentedly as he squatted down, drawing
at a cigar and occasionally having a swig of Schnapps.
" If all the bloody Huns were as decent, we could
have a cushy time out here, hurt nobody and let
the Kaiser and our brass hats fight it out amongst
themselves. But, of course, that bloke over there is
civilized, he's lived in America ! "

" And d'ye think America is a civilized country ? "
broke in Rodwell. " You must be off your nut, old
son. Of all the uncouth, primitive-minded peoples,
the Americans take the biscuit. They are like South
Sea Island niggers, who, when they get a pair of

trousers on and can run to a bottle of gin and a
second-hand gramophone, think they are as good
as any modern white man. The Yanks are just the
same. All their so-called culture is mere skin-deep
veneer. They are loud-voiced, brazen-faced, boast-
ful, ranting and obstinate. They are actually as
crude as Irish peasants from Galway," with a swift
glance at O'Donnell.

"I dunno, you blokes do like to ride the high
horse with your opinions," cut in Oldham quickly,
before O'Donnell had the chance of seizing the
opening. "I know nowt about Yanks. All I do see
is that we are going to have a quiet day, because a
German lived in America and knows our lingo!"

"Eh, mates, listen to that!" broke in Maddocks.
A preliminary strumming from the German sap,
and then the sweet, pure notes of a violin wafted
in the summer morning. Schubert, Beethoven and
then the lilting tunes of Strauss came to our ears.
For a brief space of time we felt as if the dirt, dreari-
ness and hardship of war were but a forgotten
nightmare, and we had been wafted away to awaken
into a fresh world, where bliss, harmony and colour
held sway.

"Bryvo, boys!" yelled Snewin approvingly.
"Give us some more," as the player ceased.

"Good, eh?" came the Yankee voice again.
"Johann was a *künstler* in the Adlon Hotel orchestra
in Berlin!"

The player tuned up again and treated us to some
Hungarian Tzigane tunes, but just as he was getting
into stride some bilious-minded trench-mortar man
somewhere in our front line, attracted by the music,
thought it a fit opportunity to lob a stream of Stokes
shells across and mar our peace.

"Blast his bloody eyes!" ground out O'Donnell.
"That's put the lid on it!"

The playing ceased. The German mortars began
to retaliate, and war, thrust aside for a fleeting
minute, reasserted its fell ubiquity. However, as

far as our two opposing saps were concerned, martial activities, by common consent, were vetoed, and we spent the day in comparative safety and comfort.

Late in the evening, as shadows began to lengthen and Very lights commenced their nightly display, our German-American hailed us again, wished us good luck and informed us that the Bavarians were on the way up.

" All right, old cock, good luck, and give 'em my love ! " sang out our irrepressible Marriner. In due course another section came up to relieve us, together with Mr. Walker on a tour of inspection. He was very amused when informed of the incident. Having handed over, we ambled back to our funk-hole and journeyed down into the Land of Nod. The Bavarians were in all right. The whole night long the noisy activity of their cursed mortars, banging and crashing through trench and traverse, made sleep impossible, and the sector positively hideous to us.

VI

On this frontage sniping is very rife just at present, and friend and foe alike have some smart men busy at this nerve-racking pastime. In certain spots in our front line where it is possible to obtain a glimpse of the enemy trenches and a commanding view of the shattered waste in between, little shelters have been made at the bottoms of the parapet walls where the marksman can crawl in, lie full length and take aim through a loophole protected by a steel shutter. A piece of blanket drawn across the entrance prevents keen and watchful enemy observers from spotting the firing-point, by spotting the light seeping in from the trench.

Yet with all these precautions, the number of victims the enemy marksmen manage to make is astonishing.

I saw one such incident myself. Turner, the hefty

Rhodesian, an experienced battalion sniper, had been sent up to us, to deal with a very troublesome Hun marksman who has been taking heavy toll of men these last couple of days. He nearly got Marriner this morning, when that cheerful rogue was crossing over an exposed bit of trench-line wrecked in the early morning strafe on some mysterious errand bent.

I was on the *banquette* on sentry, when Turner ensconced himself in the sniping-hole below my fire-step.

A little later the ping of an enemy sniper's rifle broke the morning stillness like a whip-crack, to be followed immediately by a quick burst of Lewis-gun fire from down the trench.

Sergeant Wilson came along, and looked into Turner's hole.

" Did you spot him ? " I heard him query.

" I think so, Sergeant. He is in that clump of bricks, near the big shell-hole, about a hundred yards away. I'm waiting for him to move."

"All right, try to get him if you can, Turner. I'll have the Lewis trained on that spot and I'll give the artillery the wire ! " So saying the sergeant straightened up and moved off, leaving Turner to his own devices. Some time later I heard the sharp bark of his rifle, followed immediately by one from the hidden Hun sniper. I ducked below the bags as a precaution, but no bullet came my way. The morning wore on in perfect quietude, nothing stirring. The trenches had become sleepy hollows of relaxing humans, grateful for the warmth Old Sol was so generously bestowing on them. Only occasional distant gun-fire throbbed through the summer day like far-away rumbling of drums.

Presently Rodwell came up to relieve me, and as he prepared to get on the fire-steps I asked, " What's up with that big stiff of a Rhodesian below, has he gone to sleep ? I heard him fire about an hour ago, but he has not stirred since."

"All right, have a look as you get down," answered Rodwell, scrambling up. On getting down I noticed that the blanket over the sniper's hole was displaced, and I caught a glimpse of Turner, lying prone and still.

"Hey, Turner, you lazy blighter," I cried, jerking his leg, "wake up, it's nearly time for some grub!" No response, his foot felt heavy somehow. I bent and looked closer.

"I say, Rodwell, get down here a moment," I called up, "there's something queer here with Turner." He stepped down beside me, and catching hold of a foot each, we dragged at Turner and heaved him into the trench, unresisting. We soon saw the reason. Poor Turner was stone dead. He had been shot right through his aiming eye! When he had fired the Hun must have turned his telescope on him and, noticing the chink of light exposed by the displaced blanket, had aimed carefully and had shot so swiftly that Turner died without knowing what had hit him and without stirring an inch from his position. Poor blighter! He had left a nice little farm on the rolling South African plains to come and scrap for the Motherland. This was his reward. Not even to die in the heat and clash of battle, but to be rubbed out unhonoured and unsung in the midst of a calm summer's morn when all Nature was astir, breathing of hope and fertility. He looked quite peaceful and undisturbed in death. Not a single feature marred or strained; but for the splotch of dark red where his right eye had been, he seemed asleep, his tanned features not yet blenched by the pallor of death. Many were the ways in which the Grim Reaper wielded his lethal scythe to cut down his human crop in these French fields where he held undisputed and grisly sway!

CHAPTER THREE

I

LIKE everything else in this world, at last our tour came to an end, and we marched out bound for the back areas for a protracted rest. We were relieved late at night by a battalion of diminutive, tough-looking men. The Welsh bantams, keen little fellows with plenty of guts. We wended our way through Maroc and across country and the dawn light found us in Petit Saens, our new *pied-à-terre*, a few kilometres distant from Mazingarbe ; the Platoon all billeted together in a large top floor hall. Cookers awaited our arrival, hot tea was issued and, wonder of wonders, two blankets a man—comparative luxury ! We laid down to rest our weary, tired bodies to wake up late, breakfast at ease off fried bacon and cheese and go through the rigmarole performance of the first day out of the line. Hot baths in huge vats, clean linen from the French laundresses moving about unabashed through crowds of naked men shouting and revelling in the water. All our troublesome and unwelcome parasites left us in an atmosphere of hot steam, soap and Harrison's pomade. This was wonderful stuff to deal with the lice, and when rubbed on the body produced stinging sensations in the tender parts of our anatomies, akin to electric shocks.

What relief to be free from our frolicsome lodgers without need to indulge in the constant fumble, scratch and hunt, frantically questing for the denizens of our shirts and pants. Refreshed, clean, cheerful, the Company lined up for the great event of the day— pay ! Seated at a table in the open yard Captain Sherlock, flanked by the Q.M.S., the two soldiers as witnesses standing rigid behind, as laid down by regulations, the Sergeant-Major hovering in the background smiling like a benevolent jinn, doled out 10- and 20-franc notes to the cheery throng, while further off the inhabitants and shopkeepers of

Petit Saens made ready to gather the money harvest that would presently swell their stockings.

Petit Saens looked a nice sort of spot, as villages in this part of France go. Wide main street with several *estaminets*, a few shops, clean-looking side streets surrounded by carefully tended fields and small garden plots now all abloom with summer flowers.

" I know a nice quiet place where we can get a real decent meal," said Rodwell, after we had been paid out. " Shall we go along ? "

" Certainly, let's," I replied.

Our little party assented and later on we wended our way down, past the corner *estaminet* crammed to overflowing with throngs of cheerful fellows quaffing *vin rouge* or *blanc* and beer, echoing with sounds of revelry, songs and the strumming of a piano somewhat the worse for wear, and into a little *épicerie* at the very end of the street.

We entered ; Rodwell and O'Donnell were old customers and Madame, a kindly, tidy, gentle-looking old soul, greeted them effusively, expressing her pleasure that they had returned safe and sound from the clutches of " les sales Boches, ces monstres ! "

"Ah, this time, Madame, we have one with us who can talk," bubbled Rodwell in his pidgin French.

" Ça va bien, Messieurs, voulez-vous entrer ? " and she led us into the clean, comfortable back parlour. " Reservè pour nos amis speciales," she informed me smilingly, and while we took our ease she bustled away to prepare us something nice to eat. I first made friends with her cat, who naturally occupied the most comfortable chair in the room, and then, picking up yesterday's copy of the *Journal*, I began to translate the news to the boys. Columns about Verdun, plenty regarding Kitchener's recent death and the Battle of Jutland and casualty lists.

O'Donnell and Rodwell were soon busy with their customary battle of words with Oldham interjecting occasionally and Marriner egging them on and enjoying the fun.

A savoury smell made our noses crinkle in anticipation ; Madame, followed by a little girl with plates, cutlery and table napery, entered and began to lay the table.

" Reminds me of me old parlour in Preston," said Oldham reflectively as he watched our hostess spread a spotless table-cloth, " and my old woman getting the Sunday dinner on the go ! It does seem funny to see a clean table-cloth again ! "

" Ah ! you should have been out on the veldt for months, Oldham, with sand in yer grub and next to yer skin, always on hard tack, flies in yer tea, burning sun during the day a-roasting you, shivering cold at night, never a wash fer weeks, and Woodbines at two bob a packet, chasing Boers all day, never findin' them and flopping out dead-beat at night with the blighters sniping at yer fires ! You'd know then what it's like to see decent grub again ! " chipped in Marriner reminiscently.

" Avast there with your yarns of the bow-and-arrow wars, you old scrounger. Sit down and get ready to tuck in ! " said I chaffingly as I uncorked a bottle of Barsac.

" Ho ! bow and arrers indeed ! " rebutted Marriner indignantly. " A day under fire from Boer snipers would make you change your mind. They had Fritz beaten to a frazzle as regards fly dodges and rifle-shooting. An' to think that after all these years the Boers are now fighting against Fritz and are with us. By gosh, this is a rum old world all right ! "

Madame made her appearance with a steaming tureen. Excellent soup followed by *poulet au Perigord* with all its savoury accompaniments. We did full justice to the rest of the luxuries our good hostess set before us, accompanying them with a cheerful stream of chatter and fussings. Coffee and then the wines followed, and we relaxed content and replete, at peace with the world.

Presently a well-built French soldier of about our own age, sporting the Medaille Militaire, walked into the room somewhat diffidently and stood hesitating as he caught sight of us.

" It is my grandson," said Madame, proudly giving him a gentle push forward. " En permission —mais quel horreur ! " she added, throwing her hands up and turning her kind eyes heavenwards . " He has been at Verdun for four months, and every day I have been praying ' le bon Dieu ' to keep my little lamb safe for me ! " lovingly squeezing his elbow.

He stood rather embarrassed, but I spoke a few words to make him feel at ease ; he saw that he would be welcome, sat down amongst us, accepted a glass and a gasper and soon joined merrily in our badinage and songs, beating time to our tunes as he could not sing in English. But now and again a strained, hunted look gleamed in his eye, and he became silent and morose. I tried to brighten him up and draw him out. We began to talk, and, as usual, began to relate our war experiences to each other. After a while I asked him why he was so thoughtful, and then he burst out :

" Ah, ' mon vieux,' all will become like I am before this terrible butchery ends. Just think ! I had been called up for my military service in April, 1914. In August I was with Pau in Alsace, then my regiment went into the Champagne fighting, Berry-au-Bac, the terrible winter of '14–15, when we stood with water up to our waists, then in the spring Souchez, Notre Dame de Lorette, Champagne again in September, and finally, to cap it all, at Verdun since February. I have had many comrades time and again, but to see them swept away after a little while just as chaff blows away in the breeze. And all this while through dust, din and blood of battle, weary vigils in the trench-lines, patrols, attacks, toil and weariness, not a day's rest or scratch for me ! I have become an old man overnight, my

nerves on edge and fearful of my own shadow.
Ah, Verdun! What hell upon earth!" he exclaimed bitterly.

O'Donnell and Rodwell had been following the
speech and understood more or less. They were
quite interested, while Oldham and Marriner had
been staring at us in amazement.

"What's he saying, E——?" they queried
together.

I explained, and from then onwards translated the
gist of the Frenchman's remarks, which they
followed interestedly.

"Day after day pounded by artillery, peering with
bleary eyes through the dust and smoke, the earth
rocking drunkenly, trenches flattened out and
smashed. And then the Boche attacks. Wave after
wave of grey figures scramble from their trenches
and run forward, howling like maniacs. They fall
upon us. Tr—tr—tr—go our mitrailleuses. The
enemy wavers, pauses, gaps appear in his ranks, his
men fall in heaps, and the survivors pause, hesitate,
then scramble down to cover. And the guns start
battering at us again. We are blasted out from our
trench-line by sheer weight of metal and cling on in
shell-holes, sleepless, tired, almost dead, bewildered,
sickened. Our senses reel with the din, the con-
cussion and the impact of projectiles. And the grey
hordes attack again and again! By day and by night
the struggle goes on. We fight hand to hand with
bayonet, teeth and bare hands, and they drive us
back. Then our soixante-quinzes commence to
cough. Reinforcements come up and we counter-
attack. It is a hellish nightmare, a horror of struggling figures. Knife, bludgeon and grenade come
into play. Ours fall in swathes, but we leap over our
dead and dying, careless of everything but the enemy
in front. We fight like fiends out of Hades and
reconquer the position. And then the Boche starts
all over again! Night after night, day after day this
mad saraband with Death goes on and never ceases!

Painfully strengthening a position but to lose it,
attacking to regain it. The stench, the reek of blood,
the countless unburied bodies and the heaps of wailing wounded, praying and cursing, asking for water,
shelter, protection and help, are enough to shatter
any man's sanity. We come out and go back to the
caves for a rest, but the shell-fire, the aeroplanes,
they follow us, and anon we go back again into that
flaming hell. As my *copains* disappear in this maelstrom fresh faces come up to take their places, and
in their turn, within a few days or maybe hours, they
melt away like snow in the sunshine. And I linger
on unscathed physically, but spiritually bruised and
broken! Mon Dieu! C'est pas la guerre! C'est
la mort partout et pour tous ! " with a weary gesture,
and then with new energy he continues : " But with
all this we have sworn ' they *shall* not pass,' and if it
has to take every man France has to do it Verdun
will remain ours to the very end. They may batter
and bend us, but break we shall not ! I have seen
battalion upon battalion of ours, line, chasseurs,
Moroccans, Senegalese, Legionnaires and what not,
enter the very maws of hell at Douaumont and the
Mort Homme singing as if going to a marriage feast.
I have seen the remnants come back dirty, tattered,
blood-soaked, exhausted, staggering with fatigue,
hardly able to keep on their feet, but still as game as
ever. It is like a road to Calvary, the way from
Verdun Town to the front. Strewn with the shattered bodies of our manhood, soaked with their
blood, but still ours to fight for and keep ! " His
eyes flashed and his cheeks flushed in his excitement
as he spoke.

I had always looked on the French soldier with
tolerant good-natured contempt, but the sight of this
twenty-two-year-old veteran, in his faded horizon-
blue uniform, war-weary, sickened, but with un-
quenched spirit, made me think of the brave
French chivalry of old, and I realized that their
famed martial ardour and Furia Francesa still burnt

brightly and strongly in the breasts of their descendants.

" Well, my friend, we have to see this job through before we can fling pack and rifle aside, so ' à bas le cafard ' and let us drink to success ! " I answered encouragingly.

He snatched up the glass, gulped its contents and then turned to me apologetically.

" Forgive me for this outburst. But then you understand, you know what it all means, but my people and the civilians, bah ! they cannot realize or grasp our point of view. One cannot speak to them thus ! " with a sweeping gesture, and then with nervous excitement : " After this I must play and sing." He crossed the room, sat at the piano and the lively lilting " Madelon," the French war song, burst from his lips like an anthem and the piano keys quivered and rang under his nervous fingers.

I have never heard it before or since played or sung with such ardour and meaning. As one listened to its verve and cadences it seemed as if the very spirits of departed warriors hung around, watching and encouraging the young, fresh battalions marching into battle. We all joined in as best as we could, while the grandmother and granddaughter and odd members of the household stood grouped around looking with approval at this exhibition of *l'entente cordiale* with tear-stained eyes.

" Good for you, lad ! " approved Marriner, smacking the Frenchman heartily on the back, " that's the stuff to give 'em ! "

In this cheerful atmosphere the Frenchman seemed to cast all cares aside and for the rest of the evening joined in our fun merrily.

While in Petit Saens I met Henri Picard two or three times before his leave expired and he returned to play his part and resume his post on that Via Dolorosa of Verdun. I have often wondered whether he survived the war ; most probably somewhere on the slopes round Verdun, at Vaux or Douaumont or

the Mort Homme his remains mingle with the
thousands of other unknowns in that huge grave-
yard of Frank and Teuton manhood, while his spirit,
I am certain, finds rest in the soldiers' Valhalla—
where strife is forgotten and friend and foe meet in
true soldierly *camaraderie*, able to appraise each
other's qualities at their true worth.

II

In the dark we returned to our billets talking
cheerily.

" Do you know, E——," remarked Marriner to
me, " I had no idea the Froggies were such decent
coves. The ones I have met up to now have been
crabby, windy blighters, always jabbering like a lot
of blasted parrots. But that fellow at Madame's
seemed somehow quite different and more our
style ! "

" It just shows," I replied, " that we can't judge
too hastily. Probably the Huns even have similar
feelings ! "

Activities began with the morning. Inspections,
platoon drill, rifle exercises. We spent some
restful, pleasant days. Plenty of grub, clean, with a
little cash in our pockets, a few decent nights' rest,
we began to feel like fighting cocks.

Rodwell was very suspicious about it all and said
darkly : " There is something coming off, boys.
They are fattening us up for a slaughter ! "

" Oh, well, let it come, me bhoy," answered
O'Donnell complacently. " 'Tis time we paid Fritz
a surprise call ! "

Rodwell proved a true prophet. Late that night
orders for a battalion parade in the morning, to be
followed by the inspection and an address from the
G.O.C. Division, duly reached us via the Orderly
Sergeant.

" It looks like trouble all right," remarked
Marriner darkly. " These Brass Hats don't bother

about the likes of us unless there is some dirty work
to be done, and then they become as kind and gentle
as if we were their blinking brothers. Blast the
whole lousy bunch of 'em, says I ! "

Up early next day. Platoon inspection, sergeants
and corporals dashing about chivvying the men—
Company inspection and a homily from our Skipper.
The Battalion falls in in close column of companies,
the C.O., second-in-command and adjutant prancing
about on their hacks. Crisp words of command
and off we march to halt and deploy again in close
column in a field behind Petit Saens dominated by
a small hillock. The Northamptons, Loyal North
Lancs and Royal Sussex, the other three battalions
of our Brigade, are already formed up on the parade
ground. Cars drive up with countless red-tabbed
Staff officers in them. The Brigade presents arms,
then we stand at ease. Up to attention again. A
red-faced, stout, grey-haired, white-moustached
General, his rows of medal ribbons streaking his
tunic like a rainbow, moves down our ranks followed
by the C.O., adjutant and a glittering cohort of
Staff officers. He halted to speak now and again
to this man and that, and naturally Marriner's V.C.,
flanked by O'Donnell and Rodwell's D.C.M., caught
his eyes and brought him to a stop in front of us.
He was a nice, kindly old boy, very keen to give a
word of encouragement to the men.

" Ah ! you have some capital fellows here,
Bircham," he exclaimed in a pleased voice, turning to
our C.O. " They appear to have done some damned
good work ! " He started to talk to Marriner about
South Africa, enquired as to his V.C., spoke a few
words to O'Donnell and Rodwell and then moved
on down the lines. Inspection over, we were ordered
to sit down while the G.O.C. and his Staff mounted
the hillock. From the summit of that eminence
the G.O.C. surveyed the Brigade below him and
commenced his oration.

" Officers, N.C.O.s and men of the Second

Brigade ! I am very pleased with your smart turn-
out and the good work you have been responsible
for throughout the Spring. The Corps Commander
has asked me to select my best Brigade for a special
operation, and I have chosen you. I am certain
that you will make it a success and live up to the
high reputation of your Regiments. I can say that
I place full reliance in you, and I shall tell the Corps
Commander what a fine body of men you are.
I wish you all the very best luck individually and
collectively ! " He stopped. The troops cheered,
then we fell in and moved off.

" The old twister ! " mouthed Marriner admiringly to us. " How he spread the jam on ! "

" Yes ! " interjected Rodwell bitingly from behind
us. " He's merely said what all the Brass Hats
think. Their slogan seems to run like this : ' Go
on, men, fight like hell. Tear your guts out,
scramble through the wire ! Get at the Boche.
Bash them, gouge their eyes out, kick 'em, stick
your bayonets in their bellies. Spiflicate the lot !
If you die in your hundreds what does it matter ?
We'll be all right, reaping a harvest of K.C.B.s,
D.S.O.s and X.Y.Z.s and all the rest of it ! ' . . . .
What a bloody rotten farce ! "

" Shut up, you daft loon ! " broke in O'Donnell.
" Someone has to do the job, why not us ? We can
all do with a bit av a scrap, instead of bein' shot at
like a lot of sittin' rabbits ! "

" March at ease, men may smoke," came the order.

" Put those blasted Woodbines out ! " roared out
a voice somewhere, mimicking Barty's mincing tones.
A roar of laughter swept through the ranks. Mouth-
organs blared out, the boys burst into song and in
high good humour the Battalion swung back into
Petit Saens, heads up and chests well out.

After dinner another Company parade. Captain
Sherlock and the Sergeant-Major very much in
evidence. After standing us at ease, the Skipper
spoke :

" I want some volunteers for the bombing parties ! "

A single movement and the nine members of our Section stepped out. Men came forward from the Company line here and there. There must have been close on eighty. Once one makes a start a very few ever hang back in our Corps.

" Thank you, men, that's splendid," cried our Commander, looking very pleased. " Now I shall have to pick from the volunteers. Sergeant-Major, take these names."

Carefully forty of us were chosen and placed under Mr. Walker for further instructions. We stood fast while the rest of our Company was dismissed.

Then the Skipper addressed us :

" There is going to be a big-scale raid, and you men will form four bombing parties under Mr. Walker. Your job will be to get into the Triangle ahead of the Battalion and bomb the place to blazes ! We have some days to spare, and the Triangle position will be dug here according to the aerial photographs, and we shall practise the operation until you men have a good idea of what has to be done. The assault parties will be excused all duties and will parade under Mr. Walker every morning. I need not say that I rely on you men to make a thorough job of it ! You can now dismiss till the morning ! "

We broke up and began to talk matters over amongst ourselves.

" By goom, lads ! " remarked Oldham, " looks like a hot show ! "

" A fair grand slam," said Marriner grinning, " but I like these tip-and-run raids. It gives a man a chance of putting the kybosh on old Fritz."

" Aye, but look you, Marriner," warned Oldham, " none of your mad-headed stunts. You've done 'em on your own, I know, but this time there are others with you to think about, so you just do as you are told ! "

He was referring to Marriner's daring exploit at Cambrin the previous year, when very daringly

and single-handed he had walked over to the
German line and bombed about 100 yards of
trench, wrecking machine-guns, killing God knows
how many Germans and turning the place into a
shambles. That deed had brought him fame and
the coveted Cross.

" Oh, all right, Oldham, old cock," replied
Marriner, " I'll be Mama's blue-eyed boy. But
for Christ's sake don't give us a sermon ! "

During the ensuing days we were hard at it in
the trenches we dug for the purpose. A few rattles
behind us represented the artillery barrage. We
had to break into the position at four different
points, bomb its dug-outs, penetrate as deep as
possible, run up barricades in the communication
trenches, hold these against all comers and allow
our Battalion time to occupy the Boche front line,
while the Royal Sussex assaulted the enemy on the
Double Crassier on our right. Our practice attack
was good sport, and we enjoyed the fun of it, but it
made us realize that we had a tough job in front
of us demanding all our care and energy.

On the 29th June the Battalion took the familiar
road up, and we, well loaded with grub, entered the
support trenches and soon made ourselves at home
in the dug-outs. The immediate front was very
quiet, to the south ; however, an intensive cannonade
throbbed and rattled continually like thousands of
drums.

" Well, me lads," remarked O'Donnell after
we had distributed our belongings about the dug-
out, " I expect the show will be on to-morrow
night, so we'd better make the most of it, have a
good feed in the morning and a quiet lay in—we shall
need it," he added significantly. We turned in.
The air in the dug-out was dank and fuggy, but very
soon we were asleep. To-morrow anything might
happen, so why worry ? The great thing is to make
the most of the fleeting hours, for they may be the
last. Useless to repine or fear. The moving finger

writes and having writ moves on; all our frantic attempts will not alter destiny, they merely serve to lower our morale; so apart from the natural shrinking from physical pain, which every man naturally feels, a calm, even mind is necessary. If death presents its bitter cup—well, one must drink of it, for the Reaper's scythe cuts down the coward and the brave with the same impersonal ruthlessness.

III

Next evening at dusk, rested and replete, we were chaffing while putting the finishing touches to our gear in readiness for the night's activities, when Sergeant Wilson's form appeared at our dug-out door and his gruff voice roused us with :

" Tumble up, men ! Time to get moving ! "

" Right you are, Sergeant ! " sang out Oldham, and blowing the candle stub, turned to us :

" Come along, boys, up we go ! "

" Walk up, walk up, my lucky lads, put it all on the jolly old spade and up she goes ! " chortled O'Donnell, rattling a pebble in his tin mug in mock make-believe of Crown and Anchor.

We stepped out on to the duck-boards of the support trench, our accoutrements clinking as we banged against the trench sides.

It was pleasant to come out into the open after a day spent dozing and frowsting in the stale, close atmosphere of our funk-hole. We breathed deeply, filling our lungs gratefully.

The darkening sky, with drifting fleecy clouds rosied at the edges by the rays of the setting sun, now a molten ball of fire low in the west, the warm, balmy air, a sparrow's twitter—June was closing in a blaze of glory and summer splendour.

Only an occasional harsh crack of rifle or at intervals the deeper toned cr-rump of mortar shell bursting up on the slag heap, now looming dark on our right front, marred the essential quiet of summer. Far away in the distance the continuous rumble of guns which had not stayed their booming for the past week smote on our ears like the thunderous crash of surf on distant shores. And yet, these sounds and the evidence of warlike activity notwithstanding, it would have been difficult for the uninitiated to believe that the British front line lay ahead and that a paltry hundred yards or so beyond it a wary and watchful enemy lurked.

The other groups were issuing from their dug-outs on their way to Company headquarters. With O'Donnell still humming softly we moved on in the sergeant's wake to be joined farther on by Maddocks and Unwin and the calf-faced Norfolk lad. Such was our group. Clinking and clattering we entered the dimness of the headquarters dug-out, where we could distinguish amongst the shadows the members of the three other assault parties huddled against its walls. Candles stuck in bottles stood on the table made up of ammunition boxes, and their curvetting light served to accentuate the darkness in the corners. Behind the table and facing us sat Captain Sherlock, flanked by Mr. Walker and the Sergeant-Major, their faces thrown into vivid relief by the light of the spluttering candles.

" Are all the men here, Sergeant-Major ? " asked the Skipper, looking up from the maps he had been conning over and turning to him as we took our places.

" Yes, sir, all present now ! " rapped back old Mac smartly.

We stiffened as our Commander's glance swept over us in a quick, keen inspection.

" Well, men, you know what must be done. The Triangle must be assaulted and thoroughly wrecked. No hesitation, no pause to look after casualties. The wounded must make their way back as best as they can. Quick, sharp action is wanted. Penetrate as far down the Boche trenches as possible, then build your blocks and stand fast until three red flares go up from our line, when you will retire on to the Battalion. The Battalion will occupy the Boche front line behind you, while the Royal Sussex will attack the craters and the Boche trenches on the slag heap. Is this all clear ? Jolly good luck to you all and give the enemy hell ! Mr. Walker will be in command of the bombing attack. Carry on ! "

His sharp, clipped words had the desired effect. I felt my blood course through my veins strongly, and glancing round in the semi-darkness of the dug-out I could see the men's eyes glitter with excitement and their hands grasp their weapons convulsively. It was hard to envisage that in a short space of hours many of these fellows, together with countless others from the attacking battalions, would be groaning and moaning in trench, traverse, shell-hole or stretcher, or staggering blindly through the desolation and horror around them, wounded, shattered and marred for life, while many more would lie stark and still in the finality of death. This last June night would witness anew Man's senseless power of destruction hurled at Mother Nature in a scornful gesture of defiance.

Mr. Walker, in battle order and wearing a private's tunic, stood up, whispered with the Skipper a moment, shook his hand and led the way out, we following in his wake.

Darkness had deepened. Very lights drifted fitfully on the skyline. Our artillery had begun to register and shells were screeching overhead to fall and burst in the Boche wire and on their parapets.

Oldham in front of me turned and whispered, grinning : " Roll on Blighty ! "

Zhee-Bang ! Zhee-Bang ! Zhee-Bang ! Sudden vicious swishes and a flight of Boche light-calibre shells burst on the lip of the trench, causing us to duck quickly and covering us with dirt. Apparently the Germans were beginning to wake up and were commencing to pepper the approaches to the front line. Swearing and spluttering, Marriner behind me muttered : " By Christ E——! The asterisks know something is up ! "

Our pace got brisker and finally we entered the firing-line. Dim figures crouched alertly on the fire-steps, bayonets fixed and eyes staring into the murk. The Northamptons were standing-to. Traverse by traverse, we wormed our way onwards, up a narrow gully and finally into the forward sap. On our right the Double Crassier towered above us dark and awesome like some uncouth monster. Flares were going up and down over the whole front, illuminating the waste fitfully. Crouched against the sap-head, we talked in whispers, tense with the strain of waiting.

" By God, E——! I wish the show would start. I am shaking like a bloody jelly ! " I heard O'Donnell say. Marriner, a little way farther down, was giving harrowing and bloodcurdling descriptions of previous raids to the Norfolk boy, who, with his vacant looks and drawn face, presented a faithful picture of a sheep led to the slaughter. The wind freshened . . . we shivered . . . each one of us thinking of the task that lay ahead of us. Suddenly our guns at the back broke out into a mad cacophony of sound. The rush of shells overhead and the crash of their explosions blended into one awful roar, deafened and numbed us—setting our nerves quivering. The German front line became an inferno of spouting earth vomiting red and yellow glares. Flares went up in bunches from their advanced and support trenches and their machine-guns commenced their tac-tac-tac questing over no-man's-land. We shook with excitement, straining like eager dogs at the leash. The acrid smell of cordite, the fumes and smoke, the back rush of air from near explosions, the roar of guns now merged into a mad tocsin intoxicated us. We ceased to be rational thinking men. Our only goal became the hazy red-lit hell of heaving earth, a bare hundred yards ahead, and we were eager to enter it.

" Assault party, get over the top and lie down in front ! " came the whispered order. Quickly we scrambled over, Marriner following behind me as we stooped and crawled through the gaps which had already been cut in our wire. We stumbled on and lay down in a straggling line, Mr. Walker and a runner on our left rear.

All at once hell broke loose. The Boche counter-batteries had come into action and were splashing masses of shells that fell behind us on to our front line like hail. From the slag heap sudden glares, smoke, spouts of earth, the dull sound of explosions and the staccato rattle of machine-guns came in waves of awful sound. The world seemed suddenly to have changed into a very maelstrom of noise.

Then the artillery paused abruptly. A few seconds' strange hush clapped down, smothering all the battle noises as if a giant stopper had been suddenly clapped on a pot of hissing boiling water, and then with redoubled fury it resumed its crazy roaring as it lifted to blast the German back areas flat. At the same instant a great glare lighted up the landscape for a fleeting instant with a lurid flame, to be followed by an awful crash which blinded and deafened us. An avalanche of stones, earth, bags, wire and heaven knows what else, fell and bounced all around us crazily. The mines had been sprung along our front ! ZERO !

Whistles shrilled out. With inhuman cries and tautened nerves we sprang up and, cursing, roaring, singing, scrambled forward towards the Boche like a band of fiends.

Holes, twisted wire, debris of every kind, seemed to grip and drag at me as I scrambled over the twisted heaps that had been neutral ground. Stumbling and recovering, helmet bobbing up and down, slugs pinging all round me, bewildered and deafened, but determined, I ran forward, tearing through the wreckage of the enemy position like a madman. All caution dropped from me as if it were a discarded mantle. I became intoxicated with battle lust, my one thought was to destroy everything that stood in the way. Ahead, abreast and behind me the rest of the party were running and scrambling forward with hoarse cries.

Marriner, rifle slung behind him, hands grasping grenades, overtook me, jumped on the German trench-top and, scattering his grenades before him, jumped in yelling like a fiend :

" Do them in ! Kill the bloody swine ! " I followed him. We came to a wrecked dug-out adit. From some hole in the trench a few Germans emerged, bewildered. I could just distinguish their flat caps in the half darkness. But before they had properly set foot in the trench and recovered from their surprise we were upon them with bayonet, club and trench-knife, and in a few instants we were pounding on over their dead bodies. Crash ! Roar ! Crash ! Tac-tac-tac-tac ! A noise like a million hammers in my ears. Rodwell, O'Donnell and other shadowy figures, hard to identify in the gusts of drifting smoke, were running about, stabbing, bombing and destroying. A communication-trench appears before us, we plunge down it. Bodies scrunch under my feet, unheeded. We halt, panting, before a dug-out entrance. I take a pin out of a Mills, chuck it in the canvas bag full of grenades I am carrying and sling the whole lot down. I can hear it rattle and bump down the steps, then a muffled roar, a swirl of dust and smoke, a few smothered cries quickly extinguished and the whole adit disappears in an avalanche of earth and splintered wood. Machine-gun and rifle-fire breaks out on our front. Grenade burst further down. The Boche, having recovered from his initial surprise and the stunning effect of our bombardment, is attempting to counter-bomb his way up.

" This way, boys ! " yells Marriner suddenly and, running like a madman, he vaults on the trench-top, runs down a few yards, heedless of everything about

him, and starts dropping his grenades on the heads
of the Boche further down in the trench.

" Here are the bastards ! " he shouts. " Give 'em
hell ! " Like hounds in full cry we crash through
the bays, destroying everything in our path, and
burst on a crowd of saucepan-helmeted Germans,
bewildered by the bombs and herded together. A
short fierce struggle, groans, cries. Hands go up.
We herd our prisoners over the top and shoo them
towards the British lines in charge of Unwin. I
wonder what that simple Norfolk yokel must have
felt like as he prodded over a dozen hefty Germans
onwards with his bayonet. Anyhow, he is comparatively safe for the rest of the night and out of
harm's way !

Sharp thuds further down on our left warn us that
the other bombing parties are hard at it. From the
slag heap a sudden murderous burst of machine-gun-
fire sweeps over us and I see one or two men fall. A
terrible scrap is going on up there in the craters,
judging by the sounds. The German artillery has
now shortened its range and is plastering the whole
triangle with its shells, regardless as to whether it is
held by friend or foe. Suffocating fumes sweep over
us. Bags and earth crash round, the trenches rock
like express trains to the shock of bursts. The Very
lights going up in multicoloured profusion illuminate
the scene like a gigantic Brock's display. We
advance further down carefully. A turn in the
trench. We have reached our appointed limits.

" Up with a trench-block, boys ! " yells Oldham.
Feverishly we fall to work with trench tool, bayonet
and bare hands, scooping earth, piling sandbags and
debris to form a barricade. Rodwell and I crawl up
on the trench-lip on either side and with rifles ready
we strain our eyes towards the Boche support line
just further on. The battle has now spread north-
wards, the Royal Sussex and our Battalion have
crossed the bags and are now throwing out the
Boche from his front line along the whole Brigade

front. As far as the eye reaches the horizon is a red
sullen glare splattered with gusts of dark smoke.
Machine-guns are cackling and spluttering everywhere. Nothing but thuds, noise and crashing roar
all around. The ear-drums seem to burst with the
constant thud, thud, thud of explosions. The
Germans are trying to launch a counter-attack from
their support trenches. We descry a line of straggling figures clambering over the parapets while the
thud of grenades further down the trench warns us
that the enemy is working his way up the trench as
well. They make a sudden determined rush.

A yell bursts out from the line held by the British :
" Stand to ! here they come ! " and a roar of rapid
fire breaks out. The bullets whizz by me like a
storm of angry bees rattling and plomping like hail-
stones. I fire and fire till my rifle becomes too hot
to hold and the bolt sticks and won't act. Some
Boches make a rush for the block below. The world
becomes a red haze to me. Cries, yells, groans, and
then comparative quiet. All over ! The counter-
attack crumples up and the Boche scuttles away to
what cover he can get in shell-holes and trenches.
And then Marriner loses his remaining senses. As
Rodwell and I slide back into the trench he lets out
a roar, scrambles over the trench-block and runs
down in pursuit of the retreating enemy. Neither
Rodwell nor I can resist the urge. We clamber over
the block and follow him. I slither and stumble
over a still-twitching form. Moans and wailing
cries come from dim shapes crouching and lolling
against the trench-sides. And then as I round a
corner and glimpse Marriner in the very act of
bayoneting a prone German—a whistling swish
seems to fill the world. A soul-splitting roar, a
terrible glare blinds me for the nonce. I feel myself
lifted up as if by a giant hand and flung like an
empty sack against the further end of the bay. I hit
the wall and slither down, while a cascade of earth
and bits of all kinds whizzes by and around me. I

feel as if my body is being torn asunder by red-hot pincers, breathing is a superhuman effort. I stagger up dazedly with whirling senses. Part of the trench in front of me has disappeared, leaving a huge shell-hole behind, the sides have fallen in. For a moment I seem to feel as if I have no bones left in my body.

Gingerly I begin to paw at my legs, chest, and over my body, to see if I am hit. I seem all right. But what is all this sticky liquid and gobs of flesh spattered all over me? The explanation flashes across my numbed and dazed brain. Marriner caught full tilt by a shell has been blown to fragments. I shudder and sicken at the thought, then scramble frantically over the debris blocking the trench, to find Rodwell pale and wan, crouching on its further side. " By God, E——! Are you all right? I thought we were all gone," he says shakily.

" Yes, I think I'm all right, but old Marriner is blown to bits ! " I gasp. We run back and get over the barricade.

The Boche shelling gets worse as we get back to the block where the rest of our party are standing alert and watchful. Fighting was getting heavier all along as the Boche gradually began to push our fellows back. His machine-guns were sweeping the trench-top, their slugs pinging and whizzing unpleasantly. The triangle by now was a mere wreck of broken trenches, heaps of burst sacks and earth, gaping holes and splintered wood. Anxiously we peered back for the three red signal lights. A shower of grenades over the barricades ! Blam ! Blam ! Blam ! we retaliate. We hear movement, tinkle of accoutrements and croaking whispers. The Boche is near us. At the same moment the three red lights rise up in the dark sky ! With a last shower of bombs to halt the Boche we leg it as fast as we can over all obstacles up towards the trench-line. Just about time too ! Hoarse shouts behind and the sullen burst of grenades warn us that the Germans

have got over the barricade and are hot on our heels.
" Come on, move in front for Christ's sake ! " yells
Rodwell. The Boche bombardment is becoming
heavier and heavier. The very sky seems to be
vomiting shells which burst and bounce everywhere.
Roars of bitter battle from the slag heap. It must
be pretty hot up there amongst the craters and mazes
of trenches. Panting and gasping we debouch into
the ex-Boche front line, to be greeted by a spatter
of Lewis gun-fire and a yell to halt.

" Stop your bloody firing you f——s ! It's No. 3
party ! " yells out Oldham savagely. We scramble
over a heap of sandbags placed at the entrance to
the communication-trench just as the first grenades
from the pursuing Germans lob over.

" Here they are, boys ! " cries a voice. " Fire
into the bastards ! " Trrrr-trrrr ! goes the Lewis
gun, pouring a dose of slugs down the communication-trench and knocking the foe over like ninepins.

I look around me and see a huddle of figures
crowding this trench. It is filled with a medley of
men from all our four Companies, and Mr. Walker
is urging the men to dig fire-positions in the parados.
On both flanks of the front line the Germans have
re-entered the trench and are systematically bombing
their way down, crowding us in towards the centre.
Unless some move is made soon we shall all go to
blazes or to Germany ! Men are falling here and
there, twisting and twitching in the agony of death.
Cries for stretcher-bearers rise on every hand, but
in most cases remain unanswered. It is as much as
we can do to hold on now, and there is no time or
opportunity to minister to our stricken comrades.
It is a case of all sound men to fight it out, and to
hell with consequences.

" Stick it out, men ! " encourages Mr. Walker. " A
covering barrage will be put down shortly and we
shall get back then."

I look round at him. His left arm is bandaged
and the tunic-sleeve ripped off. His face is streaked

with blood, dirt and sweat. He must have had a pretty hectic time by the looks of him!

The sound of grenade-bursts gets closer and enfilade fire from the machine-guns on the slag heap falls on us in waves and takes heavy toll.

A tattered scarecrow gripping a pistol in one hand and a nasty-looking trench-club in the other sidles up to me and whispers: " Well, E——! I think it's all up with us unless that bloody barrage comes down quick. The blasted Huns are getting too damn near! "

I look. It's O'Donnell, and in queer shape. Spattered with chalk dust, uniform in rags where the barbed wire has caught at him, face and hands a mass of nasty scratches, all caked with dried blood and dirt.

Just then an excited R.E. officer, flourishing a revolver, appears from nowhere and yells out hoarsely:

" Retire, men, retire! You are being murdered for nothing here! "

Some of the men hesitate, others without further ado begin to scramble out of the trench.

" Stand fast! " roars out Walker, and turning to the newcomer : " No man quits this position unless I get a direct order from my Commanding Officer or the barrage is put down. Dig, men, dig! "

The R.E. officer mutters something and subsides. We resume our toil feverishly. The Boche artillery continues to slam at us and his bombers get closer and closer. From his support line a hail of machine-guns and rifle-fire compels us to keep low. Things are getting serious when a hurricane of shells from the British guns falls like an awful blanket of fire, steel and dancing flame between the foe and us. The word to retire is passed down and as best as we can, hale, halt and lame, we scramble out of the Boche trench, rush through the remains of his wire and pick our way gingerly across no-man's-land, now littered with fresh human sacrifice. Gasping and panting we jump down into our own front line. The Boche fire has increased. His artillery are spraying our whole system with all kinds of crumps. Our front line has become mere heaps of tumbled earth, dead men and broken wire.

" All men of the Rifles will make their way back to the ' Garden City ' cellars," I am greeted with. I obey, I push my way through the men crouching against the trench walls of the front line, get to the communication-trench and away down towards Maroc. It is now between 3 and 4 a.m., dawn is in the offing. Objects are becoming clearer every moment. The communication-trench has been badly smashed up and parties are toiling to make the damage good before daylight puts a stop to their work. Straggling groups are still coming up it laden with many burdens. Stretchers filled with groaning wounded slowly moving down. Progress is difficult and very slow. A constant : " Mind my leg, chum ! " " Look out, there's a hole ahead ! " " Get out of the way, you big asterisk ! " " Halt in front, the rear has lost connection ! " keep impinging on my ears as I amble on.

Gradually I get moving quicker and I descry Oldham and Rodwell in front of me.

" By gosh, E——, " says the latter, " it's been pretty hot, eh ? I wonder how many poor blighters are done in ? "

" Coom on, boys, let's get a move on," cries Oldham, looking back. " Daylight will soon be here."

Crash ! bang ! Another shell burst near us.

" The bloody Huns are after us with bells. Get moving, Oldham," cries Rodwell anxiously.

The last turn. We enter Maroc High Street. Groups of men here and there, talking low, smoking nervously and marching off into the half light. Across the road, in a half-ruined house, a glare of candle-light. The dressing station ! Doctors and orderlies working like mad. A filthy reek of blood, disinfectant and iodine makes my nostrils quiver. Stretchers littering the doorway, with moaning occupants twisting and turning. Walking wounded, their bandages showing in the growing light, with drawn faces, stagger and stumble down the street towards the ambulances waiting on the main road leading to Bully Grenay and Mazingarbe.

We, jaded, tired, weary, move on with shuffling feet towards the " Garden City " at the bottom of the street, careless to the sights and sounds round us. We are all in ! We only look up when a body of German prisoners, seventy or so, swing by, guarded by soldiers with fixed bayonets. As I turn towards the broken railings leading into the " Garden City " a last incident impresses itself on my consciousness. Down the road, from the direction of Loos, comes a huge German, stumbling now and then, with bandaged eyes and hands tied behind him, and goading him on with a bayonet an excited, diminutive rifleman from " A " Company, scarce eighteen by the looks of him, with tattered uniform, helmet awry, a huge grin and shining eyes. " Caught him all on me own ! " he cries to us. " Come on, gee up, you big louse ! " It takes a lot to damp the spirits of the men of the Old Corps !

Morning is well on the way as we reach the cellars. Dixies of hot tea await us. Hastily we hold out our canteens, swallow the hot liquid, then wordlessly we get below, fling off our equipment and, dirty, weary and tired, we flop on to our packs and overcoats and are asleep in the matter of moments, seeking in oblivion that rest and forgetfulness that war denies us.

CHAPTER FOUR

I

SOME dinner came up late in the day, we stirred, stretched and came to from our blank slumbers.

As I awoke, the thunder of the ceaseless cannonade booming all along the front came dully to my ears. The batteries behind us were going hell for leather, and the ruins and cellars of the " Garden City " quivered to the shocks. Sundry heavy thuds above us apprised me that the Boche heavies were replying, searching for our battery positions.

Still weary and moody we swallowed our food, after which we began to regain our equipoise and take an interest in our surroundings. Nevertheless the after-effects of the night still weighed heavily on us.

Sergeant Wilson appeared at that moment, fatal note-book in hand. We turned eagerly to him.

" How did the Company get on, Sergeant ? " we chorused.

" Bloody terrible, lads ! We have lost about eighty men. Some good 'uns too. Over two hundred and fifty casualties in the Battalion, and we took ninety-six lousy prisoners ! Major Barber has gone, so has ' B ' Company's Sergeant-Major, lots of good N.C.O.s and plenty of men ! Mr. Walker is hit in the forearm, but has refused to quit and is carrying on. I see poor old Marriner's gone west ! "

" Yes, Sergeant, blown to bits in front of my very eyes ! " I answered feelingly with a shudder. " My tunic and trousers are smothered with his blood ! "

" By Christ ! " Rodwell gritted his teeth savagely. " To think that a fellow like him, a splendid pal, a chap one could always count on and as brave as a lion, should go west like this, while thousands of useless blighters at Home are busy blathering about patriotism, talking big from their club arm-chairs and the pub parlours, raking in money in safety all

the time, patting themselves on their backs and
living at ease! Somehow it seems all wrong!"

"Aye, but it can't be helped," answered the
sergeant philosophically. "I am very sorry you
have lost your pal, and the Platoon a man we could
hardly spare, but what can be done? Anyhow, we
have given old Fritz something to get on with.
You men get cleaned up a bit, Mr. Walker is coming
round presently and I can tell you we are going out
for good to-night." And with that he left us.

"Thank the Lord we are leaving this blasted hole
at last!" ejaculated Rodwell feelingly. And we set
to, busily removing the battle-stains from clothes
and arms, in a very subdued and unusually silent
mood. Marriner's recent death damped our spirits,
we felt his loss keenly. A lovable scrounger, reckless
and feckless, uncouth, when judged by the standards
of " nice " people, but worth a whole heap of those
comfortable and complacent burghers who fondly
cherish the delusion that they are "those that
count." Irreverent and foul-mouthed as Marriner
may have been, I am certain that when weighed in
the scales of Divine justice he had more chance of
leading the way into Paradise than those hosts of fat
and self-centred "respectable" people who pose for
the opinion of their neighbours and live "righteous"
lives because they dare not do otherwise. His pieces
are scattered in the rubble of that French coal heap.
No grave enshrouds his body. Only on the honoured
scroll of the Regiment's glorious hosts of the dead
does his name find an abiding-place. But the
memory of his vital personality lives on in the hearts
of those who knew him and were his friends.
Marriner, V.C.! A soldier, a man and a real pal.
What better epitaph can you have?

"Do you know his address, O'Donnell?" I
enquired.

"He came from Salford, Manchester, I think.
Sergeant Wilson knows. Anyhow, it's no good us
writing to his people. We can't very well tell them

how he met his death. Mr. Walker will do it and put it nicely ! "

In due course Mr. Walker appeared. He looked pale and wan and a little tired, his hand was bandaged and thrust through his Sam Browne cross-strap.

" I hope you fellows are quite fit," he said on entering our cellar. " I am very sorry about poor Marriner. It is a great loss to the Company. He died in making our show a success ! I am very pleased with you all for last night's work, the bombing parties were splendid. I have also some cheering news to give you. While we were busy holding up the Boche up here at dawn this morning the British and French attacked the Hun in the south on a big front, and first reports state that they have broken through ! "

" Hoorah ! " yelled O'Donnell. " That's something to pay for our do anyhow. Hope we drive them to hell out of it this time, sir ! "

" Well, we all hope so," said our Platoon Commander with a smile. " We shall be going back to Petit Saens to-night and then to the south very probably." He looked over our arms, etc., and left us.

" Aye ! " growled Rodwell gloomily. " Everyone is full of beans when a new show starts. Do you remember Loos last September ? We drove them back all right on the first day, and then we were shot to bits on the Hulluch road ! Yes, we'll go out all right. Fresh drafts will come up, make us up to strength and then into the blood-bath again, with the Army Commander's compliments. I expect our G.O.C. is bloody pleased over last night's do. He'll be counting the ninety-six prisoners we took twice over, writing his reports and observations in triplicate to G.H.Q., and all the lads that went west will be dismissed from his mind as the necessary price of war ! Just pawns to be shot back in the box when finished with, that's all ! "

" We'll never get another like old Marriner," put
in Oldham regretfully, " but we have got to grin and
bear it, boys ; grousing won't help ! "

As darkness fell the remnants of our Battalion took
the road back to Petit Saens, speeded up by a
shower of parting shells from the Boche, who
pestered us with these unwelcome bouquets all the
way down to Bully Grenay.

II

A drink of hot tea from the field cookers as we
trailed in, and then into our previous billets for the
night.

Feverish bustle fell on us with the morning. A
complete renewal of uniforms which were badly
needed. O'Donnell looked like a scarecrow. I
was in no better plight, and Rodwell's clothes
would have disgraced an Oriental beggar, so ragged
and filthy were they. Arms and equipment were
handed in and properly overhauled and the day
passed in ceaseless activity.

A large draft came up in the afternoon. Not a
very impressive lot this time ! Mostly lads of
nineteen, and with little training. With them came
fresh rumours of the battle raging in the south down
by the Somme. It appears that things are going
on well there and that a proper break through in
a big way seems likely.

When everything is over we wend our way down
to Madame's *épicerie*. She is very sorry when she
hears about poor Marriner and is extra specially
nice to us. After an extra special dinner we take our
final leave with mutual regrets.

The civilians in Petit Saens seem very bucked by
the war news, there is a feeling of optimism and
expectancy in the air.

In the crowded " estams." everyone is talking of
our late stunt and the Somme battle.

" We'll knock them stone cold this time, boys ! "

cries O'Donnell, " and if we get down there, by
heck, it's up to us to make them pay for poor old
Bill Marriner ! "

" Aye to that," answers Rodwell heartily ; " as for
the first part, ' wait and see,' as Asquith says."

We turn in early. We'll need all the rest we shall
be able to snatch. At dawn the Orderly Sergeant
rouses us. " Come on, show a leg ! Hand in the
blankets, get everything packed up. All Company
stores to be shoved on the carts at eight." Scurry
and preparations on all sides. A hurried breakfast,
then we roll up the blankets in bundles of ten, clean
the billets, load up the carts and stand ready to
fall in.

Pipes are droning and skirling down the street,
we turn out to see one of the Jock battalions complete with transport and mounted officers swing by.
The men look hardy, bronzed, fit and cheerful, and
make a fine picture with their swinging kilts and
tam-o-shanters. The French, who have a special
love for the Scots, come out on the side-walks to
speed their ancient allies with words of good cheer.
The Division is on the move, the Munster Fusiliers
follow the Scots.

" Down to the Somme, me bhoy, to give old Fritz
socks ! " chortles O'Donnell. " Yus, and to get
blankety well cut up," rejoins Snewin.

We fall in. The Battalion moves off down a main
road and in a new direction. It's a nice, mild July
morning and everyone is cheerful. The raid is
already a thing of the past, everyone is looking
forward to the future confidently. Songs break out,
mouth-organs blare, gaspers are lighted up here
and there and our feet come down steadily and
rhythmically as we eat up the miles. Kilometre
after kilometre down the long straight *pavés*, the
fragrance of grass and new-turned earth coming
sweet to our nostrils.

But for the heavy packs galling our backs it would
be a pleasant jaunt. We halt to eat our dinners by

the wayside straight from the field kitchens, and then on again in the hazy heat.

The day gets warmer and warmer. Sweat runs down our faces and chafes our legs, arms and shoulders, the dust and heat make us dry and thirsty. Our packs become heavy loads. So the long column marches on through the sultry afternoon and men fall silent and tramp on doggedly, heads hanging forward.

" One more river to cross," breaks out Snewin behind us. The column takes it up. Shoulders go back and we swing on with new verve. We breast a slight slope and enter a wide main street lined with low houses, shops, *estaminets* and with civilians looking on expectantly. Our first stage, Mar-les-Mines.

A sharp order. The column comes to a halt. Our Company falls out on one side of the road, packs are taken off and the men sit down. The other Companies move off in various directions. A bit of rest at last while billets are found. We start talking cheerily and light up. Alas, my rest comes quickly to an end.

" E——," calls out the Sergeant-Major. " Leave your pack and rifle and come along ! "

I double up, wondering what dirty job old Mac has in store for me.

" Go up that street," he says, pointing to a side turning, " and find billets for the Company. One house with a mess room for the officers, one for Company office, the Q.M.S. and myself, and about one section in each of all the available houses. Here you are," handing me a slip of paper and a bit of chalk. " Write the Platoon, Company and number of men on every door, and don't be all day about it."

" Right you are, Major, can I have someone to help me out ? " I query, looking towards O'Donnell and Rodwell.

" All right, take your blinking pals along ! " growls Mac.

O'Donnell and Rodwell join me and we plunge up the street and amongst a vociferous crowd of French females.

Every house wants officers naturally. They pay 5 francs a day each—rank and file only 1 franc! And the women try to bargain hard. I have dealt with Indians and sundry Asiatics, with Sicilian curio sellers and others, but never have I met anyone to compare with a Frenchwoman when it comes to a bargain.

With cajolery, artifice and bluff we get through the job quickly. I nail a corking billet for ourselves and Oldham. Real beds, with clean sheets for once, a real stroke of luck!

The Company cookers clatter up and park in the open at the end of the street. The troops move in and all is bustle. Fatigues fall as thick as leaves in Vallombrosa, but our billeting job saves us a lot of dirty work and we three are left to our own devices, so we begin our usual explorations.

The French civilians here are very cheerful and display a more than ordinary cordiality towards us. Apparently the offensive is going on well, and the fact that we are on the way down to the battle makes the Froggies amicable and pleasant. We move about with sundry pats on the back and cheerful smiles from them.

The place is crammed with troops all cheerful and bucked at the prospect of open warfare, all is suppressed excitement and eagerness. We spend a roaring evening in the "estam." playing cards, quaffing wine and free for once from arguments. Early to bed to enjoy the unusual luxury of sheets.

Madame in *numéro* 9, our billet, is a friendly, cheerful gossip. As we come in she invites us into her neat parlour, regales us with excellent coffee, begs some of our tinned rations to send off to her husband, a prisoner in German hands, and plunges into detailed accounts of local scandal and events.

" Ah, Messieurs! For many days now have the

brave soldiers marched in at night to move off on the morrow, on their way to drive the ' sale Boche ' out of our beloved land, and right well we have welcomed them, the brave ' garçons,' but you understand there are things that must not be done. But some of my neighbours ! Oh ! la ! la ! '' throwing her eyes skyward and gesticulating excitedly. " What a scandal ! What a disgrace to our village ! That Madame Boncour ' au numéro ' 25, a shame to all of us ! Her poor husband, ' un bon homme, vous savez,' away on garrison duty on the Loire, and this wretched, abandoned woman here sharing her couch with a different bedfellow every night ! ' C'est incroyable ! ' This harpy, this Circe, casting her evil spells on the soldiers ! ''

We burst out laughing.

" Ha, what a chance poor old Marriner missed ! " mused Rodwell reflectively.

" Bother Madame Boncour ! " remarked Oldham forcibly. " We'd better turn in, lads, we shall be padding the hoof to-morrow," saying which he led the way to bed.

" Come on E——," invited O'Donnell, " let's look at this bally Spellbinder, no use asking Oldham, he is a respectable married man ! "

" Aye, boys—now don't make fools of yourselves," he replies good-humouredly, " I am going to kip right away ! "

The two of us wended our way to *numéro* 25, but a glance at the chalking I'd done on the door halted us in our tracks. I'd billeted Rodway, the Crown and Anchor King, and three other old soldiers from No. 10 Platoon, so Madame would be very much occupied and visitors would be decidedly unwelcome.

We never had the pleasure of beholding this modern Jezebel plying the ancient game, and thus had no opportunity to test the efficacy of her charms except to hear from Rodway that " she was the goods," for next morning after a hurried breakfast we were on our way again and Mar-les-Mines was

left behind us. Knowing the French temperament,
however, I wonder how her husband met the gibes
and mockery that must have surely greeted his
return ! The French are extremely touchy on this
point. One can play up a Froggie in many ways
without much harm. But once the label " cocu "
has been fastened on any man, his life is not worth
living. He appears as a figure of fun and scorn to
the world around him, and once the iron bites deep
he may become quite dangerous. A short march,
and then we piled into railway trucks and off we
went to fields afar and pastures new, down to the
smiling fields of Picardy.

III

All day and through the night we crawled on,
halting at sidings, shunted about. All I recollect
is crowded quarters, heat, the sweaty smell of close-
packed humans, sundry canteens of tea, songs,
laughter, card playing and dozing, with the rumble,
rumble of the wheels continually seeping through
my sleep.

A jerk woke me up in the early murk of morning,
the train had stopped. O'Donnell, like a great
elephant, trod on me as he scrambled forward to
push at the sliding doors. Glorious sunshine
broke upon us and we discovered green, cool-
looking woods all round. We scrambled out, glad
to leave the fugginess and stale air of the trucks.
An alfresco breakfast of strong tea and crisp fried
bacon from the cookers, and we fall in. To our
eyes, accustomed to rest on the dreary surroundings
of slag heaps, destroyed villages and wreckage of
all sorts, the greenery and forest odours seem like
a slice of Paradise. We enjoy the fragrant moment
to the full. The chirping of birds flitting and
fluttering through the trees, the rustle of leaf and
branch swayed by the warm, gentle summer breeze,
the sun's rays piercing through the foliage and

splashing shafts of light here and there. It soothes
our spirits, brings an indescribable sense of repose
to our beings coarsened and blunted on the anvil
of war.

Eventually we fall in again and march off in the
best of humours. Round the corner a small railway
station and a collection of cottages. "Candas"
reads the direction board, as we swing by.

"Ah, this is a nice break, E——," sighs
O'Donnell contentedly, "just like a picnic. I wish
it would go on for ever!"

"Yes, it's the lull before the storm breaks," cuts
in Rodwell. "We'll get our bellies full in a few
days, don't you worry."

Whistling and smoking, we tramp on in these
sylvan surroundings.

Two hours later we march up a tree-lined road
and into a sprawling village of whitewashed houses
with thatched roofs, and a wide, unpaved dusty
street criss-crossed with deep wheel-ruts. Flesselles,
a quiet rural backwater tucked away from the
main stream of life, war, death and turmoil.
Barns, stacks, sheds, peeped here and there. Stray
hens clucked and scampered about. The bray of
a donkey came to my ears. No doubt industrious
peasants are busy at their work as hardly a soul is
to be seen.

The battalion broke off to its appointed billets,
and my Platoon swung through a big doorway and
into a large farmyard surrounded by buildings on all
sides. The familiar midden in the middle with its
sour, steamy manure odour. Pigs grunting and
scuttling about, hens pecking busily in the garbage,
bits of straw everywhere, a heap of rusty farm
implements stacked against a crazy-looking shed
leaning drunkenly by the farther wall.

We march through another doorway and enter a
semi-dark chamber filled with wire beds. Off
come our packs and equipment and we relax thank-
fully. A babel of voices makes itself heard.

Sergeant Wilson comes along as we settle down. " No parades to-day, boys. Just take it quietly, we move off again to-morrow ! "

" Well, that's that ! " remarks Rodwell. " Another island of quiet before the blue-eyed boys grapple with the tyrant foe ! Come on, E——, let's have a look round ! Drop your blinking note-book, you Irish madman," as he notices O'Donnell fumbling in his haversack for paper and pencil. " No writing, only looking to-day, come on ! "

" All right, you half-baked lawyer ! " answers O'Donnell, good-humouredly. " Have yer way ! Lead the way, E—— ! "

We stroll out in the yard, idly watching our comrades busy at sundry jobs. One is already washing under the pump, watched with amazed interest by a couple of dirty urchins. A wizened-faced, elderly Frenchman, dressed in better clothes than the average labourer, evidently the *proprietaire*, is flitting about anxiously scanning the soldiery. I approach him and enquire in French what his trouble may be.

" Oh, thank God someone understands me at last ! " he cried with a sigh of relief. " I am looking for the officer. I want him to place a guard over my cellar ' en bas ' ! " indicating a door at the side. " I have a little wine stored there and, what do you think ? The men of the Battalion that rested here yesterday went down the cellar and looted four bottles ! " he said bitterly.

I laughed inwardly. I could imagine the feelings of chagrin and anger agitating his soul. To a thrifty French peasant such loss seems worse than having a couple of teeth extracted. His avaricious being shudders at the thought that someone has been able to trick him so barefacedly.

" What the dickens does he want, E—— ? "

" Only a guard to look after his confounded wine."

" Well, let him look for one. Leave him alone," said Rodwell crossly. " It's nothing to do with us."

" Wait a minute, I'll take him over to old Mac.

He'll fix him ! " and, turning to the Frenchman :
" Come along, Monsieur, I will take you to our
Sergeant-Major. He will advise what can be done
about a guard ! "

" Merci, Monsieur," he replied. " You are very
kind, I will not forget ! "

" You are a chump, E——, to waste your time
over that scarecrow ! " said Rodwell disgustedly.
" What do you think you'll get out of it ? "

" Oh, perhaps a bottle or two. Anyhow, it won't
do us any harm ! "

" Bottle of wine, eh ? " he answered sarcastically.
" I can just see it coming. Have you ever heard of a
Frenchman who gives away something for nothing ? "

" Oh well, never mind ! If he goes and sees the
Skipper we might drop in for a guard. So we'd
better try and head them away from that somehow ! "

" Sure, E—— is right ! " chimed in O'Donnell.
" Let's take old skin and bones along to Mac ! "

The Sergeant-Major shared a dark-looking den
with the Q.M.S., and the whole place was a dump for
the Company dunnage.

" Major," I said, stepping in, " here's a Froggy
wanting a guard over his wine-cellar ! "

" What ! " roared out old Mac, glaring about like
a tiger. " Does he think we are a lot of blasted night
watchmen ? You just tell him it can't be done. Let
him mount guard himself, or go to hell for all I
care ! "

" What does the Sergeant say ? " queried the
Frenchman, anxiously hopping about like a cat on
hot bricks.

" He will see the officer and inform you," I
replied, as a brilliant idea flashed across my mind.
" I am the interpreter, and will come presently and
tell you what the arrangements made are ! "

" Ah ! Merci, Monsieur ! " he replied gratefully.
" You are very kind," and ambled off to keep a wary
eye on the cellar.

" Hey, E——, what are you up to at all ? " asked
O'Donnell as we still lingered near the Sergeant-
Major's door. " What do you think you are going
to do ? "

" Let's find Oldham, and I'll put you wise ! "
I answered, winking and grinning.

We found old Oldham and then I propounded the
scheme.

" Look here," I said, " we are marching off in the
morning. No guard will be put on that cellar, unless
we find an unofficial guard ! "

" Have you gone dotty ? " enquired Rodwell.
" D'ye think I am going to waste my time guarding
a lousy cellar just to oblige a confounded Frenchman ? "

" Now, look here," I explained, " that cellar is
full of wine. The lads in the Company could do
with some, so could we. Suppose we mount a guard,
and I tell the Frenchman that some cases with rations
are to be put in the cellar if a guard is mounted, and
that I have to have free access to them, what's to
prevent my filling them up with bottles and carrying
them out under his very nose early in the morning,
eh ? "

" Eh, lad," remarked Oldham admiringly, " you'd
make a high-class burglar ! "

" Well, Oldham, you are an N.C.O., you'll mount
the guard and be in charge."

" Eh ? I'd get court-martialled if I got found out ;
talk sense ! "

" I'll tip old Mac the wink, and you know how he
loves the Froggies. Leave it to me ! " I answered.
With that I ambled into old Mac again.

" Sergeant-Major, my pals and I have agreed to
look after that cellar for the Froggy," I said, keeping
a straight face. " Will it be all right ? "

Old Mac looked at me for an instant with astonish-
ment, and then :

" God help that Froggy if you blokes are going to
guard anything ! " he said feelingly. " You can do

what you like, but mind, this won't take your names
off the duty roster ! "

" Can I have some empty cases, Sergeant-Major ? "
was my next question.

" What are you going to do with them ? "

" Store them in the cellar till the morning ! "
I answered with a grin.

A light broke in the Sergeant-Major's mind, the
Q.M.S. leaned forward interestedly.

" Well, of all the cheek ! " ejaculated old Mac.
" Still, these miserly Frenchmen deserve what they
get. All right, E——, take the boxes. I don't want
to hear anything else ! "

I sped back to the Frenchman.

" There will be one sentry put on for the day," I
said to him, " but during the night you will have to
guard the cellar yourself. Also, it is asked whether
ration-boxes can be stored there until the morning ! "

" Certainly, Monsieur, I am very grateful, and I
hope you will accept a small bottle of champagne ! "
he answered. " For the night I do not mind, it is
in the day when wine disappears ! "

I now elaborated the scheme. Oldham solemnly
placed Rodwell on guard by the cellar door, of
course in fatigue order, then getting hold of
Maddocks, Snewin and O'Donnell we collected
two empty bully beef cases and solemnly staggered
with them down into the cellar, the Frenchman
hovering in the background. The cellar ran under
the whole building, and was lined with crates and
bins holding thousands of bottles and with huge
vats and barrels of wine. A veritable toper's delight !

The Frenchman was extraordinarily generous. He
actually gave me a bottle of " bubbly " for myself
and treated the " guard " to another.

For a while I left matters thus. The men slept
most of the morning, their repose only disturbed
by a foot inspection. In the heavy, sleepy hours of
the afternoon, while M. le Propriétaire, his soul at
rest about his precious wines, was busy on his lawful

occasions, I slipped down the cellar, which O'Donnell was now guarding, and filled up the empty ration-cases with champagne, Chablis, and whatever I could lay hands on. Seventy-two bottles in each case just gave room for the lids to be rammed home and fastened down.

Leaving everything ship-shape, I returned above.

Night fell, candles were lit and cards came out. For several hours we indulged in rummy, till at length the Orderly Sergeant came around to douse the lights and inform us as to the next day's orders, after which we lay down on our pellets and sank into the deep sleep of healthy men.

We roused at four and prepared our equipment and arms for the march. In the hurly-burly I got my fatigue party ready, and with Maddocks, Unwin and Rodwell made for the cellar.

The Frenchman was already astir and alert, keeping a wary eye on the bustling troops.

" Ah, bonjour, Monsieur ! " I greeted. " Will you permit us to go down the cellar and remove the store-cases ? "

" Mais oui ! I will fetch a lantern and light your way ! " he replied. He soon reappeared carrying a smoky storm-lantern, and down into the cellar we went. A couple of the boys to each box, and the two cases, heavy with their precious cargo, were hauled up carefully, while I chattered to the *proprietaire* affably.

As we came out I said to him casually : " It were better to lock the door now. You understand, in this confusion it would be easy to slip down there for a little wine ! "

" C'est vrai, Monsieur," he replied. " I shall do so now, and thank you for all your kind help ! "

In triumph we entered our quarters with the cases. These were soon opened and the booty distributed throughout the Company. We did not forget old Mac or the Q.M.S., and a few bottles were passed on to the Company Officer's batman, to reach our

Skipper as an anonymous contribution to the mess. Presently breakfast, then a quick inspection, and out we moved in the glorious morning sunshine, the proprietor at the door watching our departure and waving good-bye.

In the best of spirits the troops swung out on to the main road, and soon Flesselles was behind us.

Away from Flesselles the story of the wine became common property in the Company, and many were the conjectures as to the Frenchman's reaction when he discovered his loss.

" I reckon old skin and bones will have a fit and die on the spot ! " chuckled O'Donnell.

" God help the next lot of troops that billet there ! " observed Rodwell. " He'll keep even his pigs under lock and key, and will make 'em pay for water, to make up on the wine."

" Serve the lousy miser right," cut in Maddocks. " He was mingy over a couple of bottles, and now he's lost more'n hundred ! Ha, ha, ha ! "

We marched on cheerfully, each man with a bottle of wine in his pack, worth more to us than the famous field-marshal's baton legend says may be found there !

A bend in the road and we presently debouched into a main road, and all our sylvan peace was left behind. As far as the eye could see along its tree-lined length there was a continual stream of traffic moving in two directions. In the warm morning sun the scene was unforgettable and interesting.

Here was one of the main arteries leading away to the front.

Motor-lorries loaded with stores tore past. End-less lines of troops tramping on. Guns, guns and yet more guns. Field artillery harnessed to mules clattered by, huge howitzers with caterpillar tractors, their squat snouts pointing skywards, rumbled slowly on their way. Motor-cyclists dashed by in a swirl of dust and noise. On the other a continual stream of ambulances, empty lorries and, once or twice, groups of German prisoners with their escorts. Dusty-looking, some trudging along dejectedly, others with I-don't-care-a-damn air. Tall, short, stout and lean, in caps, bareheaded, steel-helmeted, on the whole, hefty-looking brutes. Some had hopeless, frightened eyes and puckered brows. They must have had a hell of a time, judging by their appearance.

The sight bucked our fellows immensely. Here was tangible proof that the battle was going on well. These groups of prisoners meant that our lads were on the move all right!

The long stream of ambulances pointed the same moral, but as their inmates were out of sight we did not look too closely on this side of the question.

A dull, continual rumble came to us from over the far horizon. We were getting nearer and nearer to the realm of Mars. But, above all, one thing stood out.

These long columns of fresh troops seemed keen. They moved with a swing, an eagerness that betokened confidence. Songs were echoing down the long *pavé*, and an air of exhuberant optimism could be discerned.

All morning we tramped, sometimes halting to let heavier traffic go by. We passed many glades and nooks, all alive with troops bivouacking and throwing sundry questions as we swung by.

" It looks a big thing all right," said Rodwell. " The troops are as thick as ants, and we must be miles behind yet."

" Old Fritz doesn't seem to have much aircraft floating about," cut in O'Donnell. " Just fancy all this traffic in daylight on the Ypres salient ! "

He had hardly spoken when the hum of motors in the sky caused us to look upwards at three machines sailing majestically in the blue, white and dazzling in the sun's glare. We could faintly discern their red, white and blue rings. Ours ! Bent on some errand or other. No wonder the Boche was keeping low! They slowly disappeared over that far horizon, where guns muttered and men laboured bloodily.

For hours our feet beat in rhythmical unison, and we moved up that interminable highway, dusty, thirsty and sweaty, but full of vim and vigour, for the varied busy sights around us, the traffic, the troops, the guns, all proclaimed in unmistakable terms that the British Army, after two weary years of position warfare, undermanned and out-gunned, was at long last leaping forward at the enemy, fresh and dauntless, its ranks filled with the best material that a soldier can wish for—enthusiastic, high-mettled young men, whom love of country had summoned from the four corners of the world.

This highway was a veritable processional route of the British race. The ceaseless stream of Yorkshiremen, Welshmen, Scots, Irish, South Africans, men from Cornwall and the Fen Country, battalions of short, sturdy fellows from the great industrial centres, ploughboys, miners, clerks, students, labourers, pioneers from rough Colonial backwoods and the products of public school and Varsity, marching cheek by jowl in a comradeship cemented by a common purpose and a mutual respect, welded these representatives of the various rungs of our social ladder into a vital, harmonious whole such as the wild, fantastic theories of political tub-thumpers, social reformers and scatter-brained and unbalanced dreamers and theoreticians will never achieve. For this mass of Britain's splendid youth, marching onward into battle with a song on its lips and a steadfast courage, represented reality and all that was best in our race, and hall-marked the age-old truth that the way to the stars lies through selfless sacrifice.

This vision of radiant manhood tramping undaunted towards the life-searing heat of the flame of conflict, impressed itself deeply on my receptive mind, and has ever remained a symbol to strive after. . . . Unity born of understanding, achievement through mutual striving ! This the pregnant message that those about to die flung to the legions that would follow them. Will it ever be understood, I wonder ?

The sounds of the cannonade became plainer as we forged ahead. The sky became overcast with clouds, the atmosphere heavy and clammy. In a whirl of dust we swung off the highway into another group of mean-looking cottages huddled together on the edge of the high road. Wherever the eye ranged, troops, ration-carts, dumps, horses, guns, the very workshop of Ares and Vulcan ! Whistles shrilled out, companies deployed and the Battalion halted.

The usual helter-skelter, orders being bandied about, and the Platoon moves into a cleared space, squats down and waits for its dinner.

" Phew ! It's bloody hot ! " ejaculated Rodwell, while O'Donnell, grumbling like a soul in torment, is hiked off by the Orderly Corporal to fetch the stew dixy from the cooker.

Dinner is soon over, we relax where we are, lying content for the nonce to forget everything and wallow in that pleasant feeling of utter comfort that overtakes a fellow after a particularly warm and weary march.

Sergeant Wilson appears amongst us, and we cock a wary eye on him.

" All packs will be handed in to Battalion store at three o'clock, and your overcoats. We will march off in battle order. Ground sheets in the haversack. All spare kit will be left with the packs, which are to be stacked by platoons. Any man who wants his boots, arms or equipment seen to report to the Quartermaster at once."

" I say, Rodwell," I remark, " this looks like ' business as usual ' almost at once ! "

" I should say so," cuts in O'Donnell, who, his fatigue over, has recovered his equanimity. " I'll have to go and see old Robo. I've lost my canteen lid somehow, and my trench-tool handle is split ! "

" Come on, then," I said, rising. " Might as well tap him for a new ground sheet, mine's part worn ! "

We rose and strolled across to where, by the battalion transport, the Q.M. had set up his realm. Rodwell accompanied us. Bearding Captain Robinson, the Quartermaster, was a terrifying experience for new men, though a very amusing interlude to folk like ourselves.

The Quartermaster had been a regimental character for many years. Big, stout, red-faced, with a voice like the roar of a wild bull, he loved to terrify the unlucky wight who came to him for odd necessaries. However, he was all bark and no bite, and a jolly good fellow once one knew his little ways.

As we approached his temporary office, made up of bully beef and biscuit cases, ammunition-boxes and sundry tarpaulins, with the whole regimental litter strewn all round, carts, mules and horses, amongst these " Coal Box," our battalion mascot, a diminutive pony the battalion had captured from the Boche in the early days of the War, and a particular pet of the Quartermaster's, we heard his voice raised to the heavens.

A small group of men stood before the entrance. Mostly new draft men, uncomfortably ill at ease. Then we caught sight of Robo yelling at an undersized, trembling wretch of a man in shirt-sleeves.

" So you've lost your tunic, eh ? " he howled sarcastically, his face mottling up and shoving his chin forward threateningly. " You went to help the cooks, and left your tunic on your pack—and now it's gone," with a huge bellow. " Do you think I am a blankety wet nurse ? Hell, some of you blokes would lose the eyes out of your head and never know ! I've half a mind to get you pegged for being such a bloody fool. Here," as he saw the look of sheer frightened misery in the man's eyes, " get

hold of this," flinging him a tunic, " and GET OUT ! "
he roared at him.

The fellow made a grab, snatched the tunic up
and flew as if the very legions of hell were after
him.

We hung back, enjoying the fun. Old Robo waxed
eloquent with each of his unfortunate customers.
They certainly got their stuff, but retreated, crushed
and dismayed, vowing in forcible and unprintable
language that they'd take jolly good care to have as
little to do with the Battalion ogre as possible !
Probably there was method in old Robo's unconven-
tional system. It discouraged carelessness, and made
the men careful of their gear.

" Yes," he said, eyeing another victim contemptuously, " I'll come and tuck you in bed,
shall I ? You lose your buttons every few days, and
then have the cheek to come to me for more ! Here,
let's have a look ! Unbutton your tunic ! "

" I . . . I . . . can't, sir ! " stammered the man, a
lanky, miserable-looking fellow. " It only buttons
up at the top ! "

" What ? " roared out the Quartermaster. " What
do you mean ? "

Reluctantly the tunic was opened, disclosing the
fact that apart from the top button the others were
held on to the tunic by bits of match-sticks.

We thought for a moment that the Q.M. would
have a fit. He goggled, heaved and stammered, then :

" Oh, Lord," he yelled appealingly, towering over
the shrinking Rifleman like an avenging angel,
" what can I do with these damn idiots. Call yourself a soldier ? " he cried fiercely. " Here, Corporal,
give him a needle and thread and make him sew his
buttons on again ! " and turning to the man : " If
you ever come to me for buttons again, God help
you ! "

This encounter exhausted him. The thought that
a man in his beloved Battalion was using match-
sticks to keep his buttons on unnerved him, so when

we came forward with our requests we got them with unusual ease.

" Old Robo is all right," chuckled O'Donnell, " except with bloody fools ! "

All the afternoon we rested in the open. After tea, on Oldham's suggestion, we scouted around the houses, for as that cautious Lancastrian put it : " It's the last chance we may have for weeks of getting fresh rations. We'd better pool our money and buy up all we can carry."

We discovered a house turned into a temporary shop crowded with men bent on the same errand. A slatternly woman was busily serving and striving to understand that medley of English, pidgin-French and occasional Hindustani words that served as the soldier's lingua franca.

" Go on, E——, push in," encouraged Rodwell, shoving me forward, " chuck your French at her and get going ! "

The advantage of knowledge stood me in good stead. Yelling above the babel of sound that filled the small room, jostling and shoving through the crowd, I caught the woman's attention and proceeded to shop. Eggs, sardines, chocolate, sugar, coffee, long French loaves, some doubtful-looking *jambon* apples made up our purchases. They would serve to eke out the hard tack that we expected for the next few days.

Back to the Platoon to pack our haversacks, and just as we are about to fall in we see some tired, wan-faced and ragged-looking men appear from the highway. Manchesters, by their badges, but not of those marching up. Their listlessness and general appearance proclaims them as survivors.

We yell out to them :

" Eh, boys, is it bad up there ? "

" My God, you'll soon see ! " answers a youngster as he staggers by with torn uniform and a far-away look in his eyes. "The Hun is fighting for every inch of ground and his bloody machine-guns are murder ! This is a whole company, the rest is in front of Fricourt ! "

We look again. One officer—a full lieutenant— about five N.C.O.s and forty men or so.

" Whew," whistles Rodwell, " they must have caught it hot ! "

" Fall in ! " shouts Sergeant Wilson suddenly. We take our places. Mr. Walker appears, and at the order the Platoon, minus packs and in battle order, moves down into the high road, joins the Company and we are on the move again. The weather has changed—a few drops of rain begin to spatter down —and a storm seems to be gathering in the offing. Wheeled traffic has decreased a lot and only long columns of men, with an odd ambulance clattering by now and again, occupy the road. As we march forward the sound of continual gun-fire gets louder and louder. As usual, the Battalion is breaking into song. It is rather curious what tunes men fasten on. Observers, unaware of the waywardness and humorous streak of the British " Tommy," might deduce all sorts of wrong ideas from his chanties. For instance, " A " Company, ahead of us, breaks out into a Revivalist tune, we all take it up and sing it lustily :

> " The bells of Hell are ting-aling-alingling
> For you, but not for me,
> For me the angels are sing aling-alingling
> They've got the goods for me,
> Oh, Death, where is thy sting-alingling,
> Oh, grave, thy victory,
> The bells of Hell are ting-aling-alingling
> For you, but not for me ? "

Rain does not dampen our spirits, we trudge on, our feet ringing on the hard *pavé*. It is now getting dark. On the other side of the road columns of men, returning from the front, are coming through. Weary and worn with the stress and dust of days of hard scrapping, lousy, tattered, but confident, they have the energy of breaking into song as they march by. Pitiful remnants of splendid battalions they look. The small scattered groups, scantily officered, looking forward to rest, reconditioning and a few days of fleeting comfort.

They may grouse and grumble, but their high quality and morale are unimpaired. " The Army of to-day's all right," to quote a well-known music-hall ditty.

Darkness deepens, the rain increases, still we move on. At times blocks ahead halt us, growls and swears down the column as movement ceases, then on again.

Presently, through the gloom, houses appear here and there, and we are tramping through a biggish town, wrecked and shattered by shell-fire.

" This is Albert," says O'Donnell. " It looks as if it had had a rough house ! "

Houses here and there are mere shells, some façades still putting on a brave front, just like many people who appear prosperous and kindly but inside are rotten to the very core. We pass what must have been a factory, iron girders and bits of machinery standing gaunt in the gloom, and we swing into the square.

On one side a church badly damaged by gun-fire, with a tall spire, gapped here and there where a shell has struck, towering up into the gloom, and from the top, bent at right angles and looking down towards the ground, a huge statue of Our Lady with the Infant Christ in her arms. Notre Dame des Brebieres, famed over the whole battle-front. There's a current legend that when the statue finally crashes the war will end—who knows ?

As we pass by underneath it seems to me as if the Virgin is stretching out and blessing the columns of passing men, giving them assurance that while there is tribulation, strife and death in the world beneath, the gates of Bliss lie beyond our material horizon.

O'Donnell, reckless as he may be, but a devout Catholic, crosses himself.

We trudge through the dark, rubble-covered streets of Albert, half unreal in the darkness, and out beyond, the rain now beating at us and running down in rivulets from our ground sheets, draped round shoulders and heads. Singing has died down. The rumble of the guns is now strong, and a strange rosy glare lights the sky where it merges with the ground beyond. We are entering the immediate back area of the battle-line, and dumps, trucks, railway lines and occasional hastily-filled shell-holes are much in evidence. The gleam of candles here and there betokens shelters. Gangs of men pass by loaded with stores, and a sudden noisy crash, followed by the swish of speeding shells, marks the heavy battery positions.

We grope along for another hour or so on unfamiliar, gradually ascending ground. Go up one dip and down another. Dimly we make out clumps of thick trees, thickets and small woods.

" Where the hell are we making for ? " growls Rodwell crossly. " Oh, blast the rain ! "

" God only knows," answers O'Donnell, " but we shall get there all the same."

Eventually we debouch on a bare hill-side sloping down and away into a plain, and we can dimly make out the shape of trench-lines.

" Halt ! " comes the order. We do. Mr. Walker comes along and pauses.

" The men will have to lie down here till the morning, Sergeant ! " he says. And turning to us : " You will have to make the best of it and try to rig up bivouacs. Do not go very far out."

We look around in the gloom. Far away Very lights are rising and falling on a ridge that rings the horizon right round us. Behind, on the hill-side, a mass of trees sloping away towards the road we came up, and on the other, lost in darkness.

" This is a nice go," says Rodwell disgustedly, " raining like hell, no overcoats and the ground al sopping wet ! "

However, as our eyes grow accustomed to the surroundings, we notice that the whole hill-side is
littered with empty artillery ammunition boxes.

Oblivious to the rain we move as near to the
sheltering bushes as possible, quickly pile boxes
together and then, chucking our ground sheets over
us, we crawl in our improvised shelters ; and despite
the noise of the artillery strafe, heedless of the
drizzling rain, cold wind now blowing and all other
discomforts, we plunge into that restful slumber that
Nature gives bountifully as an antidote to the stress
and wear of life.

CHAPTER FIVE

I

" COME on, E——! Tumble out! Are you going to sleep all day?" I heard O'Donnell's voice question close to me. I wriggled about, flung off the damp waterproof sheet that covered me like a shroud, and sat up, my effort causing the hastily-built ammunition-box shelter to sway and rock ominously.

My first conscious impressions were a glare of sunshine, and an intermittent boom of guns that set my ear-drums throbbing. I crawled out of the shelter and looked around me. Oldham, Rodwell and O'Donnell were already astir, and I could see that the rest of the Platoon were busily engaged at their first task of coaxing fires into being.

We appeared to be on the top of a slope mostly overgrown with patchy rank grass, with bare muddy patches tramped down here and there where men's feet had trod.

Behind us, and running down the incline where the ground dipped and fell to the road, rose clumps of scrub interspersed with trees, through whose trunks one could obtain glimpses of a big white house peeping through the tangle of greenery—a country mansion of some pretence, judging by its size.

But what focused my attention and held my gaze was the view spread before me. It reminded me of a scene worthy of a Detaille or a Caton Woodville.

Dropping below my feet to a valley, and then rising gently for hundreds of yards in front, was a plain, pock-marked with shell-holes, and with irregular, hummocky remains of trench-lines, crowned in the distance by dense bunches of green clumps, and the gaunt skeletons of broken trees. Away on my right front I could glimpse the outline of a main road, with broken brickwork and a wall or two denoting a village. On my extreme right another spur with more broken evidence of houses.

The extreme horizon, blocked by scattered patches

of half-destroyed woods, with a pall of smoke and
spouts of dust crowning them, was reverberating and
pulsing to the shock of a bombardment, whip-like
cracks, trails of black smoke appearing low in the
sky. Shrapnel !

And below me the evidence of the movement of
war, strange to my eyes, accustomed to the limited
and circumscribed boundaries of trenches.

The hill-side is alive with the men of our Company
clustered in little groups of twos and threes, busy
breaking up and chopping wood with trench tool
and bayonet, lighting little fires and brewing their
breakfast tea. Others are putting up " bivvys " by
lacing two or three waterproof sheets together and
constructing frail shelters with branches, bits of
wire and ammunition boxes. At the bottom, in the
valley there is a line of gun-pits well sand-bagged ;
now and again squat ugly-looking muzzles are
momentarily visible. They are howitzers and are
chucking up shells continually. Farther up some
limbers are trotting about, and quite a motley crowd
of men of all regiments are moving about quite
freely over the battle-field and towards the rising
ground on the horizon. Another line staggers down
along the cart track that meanders away in my
immediate front and joins the road on my right.
The white bandages dazzling in the sunshine and
their uncertain gait identify them easily. Wounded
men !

" Jump along, E——, here's some tea ! " yells
Rodwell from nearby.

I turn and make for a fire where Oldham,
O'Donnell and Rodwell are busily foregathered.

" Faith, this seems a fine sort of show ! " opens
out O'Donnell cheerfully. " Looks as if old Fritz
is advancing backwards ! "

" Oh, leave the bloody war alone and have some
tea, you mad Irishman ! " interrupts Rodwell.
" Tuck in and close your trap ! "

" Well, boys, and what may this place be ? " I ask.

"It's called Becourt," answers Oldham. "Yon village on the main road was La Boiselle, the valley down there is Sausage Valley; that's Fricourt away on the right and that wood up there is Bailiff Wood," pointing, "t'other is Round Wood and there's a sunken road in betwen 'em. There's a powerful lot of field batteries out by the sunken road and the edge of the woods."

"It looks like business all right!" I answer.

Sergeant Wilson materializes from thin air.

"Listen, men. We are here in reserve. Likely to be called on any time after two o'clock to-day, so get your gear cleaned up and ready, and don't wander away too far!"

"Can we get across as far as the field guns, Sergeant?" asked Rodwell.

"Yes, if there are no fatigues!" he answered drily.

"We'll make sure about that," said O'Donnell with a look at his retreating back. "Let's run up a proper bivvy, dump our equipment and have a look round."

"Yes," I answered, interestedly looking across the torn and humped expanse before me, "this ought to be pretty interesting. The salvage people haven't touched much yet."

We found an ideal pitch for our shelter near some bushes, scrounged around for artillery boxes, and soon we had run up a snug shelter. And all the while we worked, without pause or truce, the throbbing booming sound of the guns went on, and on the horizon over and beyond the trees those geysers of smoke, earth and dust rose and fell like volcanoes in constant eruption.

Oldham presently went off to draw the section's rations for the day, while we put the last finishing touches to our bivouac. Fossicking about I dis-covered that behind the brush screening the top of the hill a deep shelter trench complete with funk-holes had been dug.

Oldham ambled back, our "whack" of the rations was stored away, and then, donning our steel helmets and with our gas bags slung over our shoulders, we descended the slope warily lest some non-com. grabbed us for some unpleasant duty or other.

The whole way down a litter of broken artillery ammunition-boxes ; empty shell-cases were scattered higgledy-piggledy and the whole ground heaving to the shock of the guns firing from the pits.

At the bottom all is frantic activity and rush. Artillery men stripped to the waist, smoke-grimed, are busy about the battery. These are 6-inch howitzers, their muzzles appearing and disappearing over the sand-bagged front of their emplacements. The whole atmosphere is hazing and teetering as if it were a solid, every time the shells speed away on their fell errands.

A Battery Sergeant-Major is yelling through a megaphone, giving ranges. Telephones are buzzing and everyone is busy. Shell-cases tinkle out as the sweating gunners unload and others ram a fresh shell in the breech.

"At seven thousand," yells an officer's voice somewhere. "Same objective—Battery fire ! "

We scramble by between two pits, pick our way carefully over a littered miniature railway line and breast the slight rise cluttered with burst sand-bags, clumps of bushes, wire and chunks of wood. Behind us shells whizz into the sky with the roar and swish of express trains.

We top the rise and move on over undulating ground, keeping at the edge of a cart track that winds over and away towards the distant sunken road and right across the battle-ground of the previous days.

"It's rum to be walkin' like this in the open," comments Rodwell, "with the lads fighting like hell a couple of miles or so in front ! "

The day is blazing hot. Over the tangle of trees

and broken houses by Albert a couple of observation balloons hang in the sky like monstrous swollen sausages. Away on our right a flicker of dazzling white high up, surrounded by the spreading cloud-lets of Archie bursts, denotes one of our planes on observation bent.

We are now scrambling over what must have been the British front-line trenches, a maze of humps and hillocks, half-filled-in ditches, mounds of faded and burst sand-bags, barbed wire clumps sticking out here and there, shell-holes, smashed trench-boards and a litter of rusty tins, pieces of equipment, broken rifles and goodness knows what else. We strike out into what was once no-man's-land, a welter of confused destruction and shell-holes.

Here all the casualties have not been gathered in yet, and horrible-looking bundles in khaki, once men, still lie in shell-holes.

We pass one close in a shell-hole by the cart track. Lying on his back, his steel helmet half concealing his blackened features. Clothing all awry, legs drawn up. Must have been hit some-where in the stomach. A storm of fat buzzing flies hovers over this poor wreckage of humanity. We hurry by, averting our faces.

" Time they took all these poor blighters in," mutters Oldham.

" Too busy collecting boots and hipes," answers Rodwell, pointing to a salvage party stacking arms farther away. " They can sell them to the Jew contractors at ten bob a bag, and the rifles can be reconditioned. As for the men, they are finished with and can wait ! "

We scrambled on past all the pitiful litter and on to that gash of chalky hummocks and dirty bags running across our front that had been the German front trench.

Here the havoc was unimaginable and stood revealed in all its ghastly details under the rays of the bright sun. A strange, mephitic, undescribable smell hung about here like a tangible pall. Bodies were numerous, twisted in all the attitudes of death. Quite a lot of ours—Lincolns, Scots, Yorks, mostly in shell-holes before the trench. This itself was practically flattened out, bags all down and destroyed, but here and there the openings of dug-outs stood unharmed.

Bloated, grey-clad figures littered the whole place. Some crouching against the sides, some lying stark and still, sightless eyes staring up at the blue vault of heaven. One dead German on a stretcher with bandages all over him, by a dug-out entrance.

And all around a litter of uniforms, torn overcoats, accoutrements, tangles of barbed wire, letters and packs of cards scattered all over.

A wrecked and overturned machine-gun with two or three dead Huns by it at one angle of the bay. A crazy direction board with big Gothic letters, " Graben II." Helmets, caps, bayonets, all the flotsam of an army.

" Good Lord ! It must have been a hell of a hot show judging by all this ! " muttered Rodwell, staring at this scene of wanton destruction with bulging eyes. " Let's have a look in the dug-outs ! "

We moved along the wrecked trench. Farther on a small group of officers and some salvage men were fossicking around.

We descended a few dark steps into a dug-out, but we quickly sought the open air again. It was a shambles of dead humanity !

Across towards the patches of woodland, that I later learned was Shelter Wood, the trail of the battle tide was much the same. It looked as if a hard fight had been waged here all right.

The dead, swollen bodies of the Germans bore mostly the same shoulder numeral—111th Regiment.

We foraged around for a while picking up a few of the usual mementoes. Most of the letters were still damp, the rain had smudged the ink and the letters were running over all the page. Still some were faintly decipherable. What misery, what heart searchings were contained perhaps in some of them. And their owners ? Mostly littering this stricken field. We picked up a few scraps here and there and attempted to decipher a few words. Both O'Donnell and I had a nodding acquaintance with German. " Liebechen," read one, " I am writing under the roar of guns which never ceases. For one week now the British have been bombarding constantly. We expect their attack at any time. We have been ordered to hold our trenches at all costs, so pray the good God . . ." and there the fragment ended. Many others were in a similar strain, and we quite visualized what a hell it must have been for them.

We continued our scouting about for some time and moved on forward, gingerly picking our way through the wreck of the positions.

" It feels strange to move in the German line like this," said Oldham, " but come on, boys, it's getting on ; we'd better go back."

" All right, I think we've seen enough to give us an idea," chimed in Rodwell. " I'm quite fed up looking at all this mess."

In front of us, and running parallel to a sunken road that seemed to run right across from Fricourt to La Boisselle, our field guns were strung out in one continuous line and were blazing away like mad, drawn up just behind sandbags and sketchy gun-pits, and many of them right out in the open, wheel to wheel. A wonderful sight seen in the broad glare of late morning, with the gun crews blackened and sweating, working with increasing ardour. And across the open ammunition-limbers were trotting up. It seemed incredible that the enemy did nothing in retaliation.

We began to retrace our steps back towards Becourt and the bivouacs, pausing now and again when something arrested our attention.

Half-way back we overtook a couple of Jocks with

fixed bayonets escorting a prisoner back, one Jock holding him by one arm. The German's head was bandaged, and blood was seeping through.

As we got abreast I heard him mutter : " Wasser, Wasser, bitte ! "

" Hey, Jock," I cried to one of his escort, " give the blighter a drink, he's asking for water."

" Och, aye, I thoct he waur mouthin' something in his unco' tongue," replied the Jock, and unstrapping his bottle, " here, mon, take a guid drink." The German drank gratefully and sighed with content.

As we followed on both I and O'Donnell plied him with questions.

He was a Württemburger from the 122nd Regiment.

" Ah, ' Kamaraden,' it has been hell," he gasped. " Some of us have been cut off by this awful bombardment in some trenches in front of Contalmaison over there for four days. No food ; no water could get to us through the curtain of fire. Choked and half-buried with mounds of our dead and wounded comrades ringing us in. And then your attacks. ' Ach ! ' " he shuddered. " Nothing can live and remain sane ! "

" Oh, well your troubles are over now ! " I told him encouragingly. " At least you know that you will survive all this ! "

" ' Ach,' that is so, but, ' dieser verfluchter Krieg.' What a pity, what a pity ! " and he shook his head.

" Ah, lad, " said Rodwell in English, as we told him what the Hun said, " we're all in the same boat. We are the victims of a wholesale murder ! "

" Come off it, Rodwell," said I, jokingly. " No ase being glum. Anyhow, we're winning ! "

" Yes, winning ! " he rejoined scathingly. " Winning what ? You mark my words, if we ever live o see the end of this, we'll soon find out how we've en tricked ! "

By this time we were nearly back on the bottom of the valley and, leaving the Jocks to move on with their prisoner, we moved up to our bivouac.

II

Back at bivouac we began to prepare our dinner. Most of the Company were at the same job, or were sitting down in groups playing cards, furbishing arms and equipment or simply talking or resting.

At the bottom of the incline where the hill met the road, the Battalion office had been established, and we caught a glimpse of Colonel Bircham's soldierly figure as he emerged with the adjutant and proceeded towards the house in the trees.

Just after dinner, Captain Sherlock, Mr. Walker, with the Sergeant-Major, made their appearance amongst the bivouacs, had a good look round and moved off. The shelling was going on with just the same fury, but by now we scarcely paid any heed to it.

Presently O'Donnell and Rodwell began their everlasting war wrangle, and for a few idle moments Oldham and I listened interestedly.

"I tell you, Rodwell," cried O'Donnell excitedly. "The Boche is about beat. Another week or two of this and we'll have him broken and on the run. Then the cavalry will burst through and we'll roll him back into Germany, by gob!"

"Sounds fine," retorted Rodwell, "and then I suppose the bands will begin to play, and we'll go back and people will come out with 'Welcome' placards, I don't think!" and then fiercely: "I wish you'd wake up, Don. I can't understand you. You've had eighteen months of this ghastly business and you still talk like the headlines in a Blighty paper. As for me, I'm sick of it all. Of the blood, the mess, the lice, the whole bloody thing. And I know that when I get back, if I do, and will try to get a job, because after this my law studies will be done for, some fat, smug, comfortable blighter, who all the time has been making money at our expense, will turn round and say : ' Ah, a job. Let me see. What experience ? Killing men—soldiering. Ah ! That is all over now, we must get back to serious work. You realize you cannot command a high salary. Ah, well, you can start as we all do. A few shillings until you are experienced, and mind we don't like the rough, free-and-easy ways of military life ! ' And that, of course, if I'm lucky. If I am not, I expect I shall wear my boots out in vain ! I feel it, this business has changed us, we are no longer the plodding easy-going fellows we were ! "

" Rubbish," I cut in, " we'll get back to normal if we only keep our heads clear ! "

" I don't think ! The more I see of it here, the more I feel as if I could chuck my rifle down, and run away clean out of it, only . . ."

" Only, Rod, old boy, you couldn't. None of us could. We'd be letting down our pals," I rejoined, " and we'd be letting down the Corps. It would be unthinkable. There's no Rifleman breathing could do it. Think of the traditions of the past, of the boys that have gone, of poor old Marriner. Look at the lads all bound together by the common spirit of the Regiment—Rhodesians, Fijians, Britishers. Why, we'll see the show through and, if necessary afterwards, we'll do a bit of cleaning up for the sake of our loyalties and the memory of our chums."

" Yes, I know," answered Rodwell, " but when you see all that destruction around you," with a sweeping gesture ; " when you visualize the mounds of the dead, the selfless bravery of our boys and of the enemy too, you get sick at the thought that those who were the primary cause of all this will let you down afterwards if they get half a chance ! "

" All right, my brothers," broke in O'Donnell humorously. " Now help me to slay a very precious and cherished darling of an old Frenchman's soul," and with a flourish he opened his haversack and

produced one of the remaining bottles of bubbly
we had.

We all laughed and O'Donnell, pouring the
frothing wine into our tin mugs, gave us a toast :

"Here's to the old Corps, from Rawlinson, our
Army Commander, down to the sanitary man—
all one ! "

"You are a lad, Don," said Oldham wonderingly.
"Fancy mentioning Rawlinson and the sanitary
man together ! "

"Why, what's the matter with it ? " queried
O'Donnell indignantly. "Sure, Oldham, me boy,
you are no philosopher. Rawly and our sanitary man
are just as useful, and they all belong to us. One is
getting rid of muck by smashing the Huns, and
t'other keeps us healthy by shifting filth ! 'Tis the
same thing in the abstract ! "

"I wonder what old Rawly would say if he heard
it," chuckled Rodwell. "I bet he wouldn't be
flattered by your allusions, Don ! "

"Ye've not got imagination ! " answered the
latter airily, lolling back on his ground sheet. "Sure
he'd understand. And what matter ? They are
both Riflemen after all ! "

"This bloody ' esprit de corps ' will be the death
of you yet, Don ! " countered Rodwell sarcastically. "Why, I do believe that if you saw a Hun
with a cap badge of ours you'd be fool enough to
scrap him to get it back ! "

"I don't know that you'd be different yourself,
Rodwell," I chimed in. "You are just as hot on
the old corps as the rest of us."

"Yes, I know," he burst out bitterly, "that's the
worst of it. This cursed sentimentalism about
playing the game has got us beat. One would like to
rebel . . . but can't ! " he added heatedly. "Damn
it ! One has to risk getting killed, going through hell
and suffering like the damned, just because no man
worth his salt can let his side down. What a hideous
joke it is to be a rational human being ! "

" Oh, to hell with everything ! " said O'Donnell grandly. " Drink, me men, and hang the consequences."

We quaffed the sparkling nectar of the champagne country and sighed with content. It chased away all regrets and dark fears and doubts, it transmuted life into something roseate, desirable, vigorous and joyful.

III

" Get the Platoon together, Sergeant ! " Mr. Walker's voice was heard round the bivouacs later in the afternoon. We peeped out. Our Platoon Officer's tall form came striding along, followed by Sergeant Wilson, fussily efficient.

" Fall in, you men, in battle order ! " came the latter's command. And accordingly, scrambling into our equipment and grabbing our rifles, we fell in.

The Boche had started to wake up. Evil-looking black gusts of shrapnel were bursting over the scrub and gnarled trees and coppices in Sausage Valley and the patches of woodland up by Contalmaison. He was throwing his stinging shrapnel shells wholesale over all those scattered clumps of trees and bushes that ran out in irregular patches from Mametz Wood to the Albert–Bapaume road— Shelter Wood, Birch Tree Wood and the other thickets.

We moved off in artillery formation down into Sausage Valley and began our forward move towards Contalmaison.

In the late afternoon sky, slightly overcast with clouds, the shrapnel was bursting with an angry red glare and a long trailing tail of eddying black smoke. The ground here was all pitted and scarred and became worse as we advanced on a gradual upward slope. Broken trees, holes, pits, smashed trench-boards, rubbish of all description, sandbags and caved-in trenches and obliterated strong points.

" Blast that cursed shrapnel," swore Rodwell as a

shell burst right over us, sending us hastily ducking for cover, the angry bullets pinging and swishing around with an unpleasant droning sound.

" Old Fritz must be gettin' the wind up," O'Donnell remarked, " and is trying to get at the working parties coming up."

We now entered a region of scrub where going was difficult. Dead men were lying flung about and half concealed. Highlanders with pale bare legs, field-grey figures. German helmets crushed out of shape. I caught a glimpse of a number on one—" 16." Presently we entered a clearing smelling like a chemical laboratory. It had been recently plastered with tear gas, and the sickly, sweetish fumes of the stuff still seeped out of shell-holes and clung to the ground, making our eyes water.

A stack of petrol tins filled with water, brought up by miniature railway trucks, manhandled all the way up, confronted us.

" Come on, boys, two cans apiece, and move on. Water for the troops farther up."

We grabbed the heavy cans and, with slung rifles, staggered away up into the unknown, over the torn and mutilated ground.

The artillery fire was getting pretty thick. The British bombardment one continuous drumming roar. The Germans replying fitfully but deter-minedly. H.E. now intermingled with shrapnel, and the going became more difficult as dusk closed down.

Now and again the long single file of men came to a halt as some obstacle impeded progress ahead.

" Mind my leg, chum," came a voice laden with pain as a man, hopping about and using an inverted rifle as a crutch, came by us.

" Is it bad up there, lad ? " queried Oldham making way for the wounded man.

" Christ ! It's positive hell above Contalmaison," he groaned back. " The Welsh have copped a proper packet. They attacked this morning and the whole place was stiff with machine-guns. Fritz has strong points scattered all over it, and our artillery don't seem to shift 'em. The whole bloody position by Contalmaison Villa is a bloody slaughter-house. The lads are lying out in hundreds ! "

Crash—whizz—bang ! A shell pitches a few yards away from us, sending up a spout of earth, followed by a shower of crashing branches and bits of tree limbs.

" Duck, boys," yells Rodwell, " here come some more ! " A series of whistles and crashes all about us. In the semi-darkness the party halts in confusion, men closing up from behind crowding on us. There are smothered curses as our tin cans bang about.

" Come on, men, push on ! " comes Mr. Walker's voice from ahead, and like a long tortured snake the line moves on. Other wounded fellows are coming down, all bloody, chalky and battered about, but cheerful.

A few terrified Germans, pale-faced, shaking, pass by us, bearing a stretcher with a groaning, bloodied figure on it in their midst. They are hatless and ragged, and their bare, close-shaven skulls give them a weird appearance. These are undersized youngsters mostly. They come by us at a quick trot, ducking every time a shell roars overhead. It seems as if their nerves are frayed to bits.

We move on in this clatter and din, anxious to get on with the job before Fritz manages to land a few crumps amongst us.

The horizon ahead, in the growing darkness, appears to be lit up by fires. A red glow hangs on the skyline caused by the continual explosion of shells from the British bombardment. The German positions must be dreadful with those continual waves of bursting explosive. How anyone can survive is a mystery.

At long last a hastily-dug, shallow trench appears before us, and a crowd of vociferous Welshmen ready to take the cans over from us. We have apparently reached some kind of support position lying due east of Contalmaison as, in the distance on my left side, I catch a glimpse of heaps of rubble, a broken wall or two and a shell-pitted, torn road, with ominous-looking bundles of khaki and field-grey lying about, and a little closer a forlorn-looking heavy gun, with broken wheel, stands still and silent, its muzzle pointing to the sky. A litter of basket shell-carriers and the wreckage of a limber are close by a flattened wall.

We get rid of our cans, question the Welsh, who seem very excited, and lay down by the trench-side for a smoke and further orders.

The roar of the battle in front comes to us in fits and starts. Very lights are soaring up in the heavens, shedding a fitful, hard, momentary brilliance.

Even through the pandemonium of the gun-fire the sharp staccato rattle of machine-guns is plainly discernible. The stream of wounded increases as the darkness intensifies. Movement, under the cloak of night, becomes more pronounced. The Welsh have now disappeared with the cans of water badly needed up there by panting, parched men.

There is a lull in the German gun-fire and Mr. Walker profits by it and orders the party to move back.

" Well, that's another lousy job over ! " says Rodwell as we put our gaspers out. " Come on, O'Donnell, get on your hind legs, ready to hop back ! "

" All right, all right ! " answers our pal, who, for some moments, seemed lost in a brown study. " All this blessed noise was just soothing me nerves ! "

" My, that Irish bloke is fair barmy," I heard Maddocks tell Snewin. " The more bloody rah these asterisk guns make the better 'e likes it. Reminds me of me old moke. The more you 'it it the longer 'e stops still ! "

" Yus, mate," answered Snewin, " the bloody Paddies 'ave all got a screw loose somewhere. You

pats 'em on the back and they'll blow yer 'ead off.
'It 'em on the jaw and they'll like yer ! ''

" All right, boys," came Oldham's voice. " Come
on, lead the way out."

The Platoon got on the move, Mr. Walker leading
the way, and Sergeant Wilson at the rear shepherded
the laggards back into line.

We moved swifter going back down the track,
through the shadowed brush, into clearings, bumping into all sorts of objects, and now and again
stumbling amongst new shell-holes.

Suddenly the Germans began to belt the whole
area horribly. Shells seemed to come from all
quarters. Shrapnel burst over our heads like a
cascade of water. Shell splinters hummed through
the air and struck with dull sucking noises into the
ground. We crouched, stumbled, scrambled on and
crouched again.

" By Christ, E——, the bastards will have some
of us before long," cried Rodwell resentfully
clutching at his steel helmet which had fallen over
his eye.

Crash—crash—whooo—whoo—crash. An extra
special dose of H.E., followed by some sharp bursts
of ground shrapnel, smote us like an avalanche.
Trees went up in the air, the fiery flash of exploding
projectiles flung a red blaze in our faces and most of
us fell flat, digging our heads down into the dirt in
that frantic subconscious effort to hide it—just like
ostriches.

" By goom ! We'll be wanting our goggles on ! "
muttered Oldham wiping at his streaming eyes.
" The bloody place fair reeks with gas ! "

In fact, the Boche must have been getting rid of
his old stock of gas shells, as he was chucking them
over with a large-hearted generosity that failed to
appeal to us. The whole area reeked with the sickly
smell of lachrymose gas and tears welled up in our
swollen eyes and ran down our cheeks. Half blinded
we staggered on under that torrent of fire and

whizzing pieces, and by sheer luck got into Sausage Valley unscathed.

"Well, we are near home now, thank the Lord," muttered Rodwell. "Look behind, E——. It's like a picture of flaming hell with the souls of the damned hurrying on."

I looked. His simile was a very apt one. The ruddy glare, the quivering air, the constant burst of crumps, the gaunt, leafless shattered trees, the broken and twisted earth, with spouts shooting upwards as a shell landed, the pits and holes, debris and the huddled bodies of the slain lying half concealed here and there, the crowd of anxious-eyed, wan-faced men hurrying on with hops, skips and jumps, heads and shoulders bent low, their dusky forms silhouetted against the greater darkness enshrouding them and now and again revealed by a momentary flash of fire, just like a vision of Hades as depicted by Gustave Doré. And the line from Dante sprang to my mind : "Lasciate ogni speranza o voi ch'entrate." It was awesome and yet held a fascina-tion and a sable grandeur of its own. But we were not fated to escape unscathed from the clutches of the Gods of destruction altogether. As we made a last spurt forward, taking advantage of a momentary lull in the shelling, some imp of perdition must have caused the Boche gunners to shift their laying aim slightly and a tornado of shells and ground-shrapnel slammed down the valley and plump into our unfortunate party, showering earth, branches and slices of hissing, murderous hot steel amongst us. Coughing, choking, our lungs filled with the acrid fumes of chemicals, eyes smarting and watering, we made a wild rush for cover. I stumbled and fell over a soft, yielding form and lay still and panting for a moment, dabbing at my eyes and frantically groping for my gas respirator.

"Haah, Christ!" came a wailing voice from behind. A chorus of heart-rending cries and wails arose on all sides. "Stretcher-bearers!" "Stretcher-bearers ! " came another urgent, frantic appeal in tones laden with all the sorrows and pain of the world.

I looked up cautiously. Rodwell was crouching next to me and he also moved. Through the eddies of the smoke we glimpsed a huddle of figures farther up writhing and twisting on the ground and Mr. Walker's tall form hurrying up.

" Keep under cover, men ! Don't move ! " he yelled as we rose to hurry forward.

" Who is it ? " I hear O'Donnell ask anxiously.

" I don't know, lad," Oldham replies. " Quite a few caught a packet, poor blighters ! "

Our two stretcher-bearers, Mr. Walker and one or two others are busy over the groaning men. The fire swings away from us and, shaken, we regain our feet and crowd forward.

Three men are past all help. Their bloody mangled bodies are laid aside, to be collected later for burial. Mr. Walker takes their identity discs and papers from Sergeant Wilson who has been rummaging in their pockets. He leaves one disc round their wrists, for their later identification.

The wounded are moaning softly. Poor Unwin, the Norfolk boy, is in sorry plight. The left side of his body is a mass of wounds from the shoulder to the foot. He caught a nasty blast of shrapnel. True to type he is silent, only his heaving chest and staring eyes denote the torment he is suffering.

" Cheer up, Unwin, you are out of it anyhow ! How do you feel ? " I query, thrusting a lighted cigarette in his mouth. " Have a smoke, old son, it'll help you ! "

" Ta E——," he gasps. " Oi'll be all right. See to the others. Oh ! " as a twinge wrings a cry from him.

" Come on, Don, get him on a stretcher, we will carry him out! " I cry to O'Donnell. But we have no stretchers, so we look around while the rest of the wounded are hurriedly attended to. One lance-corporal and another five men all more or less badly battered about, mostly leg and body wounds. Arkinstall is hit in the foot. A shrapnel bullet has ripped through his boot and the foot inside it is a mass of soggy flesh and splintered bone. The stretcher-bearers are trying to cut his boot away, and he groans with the pain of it.

We find a Hun overcoat lying in the rubbish. Rodwell and I thrust our rifles through the sleeves, and carefully we lay Unwin on this improvised stretcher and the three of us, with Oldham lending an occasional hand, lift Unwin on it and begin to move forward out of this ghastly valley.

The Platoon gets together again, the wounded aided and supported by their chums and with Mr. Walker in the lead, the party hurries on towards Becourt and the first-aid post.

The Boche suddenly ceases his cannonade as we emerge at the bottom of Becourt Hill. Carefully we pick our way past the gun-pits to the Regimental aid-post pitched in a sand-bagged shelter at the edge of the road leading to Becordel. Colonel Bircham is standing by Battalion headquarters talking to some officers as we come by with our burdens, and hurries forward as he glimpses us.

" Who is it, men ? " he queries solicitously.

" Rifleman Unwin of ' C ' Company, sir ! " I answer. " Wounded in shoulder, side and leg ! "

" Poor lad ! How are you feeling now ? Keep your pecker up. The doctor will have you away quickly. Jolly good luck and a long rest in Blighty ! " says the C.O., peering at Unwin's white face.

" Th—thank you, sir ! I'll be all right ! " answers the stricken lad gratefully.

The Colonel has a word of cheer for all the wounded. He is a great chap. No wonder every man in the Battalion thinks such a lot of him. Ever careful of the men's comforts, thoughtful for their well-being, foremost in action, always accessible. The ideal C.O., well-beloved by all who served under him, able to call on his men for any effort required of them, firing them with his example. The Battalion under his command had become a first-class fighting machine capable of meeting any demand.

The aid-post was busy. We took Unwin in, handed him over to the orderlies and, with cheerful farewells, left him on his first stage back to Blighty and comparative peace.

" His soldiering is finished anyhow ! " said Rodwell. " He won't be fit for service any more. I think his leg is all broken up ! "

" Ah, well, he's lucky," remarked Oldham. " He'll see the war out now ! "

" Yes, to drudge about as a farm labourer with a game leg," rejoined Rodwell, " at a wage that's a disgrace to England ! He's made nothing out of the war, and they'll tell him he ought to be thankful to get out of it alive."

" Oh, well," put in O'Donnell as we made our way up the hill towards our. bivouacs, " that's the way of the world, me bhoy, and you can shout yourself hoarse as much as you like, without altering it one jot. You want to be a philosopher and contemplate the world with calm ! "

" Philosopher be blowed ! " answered Rodwell fiercely. " If I get out of this senseless blood-bath alive, I'll do my damnedest to wake up these blighters who are battening on our blood and our bodies, out of their self-complacent selfish pose."

" Oh, you'll waste your time," put in Oldham drily as he picked his way carefully in the dark. " They'll just put you down as an agitator and crank ! "

" Oh, will they ? " rebutted Rodwell with heat. " If all of us, soldiers of all ranks, band ourselves together, tell the politicians, the profiteers and the little-Englanders just where they get off, and re-build an England of which we can be proud of, free from sham and hypocrisy, with real brotherhood and mutual respect throughout the social scale, we shall do the work the lads are dying out here for ! "

" Aye, it sounds fine," said Oldham, " but we'll want a man to lead us. Can you suggest anyone ? "

" Yes," answered Rodwell in a sober voice. " The Prince of Wales. He's one of us ! "

" By gosh, Rodwell," said O'Donnell admiringly. " I do believe you've said something true at last. He would be the only one who could do it ! "

We were in the bivouacs now and made our way to ours. O'Donnell, fired with Rodwell's arguments, did not know or care where his feet went, and just as he was preparing to launch into another flow of rhetoric, he stumbled and pitched flat on a low bivvy constructed entirely of waterproofs. The whole thing collapsed under him, and a horrible stream of blasphemy issued from the figure trapped underneath the wreckage. The voice of Gottschalk, muffled by the folds of the waterproof, waxed eloquent as he tried to wriggle out and deal with the destroyers of his home.

" You've done it now, Don, it's Gottschalk you've fallen on," I cried, grabbing him and yanking him to his feet. " Come on, let's beat it before he sees us. He'll have our life."

Rodwell let out a great chuckle and we hurried away into the darkness, while Gottschalk, free at last, sprang out in a roaring fury.

" Come back, you blankety asterisks ! I know you. I'll make you sweat ! Oh, hell, and now I've got to pitch this bloody bivouac in this blasted darkness ! Rot your guts, you swine ! "

We dived into our den deeply amused. It seemed fated every time that Gottschalk came within our orbit an accident happened to him.

" It'll do him good to sweat in the dark, cool his bloody temper ! " said Rodwell laughing. " Come on, Oldham, out with your bottle of booze and let's have a drink. I think we've earned one."

We lit a candle, got some sardines out and there on that hill-side, ringed round by the battle flames on the skyline, our ears full with the noise of the throbbing guns, the twinkling gleam of the stars in the dark vault of heaven looking down on us, we feasted right royally and contentedly, while farther off Gottschalk, in an evil temper, struggled to piece his bivouac in the dark, using such a flow of blasphemous epithets that would have brought a blush of shame to a Billingsgate porter's face and ungrudging admiration from a bargee.

And as we supped, our comrades around us drifted into slumber, till presently only the sullen voice of the War god raging and tearing at his human victims rose in the July night.

CHAPTER SIX

I

THE ceaseless roar of the British cannonade woke me two or three times during the night. Somehow I could not sleep, and early at dawn I was astir while O'Donnell, Rodwell and Oldham slumbered on. Larks were piping in the early-morning light as I emerged from the bivvy, and for a moment I surveyed the sleeping Battalion. It was rather chilly in the morning air. The scene immediately round seemed calm and peaceful, although the guns were growling farther away and the skyline was well besprinkled by that pall of dust and smoke that hung over the woods and coppices from the Pozieres road, right across the two Bazentins and High Wood. I scrounged around, found some wood and soon had a fire blazing merrily with our canteens full of water on it for our breakfast.

Washing was a bit of a problem as the water was strictly limited, so I had to content myself with a cat's lick by utilizing a little of our scanty supply and using my shaving brush in lieu of a sponge. By the time tea was made and some eggs and bread fried, the Company was astir.

" Hullo, E——, up early, eh ? " I turned to survey Gottschalk's sour visage.

" Morning, Corporal, had a good night ? " I enquired innocently.

" Ah, just what I wanted to see you blokes about !" he answered, ignoring my greeting. " Some lousy son of a bitch trod on my bivvy in the middle of the night, and I had a job to get it fixed up again in the dark ! "

" Hard lines. Did you find out who did it ? "

" No, but I'm Orderly Corporal to-day," significantly, " and I'll make sure that the Platoon blokes get a bit of dirty work ! "

" Ah, well, Corporal, that won't interest my Section anyhow ! " I answered casually.

" Ho, won't it ? I got an idea you blokes know

something about it," he said, eyeing me suspiciously, " and I know you have a down on me ! I've a mind to get you blokes on the go a bit."

" You'll have to speak to Mr. Walker first. We have to overhaul bombs this morning."

" Ho, I forgot ! You posh blokes are always mucking about with the orficers and the Sergeant-Major ! " he said disgustedly.

" Eh, Gottschalk, you leave my Section alone ! " chimed in Oldham, suddenly appearing. " You know you've no business to muck about with the bombers."

" All right, Oldham ! Just wait till I find the blokes that broke my bivvy up ! I'll make them sit up, the bloody asterisks ! " And muttering he moved off to look for fresh and easier victims.

" Was that Gottschalk ? " enquired O'Donnell, appearing, stretching and yawning.

" Yes, out for trouble again," I answered. " Come on, let's have our breakfast."

Rodwell joined us and we fell to. After breakfast Sergeant Wilson came for us and presently, together with the other bombers, we foregathered in the trench behind the bushes and, with Mr. Walker in charge and Captain Sherlock coming round occasionally, we got through the job of examining and detonating boxes upon boxes of Mills grenades.

The bombardment was going on as usual, but as far as we were concerned it had become an ordinary routine event hardly worth bothering about.

Mr. Walker gave us a short account of how things were going on. The French apparently are on the point of entering Peronne and have captured many villages and thousands of prisoners. On the Eastern front the Russians, under Brussilov, have attacked and broken the Austro-German front and are advancing on Cracow, and their captures of ground and men are enormous.

" There, Rodwell, me bhoy," says O'Donnell gaily, " the steam roller is moving at last ! "

" Yes, until someone throws a monkey wrench into the works, and the damn thing stops like it did before ! " from Rodwell pessimistically. " Unless we can do the job properly the other Allies will get nowhere ! "

We worked at the bombs all the morning and in the afternoon the Platoon again fell in for some more fatigue duty.

This time we wended our way up across the ground in front by the cart track to the sunken road.

Past the lines of field guns standing wheel to wheel and banging away without pause. Into the sunken road teeming with troops moving up, wounded coming down, and all the litter of war flung indiscriminately about. Heavy fighting must have occurred here, for its banks on both sides were scooped and dug as if at one period they had been used as a firing position.

Some dead mules were lying asprawl on one side, with swarms of fat, bloated flies on them, rising and buzzing when men approached. The mules exhaled a foul, mephitic odour that caught at our throats and turned us quite sick.

" My hat ! What a bloody stink ! " ejaculated Rodwell as we crossed the road and halted below its farther bank. " I thought dead men were bad enough ; but, good Lord, there's nothing to compare with mules ! "

We moved up the road slightly and came to a huge heap of Stokes shell boxes. They had to be carried up. Gingerly we grabbed a box between two of us and stood waiting for the direction order.

It was getting late afternoon and movement was increasing. While waiting we catch sight of a forlorn-looking party of dishevelled German prisoners under escort of Riflemen. We hail these latter, to learn they belong to our 16th Battalion in action somewhere in front of Bazentin.

Presently, as these move down the road, Mr. Walker orders us to take up our loads, scramble over the sunken road and plunge in the wilderness and destruction of Bottom Wood and Mametz.

Two by two we move along in a straggling line through the smashed trees, litter of branches, shell-holes and mess of the wood. With the rays of the late-afternoon sun touching up with colour some of the corners of this tortured mass of trees it makes a wonderful scene.

An indescribable smell of corruption rises up ; the air is thick with it. Bits of equipment everywhere, broken-down sandbag barricades, barbed wire catching at our feet, now and again dead bodies half concealed by rubbish and foliage can be glimpsed. And over all the din of our bombardment, the occasional crash of a Boche shell in the thickets, and far away a noise like thousands of sewing-machines, harsh and metallic, comes to us. The machine-guns tap-tapping somewhere in Mametz Wood. We come again in the open, with a bare slope rising in front of us. Mametz Wood is just beyond. Here a maze of tumbled trenches, heaped with khaki and field-grey figures. A smashed railway line, debris of all kinds, and a thin trickle of wounded men painfully oozing down.

" Come on, boys, quick across this open stretch," cries Sergeant Wilson.

We breast the slope at a staggering run.

" Blast these bloody Stokes shells," curses Rodwell. " They are bloody heavy ! "

Whizz-bang—crash ! behind us, as a covey of Hun shells sails over and bursts with dull crashes behind us, in Bottom Wood, sending up geysers of earth and shattering the trees a little more.

We plunge into another badly-battered coppice. Here heaps of sandbags and shallow trenches form a sort of redoubt and men are clustering round. In the deepening shadows I descry some sort of first-aid post. Groans and moans are rising up. Stretchers, broken men, a smell of blood. A German with a red-cross armlet is busy tending

wounded. A padre, pale-faced, earnest, is whispering to a whimpering, bandage-covered figure. A
huge sergeant of the Cornwalls comes by, his left
arm bandaged right up, minus the tunic-sleeve. He
is cheery all right, and swings a posh-looking German
helmet in his good hand.

"All right for Blighty," he cries as he goes by,
"with a souvenir for the old woman!"

"Dump the boxes, lads!" Another Cornish
N.C.O. appears and guides us to a bit of trench.
We get rid of our burdens as dusk closes down and
the noise ahead increases.

"The bastards are trying to counter-attack,"
the Cornishman informs us, "but they have had a
basinful of it to-day all right!"

"Are they still in the wood?" queries
O'Donnell.

"Yes, they still have a bit of it, stiff with bloody
machine-guns and hidden dug-outs! It's bloody
murder to get at them!"

Our fatigue ended, we move back in the gathering
dark, with the roar of the fight dinning in our ears.

Brother Boche is too busy in front to bother about
shelling much behind. His gunners are belting
Mametz Wood as hard as they can, and all we can
see and hear is the distant flash of shells, their roar
and crash and the smash of falling trees.

We return without incident across the woods,
down the sunken road, now teeming with traffic over
it, and by the artillery lines. In the dark this makes
a wonderful, unforgettable scene.

As far as I can see a line of guns, roaring, banging
and flashing, with dark figures springing about like
black imps of the pit and hoarse voices yelling orders
and ranges.

As we clear the guns a shriek like an express train
comes out of the dark, there is an awful rending
crash. We duck frantically. An enemy heavy-
calibre shell hits the corner of the sunken road and a
lurid flame springs up. It has landed on top of

some artillery stores and set them on fire. A glare lights the landscape. There is a rush and we are all frenziedly busy chucking stores away from the burning pile.

" Strewth ! " gasps Snewin. " The bloody 'Un 'as made a mess ! "

Mr. Walker, risking being badly burned, is tugging away at ammunition boxes. We all pile in quickly lest the fire gets at them. Artillery officers, men, N.C.O.s are running around, but the guns continue their fire unconcernedly.

Bang ! crash ! bang ! More shells land near, scattering stones and dirt all over us. Fortunately without effect. At length the blaze dies down, smothered by earth the lads are digging and chucking over.

A gunner major comes over to Mr. Walker and thanks him for our timely aid, and off we go cheerfully, although smoky, smudged and thirsty.

No further mishap occurs and we get back to our bivouacs safely.

" Any more juice, Oldham ? My throat feels like a lime kiln ! " asks Rodwell as he lights a candle-stub.

" Aye, two more bottles left. We'd better have some now."

And we sit in the open, munching bread and cold sausage, drinking a generous beaker of Chablis, and look over the awesome sight of the night strafe lighting up the horizon with its ruddy glare.

" 'Tis something I'd like to get down on paper," remarks O'Donnell. " I bet the Press reporters, writing their rot miles away, would give their souls to see this from our grand-stand ! "

" Yes, it looks all right from a distance, but in a day or two, when we are in the thick of it, it won't feel so bloody poetic," chimed in Rodwell drily. " I bet the lads up yonder, with all these blasted tons of iron falling around them, don't appreciate its pictorial beauties ! "

"Aye, you are right, Rodwell. Come, let's turn in." Saying which Oldham crawled in the bivvy with Rodwell, while O'Donnell and I remained a while longer under the open sky, drawn and attracted strangely by the drama of war and death being played out before our eyes.

II

Morning broke out dull. The sky, overcast with clouds, looking like a storm brewing. We are still here in reserve, although we hear that part of the Division is moving up in the front line to-day. Slowly the Germans are being pushed back, but the cost is heavy. To see the shattered remains of battalions constantly moving out makes one wonder whether the effort is worth the price we are paying for it. And yet, with the horrible, nerve-wracking experience of it all, these fellows are cheerful, happy and confident. There is certainly no doubt that we have given the Hun a very nasty jolt, and he will have to revise his opinion of our War Army.

Rodwell and I walked back towards Albert this morning and farther back in Tara Valley, teeming with bivouacking troops, saw the Indian Cavalry assemble. They are going into action somewhere. They looked a wonderful fit body of men, keen and eager. Fine horses and men, their dark faces lit up with expectation, their lances flashing. Rather incongruous, I thought, in steel helmets instead of turbans. But what can they do over this shell-pitted ground, littered with wire and broken trees ; against sand-bag defences held with machine-guns and manned by a stubborn enemy ? A cavalry attack may be a romantic affair to talk about, but ever since the quick-fire rifle and the machine-gun made their bow in war, in Europe, at least, it has been futile.

"Poor beggars ! " remarked Rodwell, looking at their long lines. " If they try to bust on Fritz he'll make sausage-meat of them ! "

" I don't know," I answered. " If they follow up an infantry attack, they may burst right through, and we'll get a chance of throwing him right out ! "

" I don't think ! " he answered. " No cavalry can attack trench lines. The bloody Staff ought to know better ! "

We watched them trotting away with jingle of harness and glittering lances, and as they disappeared in a cloud of dust we climbed back to Becourt.

A scrap dinner, and again we retired to our bivouacs, in the close, listless air of the early afternoon.

" Do you know, E——," muttered O'Donnell to me, " I've the feeling something is going to happen. It's been too cushy so far ! "

" Don't be silly. The trouble with you Irish folk is that you are too imaginative. What do you expect ? Gottschalk going mad and attacking us with a trench-tool, or the Sergeant-Major ' drumming up ' for us ? "

" I don't know. There's something in this close air I don't like. Come on, E——, let's get outside."

We crawled out of the bivouac and stood in the open. Most of the platoon were in their bivvies. Here and there a man squatted on the slope, busy at some particular task. Over the open a few limbers were trotting quietly up the cart-track towards the field-guns. The howitzer battery in the valley had fallen silent. Only the deep boom-boom of guns away on the left and the swirls of black smoke floating like low clouds away over the skeletons of the woods hinted that the grim struggle with the stubborn Teuton had not abated.

Rodwell came out and joined us, and we stood gazing away towards the few pitiful bricks that denoted where La Boiselle had been.

" Won't the contractors make their fortunes when this game is over ? " mused Rodwell. " Just think of all the towns and villages that'll have to be rebuilt ! I can just imagine the company promoters in London and Paris, Berlin and Brussels, running around with schemes and plans, gathering money hand over fist ! "

" Well," put in O'Donnell, " it will provide a hell of a lot of work ! "

" Yes, what a joke it all is ! We come and smash everything up, and then work like hell to build it up again ! My God ! If anyone from another planet were able to observe us, he'd conclude that mankind is just too damn silly for words ! " replied Rodwell with deep disgust.

" Anyhow, I should not like to be the one to turn this ground over ! " I exclaimed. " Think of the horrors that will be unearthed."

" 'Tis nothing ! " said O'Donnell. " All this will be rich land for crops, 'tis well manured ! "

" Yes, and some lousy Frenchman will be reaping rich harvests, fertilised with the blood and flesh of his betters ! Even our bodies will bring him a profit ! "

" Oh, get away with you, Rodwell, 'tis the poetic meanin' of life, for out of weakness comes strength, and fertility from corruption," said O'Donnell grandly.

" Eh, boys, look at that ! " cried I excitedly, as with a swish and dull plop two or three crumps suddenly spun out of nowhere and fell near the trotting limbers. Nothing happened. The horses quickened their trot, the shells did not explode, they only emitted a thickish trail of vapour.

" The Germans are chucking duds about, b'God ! " cried O'Donnell.

We watched another clump of shells fall a bit nearer, with the same result. One or two of the boys began to gaze interestedly.

" There's something wrong somewhere," Rodwell muttered dubiously. " You don't tell me that Fritz can have all these duds in bunches." We moved forward towards the slope when, without further

warning, the sky suddenly seemed filled with swishing sounds, and a perfect hail of these duds fell on
our bivouacs like a blanket.

Immediately all was confusion. Men sprang up
out of their shelters confusedly. Whistles shrilled.
The howitzer battery below us woke to life, and
started slamming away into the blue.

Thicker rained the hail of shells, spreading all
over the hill and peppering all the ground in
front, plopping and bouncing but still failing to
explode.

We scrambled into a mess of sandbags and ducked
down.

" If they are duds we're all right," yelled Rodwell
hoarsely. " We've only to look out for a direct
hit ! "

But now a hazy cloud seemed to rise from the
ground. Our eyes began to run with tears, and a
sharp, strange tang gripped our throats.

" Oh, Christ ! " spluttered O'Donnell suddenly.
" It's gas ! " and began to pull at his gas-mask
frantically.

" Come on, quick, get the respirators on ! " I
shouted. Luckily both O'Donnell and I had our
masks slung round us. Rodwell had none ! Quickly
I unfastened my bag, pulled my respirator out and
jerked the spare one over to him.

Meanwhile the bombardment had increased, and
the hill behind us became obscured by a thick-
looking greenish fog. We could hear the alarmed,
choking cries of men, the crash of shelters, the wailing moans of unfortunate victims of direct hits.
A clanging noise away by Battalion headquarters,
the gas alarm !

Now high explosives began to crash together
with the gas-shells. Muffled orders yelled by
N.C.O.s reached us.

" Make for the trench behind ! Stand to ! "

" Eh, where's Oldham ? " cried O'Donnell
suddenly.

" Left him asleep in the bivvy ! " hooted Rodwell at the top of his voice.

" Come on, boys," I yelled, " up we go to the bivvy, find out what's happened, and we'll then make for the trench ! "

" Right you are, away we go ! " cried Rodwell, and getting into action scrambled out of our shelter and ploughed away uphill right into the thick of the gas. We scotched him up close behind, running warily, heads low and into that tornado of explosions and hissing, plopping gas-shells.

Hazy figures loomed up indistinctly in the dun-coloured fog, staggering about uncertainly, gasping and wheezing. Unfamiliar shell-holes appeared all about us, and we had to swerve and veer around. Equipment, rifles and wrecked bivvies suddenly all round us, and we eventually found our way to ours.

It had been either hit or the concussions had shaken it down. The side composed of branches and ammunition-boxes lay piled in ruins, some of the boxes leaning crazily on to the taut ground sheets.

Rodwell nosed about in the wreckage, and suddenly yelped out : " Oldham's in here. Lend me a hand, quick ! "

I dashed to his assistance while O'Donnell frantically tugged at the waterproofs and scattered the boxes out of our way.

We got Oldham out, gasping and half conscious.

" Quick, slip a respirator on him ! " I cried, and working as quickly as we could we flung a helmet over him, and half carrying, half supporting, his limp form we plunged through the bushes and into the trench behind while the shells continued to burst and plop all round.

The trench was crowded with crouching figures in gas-masks. A few men were moaning and writhing round about. Other still and bloodied figures were sprawling in the apathetic abandon of death.

" We'd better try and get down to the aid post,"

remarked O'Donnell as we gently eased our burden down. "Poor old Oldham has got a whiff of gas, and the sooner we get him away the better!"

He began to stir, wheezed feebly and struggled to get rid of the mask.

"Keep steady, old chap!" I cried to him. "There's gas about! We'll see you all right!"

A few moments more and the strafe ended as abruptly as it had begun. We jerked up. The whole trench broke into life, and with the stilling of the noise of the shells other sounds became distinctive. Groans, wheezes, coughs on all hands. The familiar cry for stretcher-bearers and orders being passed about.

In the slight breeze the gas began to thin out, and a stream of men made for the wreckage of the bivouac.

"Come on, over to the aid post!" and Rodwell, getting hold of poor Oldham, began to move out.

We lifted our stricken chum out of the trench and back in the open and laid him down.

"Take—off—the—m-a-s-k!" he cried, struggling. "I'm ch-choking!" and a fit of violent coughing shook him.

"All right, Don," I cried, "just take off yours and sniff, see how the gas is."

O'Donnell lifted his respirator cautiously, and: "'Tis all right," he said, "the bloody gas is near gone!"

Off came our masks. Except for a slight tang in the air, it was all right. I gratefully breathed fresh air into my lungs with great relief after the chemical stuff of the respirator. Quickly we saw to Oldham and ripped the mask off.

The poor blighter was in bad shape. His face had a greenish hue, his lips were frothing, and he gave us a pitiful, agonised look from his wide-open, bloodshot eyes.

"How are you feeling, Oldham," queried Rodwell anxiously.

" Oh, gug, gug ! I am—done—in," he gasped, painfully choking and coughing. " I was—asleep— what's happened ? "

" Never mind, lad, get down to the aid post," put in O'Donnell. " Come on ! "

Again we lifted him up and staggered down with him to the aid post through the litter and wreckage of the bivouacs. The rest of the platoon were moving about, Mr. Walker, Captain Sherlock and the Sergeant-Major were going round gathering the men together.

A stream of gasping and coughing men, together with many blood-spattered figures, were painfully staggering towards the aid post. The howitzer battery below us was silent, and I caught a glimpse in the distance of an overturned limber with a heap of feebly struggling and kicking horses still in the traces. Figures were running towards them.

" The bloody Huns ! " cursed Rodwell savagely. " They've made a bloody mess of us ! Blast them ! "

We got to the aid post, crowded with men writhing in agony, retching and coughing heartrendingly. The M.O. and the orderlies flitting about busily in the hurly-burly.

" All the men who are gassed keep to the road," said a corporal, running up. " They'll go off to the casualty clearing station at once, as soon as the ambulances arrive. This way for the wounded ! " pointing the way.

The doctor came out as we laid poor Oldham down. He paused, looked at him, and shook his head doubtfully.

" Is he bad, sir ? " I asked him anxiously.

" I'm afraid so ! But one can never be sure with gas ! " he replied. " Get him away as soon as the ambulance comes ! "

A violent spasm caught Oldham. He coughed and heaved as if his chest would break, greenish-looking froth oozed out from his mouth, his arms beat about feebly, and he tried to sit up but fell back.

We were helpless to help, and had to stand by watching our poor old chum struggling feebly and painfully for his life.

" I'm through, boys ! " he gasped. " E——, there's—a—letter in my pocket—get it sent on ! Take—what's in the kit——! " Another paroxysm shook him.

The ambulances chugged up. Quickly we got our helpless pal on a stretcher inside, shook hands, and wished him luck, and stood back as the ambulance, with its pitiful cargo, moved off towards Becordel !

" Poor Oldham ! " muttered O'Donnell huskily. " There's another of our pals gone ! "

" Ah, blast this bloody game ! " hooted Rodwell. " One by one we are treading the same road ! When will it end, I wonder ? "

" Come on to the bivvy ! " I replied. " Let's see what's left ! "

A figure emerged from the dressing station. Pale and wan, with bandaged head and coughing painfully. Gottschalk ! He looked in sorry shape, poor blighter, all his cockiness absent.

" Come on, Gottschalk ! " said Rodwell, springing forward. " We'll help you to the ambulance ! " And we guided our old enemy down to where the motors were loading up these poor broken bodies on their way to life or death.

" Ta, you blokes ! " he replied gratefully. " I've got it bad ! Head all smashed and some bloody gas too ! There's some grub in me pack, you'd better get it. My bivvy is all right ! "

" Never mind, Gottschalk ! " I said cheerfully. " You'll be back again fit. Have a good rest in Blighty ! "

" Back again ? " he replied shudderingly. " No bloody fear ! This is the third time, and by Gawd, if I get over it, I'm goin' to swing the lead for all I'm worth ! "

We got him away, and wended our way back up the hill slowly and morosely.

" I hope Oldham'll get over it," I said, voicing the thoughts of the other two.

" I doubt it ! " Rodwell answered despondently. " Looks as if he caught a heavy dose of gas. I've seen too many of 'em, and seriously I hope he goes under. It'd be agony to linger on with burnt-out lungs, always sick and weak and helpless. This bloody scientific warfare is inhuman. They are not content to use honest-to-goodness cold steel and hot lead. They are resorting to filthy methods a savage would be bloody well ashamed of. And then they have the cheek of blathering about the romance of war ! "

The whole hill-side was in a fearful mess. Bivouacs all scattered and broken, arms and accoutrements all over the place, shell-holes pock-marking the ground and heaps of branches, shattered trees and uprooted bushes.

We now learned that the Company had suffered grievously. Sergeant Wilson was wounded, nine men had been killed and the gas and other casualties were well over fifty—and this in the short space of half an hour when we were in comparative safety well away from the front line.

Our first care was that of retrieving our arms and equipment, and rigging our bivvy up anew. All the rest of the boys, growling and cursing, were busy at the same task.

" Hooroo ! " yelled O'Donnell, digging through the mess inside the bivouac.

" What's up, you lunatic ? " queried Rodwell crossly, as he dragged a ground sheet clear.

" Our last bottle of wine is safe and sound ! " replied Don, waving our remaining bottle of champagne, relic of Flesselles, aloft. " Thank all the gods for this marcy ! " he added piously.

Our bivvy at length was mended, and, gathering poor old Oldham's gear, we went down to the Sergeant-Major to hand it in. Old Mac was very busy, getting the Company into shape again.

" This is Corporal Oldham's gear, Sergeant-Major," I said, piling it all together before his den.

" Oh yes ! " he replied. " Poor blighter's badly gassed. You'd better take the section over, E——. I'll speak to Captain Sherlock and put you in for a stripe."

" No thanks, Sergeant-Major," I replied hastily. " I'll run the section until we get another corporal, if you don't mind. I prefer remaining with my pals."

" All right, all right, E——, I understand," he answered. " By the way, you three may be wanted presently."

" What's the matter, Major, dear ? " O'Donnell queried anxiously. " You're not giving us more dirt, are you, now ? "

" Get away with your blarney ! No, but it's something special. Captain Sherlock will tell you by and by ! "

We withdrew, wondering what was about to befall us.

" I don't like it," muttered Rodwell. " You may be sure that old Mac wouldn't pick on us for nothing ! "

" Well, it's not a fatigue, anyway ! " replied O'Donnell brightly. " So that's all right."

" Perhaps they'll be after sending us on a course ! " he opined hopefully.

" Course be hanged ! Talk sense. How can they send us on courses when we are lying here as reserves for the front line, and the Company is short of men ? "

" Come on, boys," I put in. " I've got to find out what we've got in the Section, and draw our rations ! "

We returned to the bivouac and I got busy. There's only Maddocks and Snewin and our three selves in the Section. However, I managed to scrounge double rations, so everything's all right momentarily.

Late in the day we are called to Company headquarters. We put on our equipment, grab our rifles and go down. Captain Sherlock talks to us :

" You men are wanted to make up a bombing group the Battalion is lending to the Loyal North Lancs. So draw two days' rations and report to Battalion headquarters as quickly as you can."

We salute and withdraw to call on the Quartermaster Sergeant.

" Hallo, we are in for some dirty work, lads ! " murmurs Rodwell. " Some other hare-brained stunt, I bet ! "

" Never mind, Rod," O'Donnell rebuts. " All in the day's work, me boy ! "

We get our rations and go to Battalion headquarters and join a group of men from the other companies. A subaltern in spectacles takes us over and the C.O. comes out.

" I hope you men will give a good account of yourselves," he says, " and don't forget you are Riflemen ! "

A few instructions, and off we go to the North Lancs, who are lying in Scott's Redoubt.

Darkness is falling as we move across the open, down Sausage Valley, up over a welter of smashed trenches, till finally we reach our destination. We scramble down a deep, sand-bagged trench and arrive at the North Lancs' headquarters. Our subaltern goes in while we stand by idly chatting with some of the " Loyals " standing round.

" What's goin' to happen, chum ? " I ask a dark, thick-set lance-corporal.

" Ah dunno ! " he answers. " We are to move oop later somewhere. Reckon we're going to attack."

" Come on, Rod, and you, E——," says O'Donnell, " we'd better finish our bottle of wine while we've got the chance ! "

We edge off into a bay, open the bottle and gulp down the golden liquor with relish.

A tremendous bombardment has opened up forward. From the trench-top we can see the shells whirling and bursting away in the wood. Flashes and reddish glares spring up, accentuated by the falling darkness.

" Come on the Rifles," yells a voice. We finish our wine quickly, and Don throws the bottle away with a regretful gesture. " There goes the last of it ! " he says with a sigh. " When shall we see more ? "

We rejoin our party, and our officer takes us aside to explain things.

" The whole line is going to attack Bazentin le Petit Wood, and our bombing party has to operate with the Leicesters of the 110th Brigade. We are going up to them now. Our job is to open the way to the railway track crossing the wood. We begin the attack at 4 a.m. We shall attack the German trench at the edge where the road from Bazentin joins the cutting and then push on until we reach the railway line. Get over the trench and lead on."

We scramble out, and with a sergeant of the Loyals in the lead we made our way forward towards the front line over the bare ground lying between Mametz Wood and Contalmaison.

III

The whole place was stiff with troops, and we came across men lying in shallow trenches every few minutes. The whole thing was rather confusing, as apparently these men belonged to units of the 21st Division. However, enquiries here and there gave me a hazy idea. The 3rd Brigade of the 1st Division was away on the left flank below Pozieres, and somewhere in front of Contalmaison Villa. The 110th Brigade from the 37th Division had been sent up to reinforce the 21st Division and lead the attack on this side of Bazentin le Petit Wood. The Loyal North Lancs had been borrowed from our brigade to support the attack, and had scrounged bombers from the other battalions in the Brigade to lend to the Leicesters leading the attack.

" Sounds like a bloody pawnshop," grumbled

Rodwell to me, as we stumbled along in the wake of the North Lancs' sergeant, " but, by Christ, the pawner, as usual, loses. We are the bloody interest Fritz wants, all right."

" Eh, Rod, you are thinking of Shylock and his pound of flesh," chortled Don. " You are getting mixed—that's in Shakespeare."

" It may be so," retorted Rodwell, " but the result is the same. Heads they win, tails we lose ! "

" Stop your jaw there ! " whispered our guide fiercely. " We are near the front line ! "

Down into another trench crammed with men and along a squelchy, muddy ditch and halt by a shrapnel shelter. Some headquarters of kinds, evidently. Except for the pounding of our guns things are fairly quiet. A few Very lights are going forward from the German trenches in front of the wood, and away in a sort of semicircle to our front and left. The ground slopes up on our left, but is fairly level on front and right, and away on this side looms the wood now and again revealed by bursting shells.

" Is this the bombing party ? " demands an officer's voice from the shelter.

" Yes, sir," answers the guide, halting us.

" All right, sit down ! " We squat while our officer brushes by and enters the shelter.

" So long, lads, good luck ! " says the Lancashire Sergeant, and having handed over disappears in the darkness.

Some Leicesters are in the trench with us, and O'Donnell enquires from one.

" Ehi, chum ! Where's the front line ? "

" Front line, I dunno," answers the man in the flat drab voice of a yokel. " Oi come up to-day, and don't know where Oi be at all ! " and begins muttering to himself.

" Lord save us," breathes Rodwell disgustedly, " what are we with, a blooming farmyard ? We only want a few roosters here ! "

Another man edges up, peers at us and says : "Why do you wear black buttons ? "

"Oh," answers O'Donnell, "don't you know? We are in mourning for Fritz over yonder ! " and cackles like a madman.

"Eh, lad," says the first voice, "these be daft fellers we've got here ! "

"Here, let's have a look over," I cry and scramble and peer over the parapet. Apparently there is another trench in front of us held by these troops, for the occasional plop-crack of a rifle being fired towards the wood can be heard. Beyond it about two hundred yards of bare ground, looking ghostly and mysterious in the momentary flash of falling flares, another shadowy trench—the enemy's—and the wood as a background.

Our officer comes out and comes amongst us, and moves forward.

"Lead on a little way, Sergeant," he orders. The Sergeant, out of our "A" Company, leads on past the shelter and we follow into a sort of emplacement, built up with sand-bags.

"All right, men, sit down, while I explain what you have to do," says the Officer, and our little party of fifteen men sits down in a group and listens attentively.

"We are going up into the front line presently," commences our leader, "which is held by the 8th Leicesters. At 2 a.m. our guns are commencing a bombardment of the German front line, which will last till daylight, then they will lift and we shall attack. Our job is to lead the front of the attack, and push on into the wood and bomb machine-gun nests till we reach the railway line about four hundred yards inside. We will dig in there with the Leicesters and then, when the following battalions straddle over us, our task is done and we shall withdraw back with the 8th Leicesters and afterwards go back to our unit. The Huns are holding a trench about one hundred yards in front of the wood ;

that's their front line. They have another support
line at the edge of the road, and then God knows
what defences inside the wood. Once inside the
wood our artillery will lift well over and drop
shrapnel on to the railway line and beyond, so take
care not to run too far forward. Is it all clear ? "

" Yes, sir," we chorused.

" Very well, then. See that you have plenty of
bombs, about twelve each man. Some Leicesters are
detailed to follow us up with more boxes. We shall
draw all spare bombs here and then make our way
forward and you can lie in the front line and sleep a
little if you can. We must try to do our best, as the
success of the move lies in scuppering the Hun
machine-guns."

He ceased and we began to overhaul our arms in
the semi-darkness.

" I still have a magazine full of cartridges for my
automatic," said O'Donnell, producing his German
pistol and fingering it lovingly. " 'Tis a fine bit of
iron she is in a scrap ! "

" It looks to me as if we are in for a basinful all
right," I said. " I don't like the idea of scrambling
about in the wood. I bet the Boche has some nice
trap all ready for us ! "

" Yes, boys," said Rodwell very soberly, " we
are in for a nasty show, and for God's sake let's hang
together. We don't know any of these other fellows
and we'll have to rely on ourselves. One for all and
all for one, eh ? "

" Sure," I chimed in, " if any of us go down, the
others will have to help if they can ! "

" Now don't get gloomy," put in O'Donnell
cheerily, " we've seen enough of these shows and
so far we're all right ! "

" Aye, but luck does not hold out for keeps,
Don," replied Rodwell seriously.

" Well, it can't be helped. What will be, will
be ! " I said resignedly.

" Come on, let's draw our bombs," and we went

back to the shelter. An officer and sergeant of the Leicesters doled the Mills out and our party was ready to move. In single file we crawled with bent backs along a half-dug narrow gully and presently emerged into the front line—a hastily dug trench with very sketchy bays, no trench-boards and with clinging dank mud at the bottom.

Holes were dug on the parapet side, just sufficient for a man to shelter into. The whole trench was alive with men of the Leicesters, sleeping in clumps at the bottom, and it was difficult to move along without treading on them. Now our party was split up. We three, a lance-corporal from the Sussex and the officer together. The sergeant and four other men farther off and another group under a corporal farther away still. Our little group moved on for a while and then came to rest by a Lewis-gun section. A subaltern of the Leicesters handed over to our sub., who apparently had to take charge of this group of Leicesters as well.

" When Zero goes, men, you go forward and the Lewis-gun will follow you for covering fire," said the officer. " Now make yourselves as comfortable as you can until the barrage starts."

Again we settled down. The night was fine, stars were shining in the heavens, their twinkling points like bright jewels on black velvet. The intermittent bang-bang of guns boomed all over the front except on our sector, which had suddenly got uncannily quiet. The Boche was lying doggo. Not a shot from his trenches, although doubtless his sentries were on the alert.

We three, squatted in an angle, chatted desultorily for a few moments, then gradually fell silent. O'Donnell was soon sleeping peacefully, all humped up as if he had not got a single care in the world. Rodwell was nodding off, jerking into wakefulness every few minutes and looking around with startled gaze. I was tired, but sleep refused to woo me. I sat on, thinking of the coming attack.

Would I survive, or would I lie in a mangled heap at the edge of the trees to be trod on and stamped in the earth by the feet of the charging lines ? How many of all these hundreds, deep in slumber around me, would be walking the earth twenty-four hours hence ?

That nameless dread of machine-guns that had been mine since that awful July day last year when I lay quivering in the open at Hooge, with machine-gun bullets beating a mad tattoo round me for hours on end, seized me for a moment. I looked at the peaceful mysterious stars shining above me and sighed. Well, useless to dwell on such subjects. One must enter into action with calm courage and ready hand—that's the only way by which survival can be ensured to a certain extent. Shaken nerves lead to mistakes, and in this game a mistake means death. Thus ran my thoughts.

I shook myself, stood up, peered over the parapet at that half-seen fateful hump a couple of hundred yards ahead, strolled over to the sentry standing watchful at the end of the bay, exchanged a few muttered words with him, and then came back to where my two chums crouched, and lay down beside them, and presently the noise of the booming guns and the freshness that had sprung in the night air began to lull my senses, and gradually I, too, fell into uneasy slumber, waking at intervals when O'Donnell, who was always restless in sleep, kicked out and caught me in tender portions of my body.

CHAPTER SEVEN

I

CRASH! Whizz! Swish! Cr-r-ump! Bang, bang, bang, bang, crash, CRASH! A terrific thrumming din brought us to our feet with a jerk and we ran to the parapets. In the murk of late night the flashing red glares of the bursts were enveloping the whole length of the German advanced and support trench lines, throwing the scene into awesome and vivid relief. The German front system appeared as a blazing, blinding wall of terrible dancing and leaping ruddy flames. Tongues of fire licked up, rising yards into the air, and the wood became etched in crimson light. Huge spouts of earth, as if pushed by giant hands or internal convulsions, spouted high into the air continually, the undulating clouds lit momentarily by the yellow and crimson stabs of the bursts. Green and red rockets soared up far over the trees from the tortured, heaving enemy trenches. All previous bombardments appeared to me like child's play in comparison. I glanced around at the awestruck pale-faced men peering over the parapets with stark amazement and fear in their glaring eyes.

Rodwell and O'Donnell bounced up beside me.

" What a hell ! " gasped the first. " Poor bastards in those trenches, there won't be a living thing left when we get across ! "

" Holy Mother ! 'Tis as if the divil himself is flinging his burning fire slap into 'em," ejaculated O'Donnell in awestruck tones ; " 'tis a sight to remember all our days ! "

The grand overture of the artillery settled down to a steady crescendo. The roar of the whizzing shells overhead and the awful noise of the crashes made all speech impossible. We could only gaze spellbound at this proof of the might of modern artillery. I could picture the luckless Huns opposite crouching against their heaving defences, woefully inadequate to stem this terrible

blast of bursting steel and to protect their shrinking
bodies from being consumed and smashed by this
all-destroying, flaming, raging Moloch. Doubtless,
dazed and shaken beyond endurance, those unfortunates were seeking cover in their deep underground
lairs, with the foreknowledge that when this over-
whelming and stunning deluge of fire and steel
ceased, the waves of the charging British infantry
would be crashing amongst them to complete the
havoc and destruction wrought by this soulless
machine of death.

This terrific bombardment had extended along the
whole line from Pozieres, over the Bazentin ridges
and beyond. My mind could not grasp the magni-
tude of the effort, or the countless tons of lethal steel
that were being flung, like a monster hosepipe
vomiting a stream of water, at the hapless enemy.
Minute after minute the noise increased until our
ear-drums hammered like mad, and the quivering
air, laden with the acrid tang of explosives, became
difficult to breathe. My heart was thumping
heavily, rapidly. My pulses beat quicker and even
our own trenches shook and quivered and rocked
about at the shock of this tremendous burst of fire.
One's being shrunk back appalled at this display of
ferocious destructive might. I could sense the
thoughts of those around me as if this wave of blasting sound had destroyed the material world and
bestowed on me telepathetic powers. Most of
the men were gripped by unplumbed horror, and yet
at the same time uplifted to the extent that space and
time ceased to have any meaning. We were living
in a world where flames, pandemonium and death
held undisputed sway and our living bodies were as
nothing. It is impossible to clothe the scene in
adequate terms. These are subtle shades that the
pen cannot describe. Only the actual sense can
register and visualize the whole.

The tumult increased constantly as more and
heavier guns came into action, and we stood there

on that trench parapet dazed and hypnotized by the spectacle of that raging, all-devouring storm of shells all around us. When I had been gazing for some time, lost in awe and for the moment completely divorced from my surroundings, I felt a tug at my elbow. I looked round startled. O'Donnell was bawling in my ear as loudly as he could : " Get down, E——," he shouted ; " they are going to dish some rum out ! "

" All right," I bawled back, " I'll get down "— and I clattered down off the fire-step. An officer and a sergeant-major of the Leicesters appeared in the trench with rum jar and spoon and proceeded to dole out the spirit. I swallowed mine eagerly and a pleasant glow warmed me. Everybody became keyed up, and excitement pervaded the ranks. The Leicesters kept jabbering and fiddling about, jumping on the fire-steps looking over at that awful flail of fire that raked the German lines like a searing lash, slashing and whipping at their defences, leaving furrows of tumbled earth and riven, mangled bodies.

Any attempt at further rest became impossible, and Rodwell, O'Donnell and I crouched over the fire-steps silent and keen-eyed, gazing with awe at that tempest beating at the tortured ground without pause, minute after minute and hour after hour. Time had no meaning for us, only the growing light and paling stars marking its passing.

At length we felt a touch, and turning round found our Officer gesturing at us to get down. We stepped down in the trench. He shouted at us, as the din rendered ordinary speech impossible, and pointed at his wrist-watch.

" It is nearly four ! The bombardment will stop at four and we will get over. Get ready to move ! "

The moment was at hand. I gave a last look at my arms, jerked a round up the breech of my rifle, pulled tight the straps of my bombing apron, made quite sure that the pins of my bombs would pull out easily and pinned my respirator on my chest at the ready. The others were similarly engaged. One last pull at my water-bottle, my mouth felt hot and dry, a flicker of steel as we fixed our bayonets and we stood ready. The men in the trench were scrambling on the fire-steps, a few of the Leicesters came up behind us carrying loose Mills bombs in canvas buckets and the Lewis-gun team lined up. Everyone tense with excitement waited for the fateful minute that would send us tearing out into the open and towards our fate.

The guns with a last soul-blasting sound increased their rate of fire and hurled a final, awful thundering blast of shell at the heaps of heaving earth in front of us and then, as if hurled into oblivion by some unknown force, suddenly ceased.

The instant of profound silence was more impressive than all the noise our ears had been subjected to. It was gripping, staggering, awesome. I heard the piping of a lark and then the shrill blasting of whistles here and there as with a roaring cheer the lines of the attacking infantry crossed the parapets and swarmed towards the wrecked German line.

At the same time, with another terrific surge of sound, the guns, having lengthened their ranges, hurled their massed loads of death into and beyond the wood, with rending crashes.

I found myself moving at a loping run beside my two chums, dodging round shell-holes and the usual muck and rubbish of no-man's-land, and all about me in the growing light lines of men moving forward with their bayoneted rifles at the high port. We moved forward in perfect safety for the first fifty yards or so and then a sputtering tac-tac-tac began to break out from the German line. By some superhuman miracle its survivors were getting some machine-guns into action.

" Come on, E—— ! " yelled O'Donnell, " move faster, let's get into them before they start properly ! " and with a wild shout we forged forward with a rush.

II

The growing light showed things plainer. Here and there men stumbled and fell as the machine-guns took their toll, but on the whole the attack reached the trench with very slight loss and no hold up.

Trench ? There was none. Only a few holes and a flattened, humped and hummocky ditch. A few tattered, bloody and dusty horrors sprang up, hands held high. Half-buried bundles in grey uniforms sprawled about here and there. We jumped in a sort of shallow ditch filled with dead bodies and a wrecked machine-gun and lay down getting our breath back. The trench had been won without a struggle.

" Come on, men, forward," yelled our sub., waving his stick. Out of the corner of my eye I could see the line of Leicester men rise again and vault over towards the next trench by the road and the wood beyond.

As we rose again, however, we realized that the Hun defence was coming into action. A wave of intense machine-gun fire broke out and bullets began to drone. At the same moment German shrapnel started bursting over our heads unpleasantly.

Once more with a high shrill cheer the straggling wave of men hurled itself forward, to be met by a blast of fire. Unfortunates were pitching forward at every step, and flopping down like empty sacks, writhing, twisting and moaning. The ground here was a mass of holes and dead men, sand-bags and scattered, blasted bushes and wood.

" Down," cried Rodwell as a blaze of machine-gun fire plopped in front of us, sending up spurts of earth in all directions, together with the buzzing wh-a-ng of ricochetting slugs.

" Oh, my Gawd ! " cried a voice behind me in stricken, dazed tones, and one of the men carrying a Mills box crumpled and fell, bumping into me

and pitching heavily down, his helmet spinning off,
tinkling and rattling.

" Christ ! move on," I yelled frenziedly.

Crash ! Crash ! O'Donnell slung a couple of
bombs, rose and ran forward. We scotched him up
quickly and then, hurling another flight of grenades,
we slithered down within a few yards of the trench,
with a machine-gun spluttering and roaring close in
front. Trr—trr—trr spoke the Lewis behind us as,
with a last rush, we flung ourselves over the obstacle.
Blam ! snapped a pistol-shot close to me, and then
I found myself standing over a writhing German on
the ground. I had pinned him with my bayonet !
Crashes and shots, shouts and scurry all round me.
The subaltern yelling like mad—a confused splatter
of machine-guns, rifle-shots, running men, cries,
groans, the slam of shrapnel howling and whistling,
faint cheers—and the road in front of me. We have
gained the position and the wood is before us.

We re-group ourselves pantingly. The subaltern is
still with us. The Lance-corporal has disappeared.
Two men and the Lewis gun get in beside us. No
trace of the party with the bombs. Probably somewhere behind us. Groups of men are lining the
trench and more are crowding in all the time. Lewis
guns and German machine-guns are plopping and
spluttering everywhere. Farther to our left the Huns
have put down an artillery screen, and their shells
are screeching and bursting. Here they are treating
us to a heavy dose of shrapnel. Wounded Huns and
some of our boys are moaning and staggering in
near us. There is a tang and sour reek of all battle
smells about us. Dead men, hideously mangled, are
now being revealed to our eyes by the rising sun,
lighting the ground in its rays and chasing the
shadows.

The wood looms menacingly before us, just a
clump of interlaced foliage and broken, scarred
stumps, with the enemy lurking within it.

A slight pause to regain our scattered wits and

then, glancing round, the officer waves us onward.

We inch forward warily and get ready to make
another rush.

" Over by that shell-hole," yells Rodwell, pointing to the spot about twenty yards ahead. We
gather ourselves together and then make a dash for it.

Tac-tac-tac-tack ! splutters a gun at us as we
run. It misses us and down we go into the shell-
hole—just the three of us and the subaltern. The
Lewis gunners have hung back and are firing over
our heads, to keep the Huns down.

The Hun gun is slap in front of us, somewhere in
the bushes at the edge of the trees, another twenty
yards onward.

" Sling some grenades and rush it," cries the
officer as the Lewis ceases fire. " Our gunners are
about to follow us ! "

" Over she goes, boys ! " yells Rodwell and, half
standing, hurls a grenade. We follow suit, and as
they burst we yell like devils out of hell and rush.
Crashing through the bushes we just catch sight of a
couple of scuttling grey figures and reach the gun.
It's lying over lop-sided, a Boche, covered in blood,
twitching and swaying drunkenly over it. Another
flat on his back in the complete abandon of death
with knees drawn up and arms outflung. We poke
about with our bayonets. A caved-in dug-out
entrance, hidden by leaves and fallen branches, a
limb of a tree blocking our path forwards and a pain-
laden voice : " Englishman, mercy ! "

I look by the gun. A young German with white,
scared face and holding one hand up feebly is half
lying, half leaning by the dug-out, with Rodwell
standing over him with his bayonet.

" All right, Fritz," I hear him. " Get up and beat
back there, quick ! " The scared boy gets up feebly,
blood dripping from shoulder and useless arm, and
with a wild glance scrambles away in the direction
of our lines.

" Come on, men, get forward, don't stop ! "
orders the officer.

The Lewis-gun team, three men now, crashes
through. Sounds of battle all over the place. The
dull thud, thud of grenades, the rat-tat-tat of machine-
guns and the sharp crack of scattered rifle-shots
come to us from all sides. The Leicesters are attacking the line of the wood on our left, but seem to be
hung up, for all of a sudden a wave of rapid fire
breaks out from them. We move forward again now,
but very carefully, and plunge into the tangle of
trees and scrub. We inch on, grenades in hands,
crawling on hands and knees, stopping at every few
paces. Rodwell is on my left and Don on my right-
hand side, the subaltern just behind me, and farther
back the Lewis gun, its men alert and ready to cover
us with a blast of fire. Crash ! A German stick-
grenade bursts just beyond us.

" There are the swine ! " yells out O'Donnell,
and heaves over a bomb.

The Lewis opens fire quickly and we make
another rush, only to crash against a barrier of
barbed wire stretched and tangled between the trees.

" To the left," yells the sub., and we swerve round
rapidly as another burst of fire crashes out from in
front of us. Somehow we get over the wire, our
clothes tearing and the barbs scratching and pulling
at our bodies and equipment, and we run slap-bang
into another gun just behind. Germans jump up and
come at us. For a moment there is a flurry of figures,
half-seen, hazy faces loom in front of me. I push
forward my rifle and let go, working the bolt auto-
matically, and then, as I empty my magazine, slash
forward with my bayonet. I glimpse O'Donnell
flailing about with clubbed rifle, I hear the short,
sharp bark of the subaltern's pistol and suddenly
trip over the gun and fall headlong over a struggling
and kicking German, who tries to make a grab at
me. Oh, my God, as I go down I hear the stutter
of another gun close by, and a rushing, whizzing

sound of bullets, and then some more shattering crashes and Rodwell's high cry : " That's for you, you bastards ! "

Short, sharp bursts of fire and a crowd of the Leicesters break through.

I pick myself up. The Boche is moving slowly, snorting and wheezing feebly. He is done for all right. We are in a small glade with broken trees and a barricade of branches and bays before us. The splutter of machine-guns all about us. This wood is stiff with them ! O'Donnell is in rags, blackened and grimed and in an excited state, gesturing wildly. " Come on after them, we are near that bloody railway line ! " he yells, brandishing his rifle. The Lewis gun has come up, and the Leicesters are moving on our left and behind us. The noise is terrific, a blend of crashes, bursts and occasionally falling branches and huge bits of trees. We are now drunk with it all and have become utterly reckless. With cries and whoops we dash on again, breaking through wire and obstacles. There's more open space here and we can see the railway line winding like a snake through the trees with a line of sand-bags and tree branches flung down just beyond, from which the Boche is firing away. The ground is absolutely a confusion of pits, holes, ditches, broken gear and God knows how many dead men.

But by now we are only concerned with getting to that railway line, and are deaf and blind to all else.

" Have you any more bombs, E—— ? " howls Don. " I have run out of mine ! "

" No ! " I hoot back. " I've only one ! "

" Where is the carrying party ? " asks the sub-altern, glancing back. But those fellows have either got wiped out or lost all touch with us.

" Here you are, use these ! " cries Rodwell, flourishing German stick-bombs in his hands.

Plenty of these are lying about, so we grab them, stick them on our equipment belts by their hooks and prepare to make our last plunge forward.

Bang ! Bang ! Bang ! Our artillery slams again beyond the railway line, and with a last rush we forge ahead, running and zigzagging like mad under a terrific hail of machine-gun-fire, scramble on to the twisted and broken rails and sleepers and start slinging grenades as fast as we can over the barricade. We have reached our objective ! The Leicesters begin to arrive in small groups and line the barricade, firing over and through the interstices and gaps. Lewis guns begin to chatter, gradually the Boche fire dies down, and we look about us.

" Where's the officer ? " cried Rodwell.

A minute ago he was near me ; now, as I look back, I see him waving from the ground a few yards away.

" Looks as if he is hit," I cry, and dash back to him.

" It's quite all right," he says as I come up. " Get back to your post. I am hit in the knee."

" All right, sir, you are in the open," I reply, grabbing him by the arm. " Get up with us, there's more shelter." And, leaning on me, I get him up next to Don, rip his putties and trousers and smack a bandage on. He has a slug in the leg, does not bleed much.

" Thank you," he gasps. " I'll be all right. How are things going on ? "

" All right, as far as we can judge," I reply. " The enemy has retired back ! "

" There will be another battalion coming through to us now," he goes on, " and then you men will be able to get back."

Things have quietened down for the minute here. Farther on our fellows are working through the wood. I carefully raise my head over the parapet of the barricade. A welter of tumbled bags and shell-holes, a bit of a clearing and more thick woods beyond. Crowds of dead Germans, some wounded moaning in the open, between our line and the wood, waving arms feebly. We can't help them, though, until the attack goes farther, and the enemy is flung back.

" Well, I wish the next lot would hurry up," says Rodwell wearily. " It's been a tough job all right ! "

Bang ! Whan-ngg ! Crash ! Crash ! Crump ! A perfect tornado of high explosive and shrapnel shells falls hissing and bursting round our breastwork. Geysers of earth hurtle skyward, tree branches and leaves shower down, crashing and bumping. A curtain of black smoke momentarily hides the sun.

Tac-tac-tac-tack ! A heavy bout of Boche machine-gun-fire lashes out madly at us from the wood, its bunches of bullets hiss, whizz and plop all over the place.

We cower down as best as we can to dodge the deluge of fire the enemy is hurling at us.

" Down under cover ! " yells hoarsely an officer's voice farther down. " Get ready and load your magazines ! " There's a rattle of rifle-bolts, men become tense with expectation.

" By all that's holy," grates out O'Donnell pantingly, " Fritz is going to counter-attack us ! "

Another wave of heavy gun-fire falls like a curtain behind us, crashing down amongst the trees and into the road beyond, trying to bar the way to the advancing lines of British infantry, and then the counter-attack bursts on us like a thunderbolt.

III

The Boche machine-guns blaze away furiously for some instants and then, from the depths of the wood, there emerges a surging mob of big, hefty-looking Huns, yelling like the souls of the damned and rushing forward with fixed bayonets.

" Stand-to ! Rapid fire ! " the commands hurtle down our line, and we jump up, pumping lead into the assaulting Boches. The Lewis guns are blazing away madly. We work our bolts frantically. The

Germans go down in heaps in that confined space, but the assault reaches our barricade.

We are chucking bombs frantically. Men are going down. Huns appear, scrambling over the obstacle and jumping in amongst us. Now it becomes a hand-to-hand mêlée. Faces and huge grey uniforms appear before me through the eddies of smoke. I strike out and lunge. Ti-ng goes my steel helmet, I reel, stumble and fall amongst a heap of writhing figures. For an awful instant that seems a lifetime I look up with wide, terrified eyes at a gigantic, steel-helmeted, red-faced Hun plunging at me with a bayonet. The thought flashes through my numbed brain : " This is the end," and I await the stroke that will send me to oblivion with terror-sickened soul, when there is a flurry, a figure hurls itself like a battering-ram at the Hun. A terrible yell goes up and my assailant disappears in a shower of blood and crashes down against the sand-bags, tearing at his stomach, with heels drumming and kicking at me. There's a wild scramble all round. I jump up, grab my rifle and lay about me blindly, madly. Men fall, rise, come at me, melt away. A pistol snaps in my face, I hear a gasp beside me and down goes the khaki-clad figure of my saviour. Some more confused struggling, O'Donnell's voice hooting like a banshee, a rush of khaki figures, which suddenly appear from nowhere, roaring and stabbing at the Huns. I find myself on top of the barricade, yelling inanely, amid a roar of Lewis-gun fire, smoke, explosions, while the survivors of the counter-attack run off, falling and stumbling to the shelter of the trees, leaving a trail of dead and mangled, moaning figures behind them in the open.

The air is trembling with the burst of British shells falling amongst the trees screening the Huns. A roaring cheer goes up behind me. We've beaten the counter-attack ! But at what a cost ! Our position is heaped with mounds of slain and quivering, wailing wounded. I come back to reality and stagger about, looking for my chums.

New troops are constantly coming up in groups and sections, jumping over us and plunging beyond into the wood, from whence comes a clatter and stutter of machine-guns and the dull thuds of bomb explosions. Everything seems unreal—just like a dream. Streams of prisoners are being collected and sent off under escorts. Big, hefty-looking Prussian Guards, Jaegers, men from the Lehr Regiment, quite a hotch-potch of various units mixed together. The Boche must have scraped together all the men he could lay hands on and flung them recklessly into action in a desperate attempt to hold up our advance. Most of them, although grimed and blackened by battle, bloodshot of eye, tattered and torn, look well set up, nothing like the figures of fun of the comic papers. They have fought hard and well, and the tale that they must be driven into action at the pistol point is just moonshine.

O'Donnell sidles up, the light of battle still glinting in his eye, his bayonet all spattered and streaked with blood, steel helmet at the back of his head and his clothing tattered, and rent and covered with chalk, mud, and brick dust.

" By the powers, E——," he gasps, " it's been a tearing, raging time." And then, looking round : " Where's Rod ? "

I come to with a start. The last glimpse I had of Rodwell was in the flurry of the attack. We begin looking round. Shells are still bursting fitfully, but the Boche curtain of fire has ended. Having failed with the counter-attack it looks as if they are content to concentrate in the defence. A furious cannonade has broken away on our left flank on the ridge covering Martinpuich, and also on the right, where they are attacking Bazentin from the other side. No trace of Rodwell amongst the men lining the barricade and busy putting themselves to rights. The cries of the wounded rising on all sides are pitiful and heartrending ; this slaughter-house is beyond description. The Leicesters have been cut to ribbons and the survivors of our attacking waves now lining the railway are but a pitiful reminder of that unfortunate battalion. Stretcher-bearers are busily tending the wounded, who, when possible, are scrambling back as fast as they can into the conquered woodland behind us, and to safety and care beyond.

And then we find Rodwell lying amongst a confused pile of dead men, mostly Huns, at the point where I had been overwhelmed and flung down.

" Oh, pitiful Mother of Sorrows ! " cries O'Donnell in a cracked, stricken voice, running forward and dropping down. " Here he is ! "

Suddenly I recollect that furious, lunging figure that had crashed out of nowhere at the crucial moment when the Boche was about to stick me. It had been my poor, brave pal who had snatched me from the very maw of death—and had paid the price for me !

We two, stricken with sudden, searing sorrow, bent over him. He was still alive, breathing stertorously, with eyes closed. An awful bloody wound on the side of his face just below his left temple gaped, blackened and scorched, and blood was seeping and spurting out every time he breathed.

Tenderly I wiped his forehead with hastily damped rag, while O'Donnell, shaking like a leaf, fumbled for his first-aid bundle, kept in the special pocket on the front hem of his tunic. At our touch poor old Rod's eyelids fluttered and his eyes opened, and he gazed up at us with dawning recognition, struggled to speak, spluttering painfully and expelling blood.

" All right, Rod, boy," I cried encouragingly, " keep quiet and we'll have you out of here in a jiffy ! "

" Don't move me ! " he gasped with an effort, his

voice choked with the blood welling into his mouth.
" I—am—done for ! Ow ! Give me water ! "
And he rolled his head helplessly in pain.

O'Donnell lifted his head gently, while I unfastened my water-bottle and put it to his lips. He
swallowed greedily for an instant and then, feebly :
" Lay my head down—everything—is—spinning ! "
he muttered thickly. " Good-bye, Don—E——.
It—had to be—I always knew it. Oh, God ! My
head ! "

" Pull yourself together, Rod," I cried wildly.
" We'll bandage you and get you away ; you'll be all
right." But as I gazed at his poor shattered face
I knew all would be in vain. Our poor old chum
had been shot at point-blank range by a pistol. The
bullet must have ploughed through his left cheek-
bone, for as O'Donnell and I essayed to apply the
field dressing we saw with horror that it had broken
the cheek-bone, made a horrible cavity of red,
mangled flesh, with gouts of blood seeping up, and
had carried away part of his ear. Only his vitality
had kept him alive at all. He spoke painfully once
more : " Look after—yourselves—boys—and try to
bury me—decently——! " A tremor shook him,
his head lolled back—his eyes rolled. He muttered
incoherently : " Slaughter—the Old Corps——"
and suddenly stiffened and then went limp, while
we two grief-stricken, heedless of the war, of battle,
the burst of shells, or the wails of the stricken
men around us, watched the great soul of our pal
wing its way free to soar to realms beyond our ken.
I stood thus petrified, grasping the hand of the pal
that had saved me from oblivion and in so doing
had forfeited his own life, full of purpose and
promise. O'Donnell was mute, filled with the
sense of our loss, and we two, who had learned to
look on death unmoved, bowed down and wept,
while round us the din of conflict waxed louder as
the Boche began to plaster shells again on the railway
line.

"Come on, Don," I cried at length, realizing our position. "Empty his pockets. We can do no more."

"By Christ!" he answered in a low, fierce voice. "We can't leave him to be trampled and heaved about like an old sack. Come on, E——, let's try to cover him up."

We lifted the poor body and painfully we carried him to a shell-hole below and close to the barricade of bags and wood and there we laid him, painfully scooping earth and debris over him, until at last we covered his poor remains up, and then we stuck a rifle over the improvised grave with a hastily-scribbled line on a bit of white bandage O'Donnell produced, and wrote on, with indelible pencil: "Rfn. Rodwell, D.C.M.—2nd K.R.R.C.—lies here —*Ave!*" And then, our task over, we busied ourselves aiding the pitiful, broken wreckage of men we could get at.

The sun rode high in the heavens now. The air was full of shrapnel exploding over the position. Over on the left flank a huge pall of black smoke had appeared. Men were still coming up forming and going beyond into the wood. A steady stream of wounded, both ours and Fritz's, kept streaming up. We, weary, hot, despondent, still stood at our posts with the remainder of the Leicesters.

The day wore on thus. O'Donnell had become silent and morose. Both of us were brooding over Rodwell. We felt his loss far more keenly than poor old Marriner's or Oldham's. He had been one of us, sharing our same view-points, and beneath his veneer of sarcasm and biting comment a brilliant, vibrant mind which might have made its mark—and now he had crossed into that mysterious bourne at the very dawn of life!

"Come on, Don; shake up, old boy, no use pining!" I said, turning to him.

"Oh, E——," he replied feelingly, "I'd have rather gone meself. Poor old Rod!"

" Well, he died as he would have wished, quickly and in the moment of victory."

At length a Leicester officer came up to us : " Oh, you are the men from the bombing party ! " he said. " You can make your way over there," pointing to the wreckage of the trees behind us, " the rest of your men are there ! You can go back to the North Lancs ! "

" Very good, sir ! " I replied. " Come on, Don," and, unfixing our bayonets, we began to run back in rushes, with that cursed shrapnel hot at our heels. The whole area here was a vast charnel-house. Amongst the trees festoons of broken barbed wire, *chevaux de frise* blocking our way, shell-holes, piles of dead in all attitudes, overturned machine-guns, with their dead German crews around them. A dead Boche hanging on a tree branch. Evidently a sniper shot at his post. The sergeant and two other men were all the survivors of our contingent of fifteen. We reported, sat down for a few minutes in this litter of death, and presently, when things seemed to have calmed down in our immediate neighbourhood, the sergeant rose up, looked around and then remarked : " We might as well clear out from this bloody mess. Follow me in single file ! " And away we went, scrambling and dodging between shell-holes, out through the wood, past the scene of our early exploits, back into the jumping-off trench, and so back to Scott's Redoubt. Lines of men laden with water, ammunition, sand-bags, boxes of bombs, barbed-wire rolls, were coming up at a quick pace, eager to get ahead and get the job over. The British guns were going hell for leather, and stray bits of news came our way.

" Bazentin is taken." " The Munsters have reached the switch line." " Thousands of prisoners." " The Huns are beating it." " The 110th Brigade is cut to pieces."

Back in Scott's Redoubt we get some lukewarm tea. Our Sergeant reports to the North Lancs headquarters and then comes back and tells us we can rejoin our Battalion at Becourt.

Evening, lit up with a glare of shell-fire and thousands of Very lights soaring up in all directions, has fallen by the time we reach our own Battalion and halt by the headquarters.

The Adjutant comes out, the Sergeant reports to him and we are dismissed to our Companies, and we two silently make our way up the hill and to our bivouacs.

"Come on, Don. We'd better see old Mac and hand in Rod's gear ! " I say.

"All right, E——, I suppose we'd better ! " sighs O'Donnell despondently. His mercurial Celtic temperament is at a low ebb just now and he seems distraught and moody. Poor Rodwell's death and the severe experiences of the morning have damped his usually boisterous spirits. We fumble about in the bivvy, gather Rod's scanty effects and then go down to see old Mac. Most of the Company are away on some carrying party. The thunder of the guns is echoing away, and from the brow of Becourt Hill the whole horizon seems to be nothing but a plunging and wavering sheet of fire. The fighting has intensified with the fall of night, and Briton and Teuton, locked together in combat, are fighting grimly and stubbornly for the mastery. Thousands are being hurled into eternity on these stricken fields, and their acts of bravery, self-abnegation and devotion to their duty, their pain and their labour, their defeat or triumph, hidden from the gaze of mankind by the cloak of night and stress of action. Their generous young blood is cascading in streams, to be sucked by the dry, greedy earth, unknown tragedies of cowardice and bravery are taking place in that boiling cauldron ahead, and one can but stand mute and wonder !

Old Mac saw us coming towards his shelter, where a candle guttered and blew about, fitfully casting alternate stabs of light and deep darkness within.

" Well, boys, was it pretty bad ? " he queried, giving us a keen look. " Wait a minute, have a swig at this ! " handing me a pannikin of rum. I swallowed a little and passed the rest to O'Donnell, who drank it greedily.

" Pretty bloody, Sergeant-Major ! " I answered. " Poor Rodwell has gone, here is his identity disc."

" I am sorry to hear that, lads ! " ejaculated the Sergeant-Major kindly. " It seems as if in this bloody game the best have to go first. I expect we shall be on the move soon. The 3rd Brigade attacked this morning and got a hell of a rough house. The Munsters and Welsh especially. But they have made some ground up by the German switch line. There'll be a draft coming up to-morrow. Cheer up, boys, and go and have a sleep."

" Thanks, Sergeant-Major," I replied. " I think we can do with one. Come on, Don."

We picked our way to our bivvy, got in anyhow, flung ourselves down and, despite everything, weariness conquered and we fell into exhausted, dreamless slumber.

<h3 style="text-align:center">IV</h3>

" Rouse up, Don ; let's get the grub going ! " and I shook him. Morning was already high, the Platoon were busy and the routine boom-boom of the artillery reverberated everywhere. O'Donnell crawled out of the bivvy, stood up and stretched himself.

" My God, E——," he yawned, " I feel done in and filthy. Better go down to the quarter bloke and see if we can get some clobber. Look at my trousers ! "

Both of us were in a sorry mess. Puttees, tunic, trousers, all rent and tattered by the wire, caked with dried blood, dust, filthiness of all kinds. Our faces and hands blackened, dirty, drawn. O'Donnell's blue eyes gleamed like pools in a mass of muck, long trails of sweat-lines criss-crossed his cheeks, a bristly stubble of gingery hair adorned his chin.

"Yes, we can't even eat like this, old boy. Let's get down to the battery and scrounge a bucket and some water first."

We plunged downhill and scrambled amongst the gun-pits. For a wonder the howitzers were silent, but the gunners were pretty busy packing up gear, cleaning and doing the countless odd jobs that these lethal weapons need to be kept in good trim.

"My Gowd!" cried a Cockney voice as a gunner, catching sight of us, paused to stare in amazement. "Wot the 'ell are you? Freaks from Barnum?"

"Worse than that, chum," I replied. "Have you got a bucket of water? We can do with a good wash!"

"Yus, yer need it!" he cried decisively. "Get behind there, but 'urry up. We are pullin' out presently further forrard! Where 'ave you blokes been?"

We thanked him gratefully as he shepherded us to a dug-out behind the pit and poured out some water into a canvas bucket. What a delight to plunge our aching dirty faces into cool water. To revel with soap and free our arms, chests and whatever parts of our bodies we could get to. Off came our tunics, shirts, puttees and trousers, and, stripped to the buff except for our boots, we lathered ourselves and as best as we could removed the sweat and dirt of battle. Both O'Donnell and I had scratches all over our bodies, where the wire had caught at us, but these were of little moment. And while we scrubbed and splashed we gave the group of gunners gathered round details of yesterday's fight.

"Strewth!" said our cockney friend, "I allus cussed the bloody guns, but cripes, thank Christ I'm not a bloody foot-slogger!"

The wash and sponge down lightened our spirits. O'Donnell began to regain his old verve and chatted cheerfully. A gunner corporal offered us a steaming canteen full of tea after we had dressed and life began to look rosier.

We gave the gunners odd bits of souvenirs we had in our pockets, brass eagles of German helmets, shoulder straps we had cut off Hun tunics, and presently we quitted the battery.

"Quite a decent lot of chaps," said O'Donnell as we climbed back up the hill. "Be God, that wash has done me a power ov good! Poor old Rod, I can't quite believe he's gone. It seems as if he were just ahead!" he added with a regretful sigh.

"Well, old man," I put in, "we've got to soldier on. He is all right now and all we can say won't alter things!"

"Yes, you're right. There's only two of us now. I wonder who'll be the next?"

"Don't you start thinking of that, you blasted Jonah! Come on along to the quarter bloke!"

Captain Sherlock and Mr. Walker were by the Company headquarters as we arrived. We saluted and paused.

"I'm sorry to hear about Rodwell," said the Skipper very kindly to us. "I knew you three men were very close friends!"

"Yes, sir," I answered, "he gave his life for me!" and in a few words I told him what had happened.

"A splendid chap! What a great pity!" muttered Mr. Walker. "A very reliable man, too!"

"Well, you fellows, cheer up," the Skipper continued, "things are going well, and who knows, the end of it may not be so far away! You'd better see about some clothes," he added looking at us; "you certainly need some."

Luckily the quarter bloke was able to make us up, and clothed and more or less in our right minds we got back to the bivvy.

"I say, E——," said O'Donnell, "there'll be some new men to this Section. The draft will be here presently. We'd better get Maddocks and

Snewin in with us, we know them. You never can tell what bloody fish might come up with this lot ? "

" Yes, we'd better go and ask them."

We found them wrangling with some men out of 10 Platoon.

" Yus," was hooting Snewin, " you blokes fair gives me the creeps. There ain't no one in the Batt. like Mr. Walker, and you can swank as much as yer likes. We knows 'im and wouldn't swop 'im for nuffink. Any'ow he wouldn't own such a bloody measly lot of coves as yer Platoon is ! "

" Eh, Snewin," I cried, coming up, " haven't you enough with one bloody war ? Do you want another one ! "

" Ah, these blokes fair make me sick ! " he spat disgustedly. " They was talkin' as 'ow old Walker wanted us slaughtered on the Triangle do, and was too thick-'eaded to retire. We knows better'n that ! "

" Never you mind," I replied easily, " old Walker can look after himself. I want you and Maddocks. Come over here ! "

" What's the game ? " asked the latter suspiciously. " What are you blokes up to now ? " as they followed us.

" Well, we were thinking that perhaps you two would like to barge in with us. There will be some new chums come up into the Section, and maybe you'd rather keep in with the fellows you know ! "

" Yus, that'll suit us to the ground ! " said Snewin cheerfully. " We'll break down our bivvy and make a bigger one for the lot ! " and away they went.

" That Snewin reminds me of old Marriner," remarked O'Donnell musingly. " They seem both decent sort of blokes and will keep us amused." And so another field partnership—doomed, alas, to be of very short duration—started. When I think how in the brief space of months these friend-ships sprang up, held and stood up to the stress of circumstance, to always end under the sweep of fate's scythe just as one began to understand and appreciate their quality, I sigh with regret. Quite immaterially to the social stratus of its components, these brief friendships held far more meaning than the inane, hypocritical acquaintanceships it has been my fate to make in the ordinary course of life. Then no sacrifice was big enough for the sake of a friend—any hardship was cheerfully endured, no self-seeking motive hovered in the background.

Maddocks and Snewin returned with their gear, the enlarged bivvy was run up and at noon we shared our first common dinner.

CHAPTER EIGHT

I

"HALLO," cried out O'Donnell, "here comes the new draft." He had been sitting for some time in front of our bivvy busy scribbling in his note-book. As he caught sight of the group of men standing by Company headquarters he closed the book, put it back in his tunic pocket and stood up.

"Wonder what fellows we'll get," I remarked also, standing up and pocketing a tattered copy of *Three Men in a Boat*, by Jerome, I had been reading. "Let's go and have a look and see ! "

We strolled down and eyed the new men waiting for the Sergeant-Major's allotments to the Platoon. A very mixed bag these, we could see. A few old soldiers, but the majority just raw youngsters.

"Where have you come from ? " queried I, addressing a forlorn-looking kid, gazing round with wide-eyed wonder.

"The 'Avre base camp, chum ; we've bin there a fortnight," he replied in the nasal twang of a cockney. "Come from the 6th Battalion at Sheerness ! "

"Ha, did you ? " queried O'Donnell facetiously. "And how's me friend, Nobby Clarke ? Has he finished those blasted brick and cinder paths at Holm Place yet ? "

"No ruddy fear ! " answered the cockney. "Defaulters are still a-laying them down. I 'ave broke me back more than onst luggin' those blasted bricks about ! "

"Yes," I chimed in, "old Nobby will be still laying them down when the war ends ! "

That brick fatigue at Sheerness was a standing joke in the Corps, and the care old Sergeant-Major Clarke bestowed on those paths, criss-crossing the muddy camp, was proverbial and a terror to all the delinquents unlucky enough to be mustered for that work. In fact so heartily sick had we become of that endless toil that once a particular gay crowd of us had sent old Nobby a brick by registered post as a gentle reminder, and loud had been the laughter in the Sergeants' Mess when the redoubtable Sergeant-Major opened his parcel there one evening!

"Well, never mind me, lad," encouraged O'Donnell, "ye'll think old Nobby's fatigue parties gentle amusement before you are through all that!" with a gesture towards the horizon where shells were bursting and earth and brick dust rising and falling like huge clumps of water spouts.

Old Mac came out, eyed the draft and distributed them to the platoons. Ours, pretty badly knocked about, drew a sergeant, a lance-corporal and about sixteen men. Four new rookies for our Section and a lance-corporal. I had a pleasant surprise in the latter. A very old acquaintance of mine. Carpenter —a tall dark man in his late twenties; an actor of sorts. We had met on the Whitehall parade ground, on that day that seemed so long ago now, when, as newly attested men, we had mustered on our first journey to Winchester. We had been together for a few days at Sheerness and then I had gone off to the 7th Battalion and he God knows where, and now, nearly two years later, we were meeting again on this French field!

"Hallo, Carpenter," I cried as the men made their hesitant way amongst the bivvies, "this way, and welcome to the 2nd!"

"Why, bless my cotton socks, it's E——. How are you, laddie?" shaking my hand heartily. "I've brought something to warm the welcome with!" tapping his water-bottle significantly.

"Now that's talkin'!" joined in O'Donnell enthusiastically. "Come along, you'd better muck in with us!" and we wended our way to the bivvy, exchanging news and making mutual enquiries over common acquaintances.

Carpenter is a whimsical sort of fellow with an inexhaustible fund of funny stories and limericks, mostly unprintable, which he fires off on the slightest provocation, heedless of his surroundings. A jolly, care-free fellow, who knows all the by-ways and highways of Britain ; who can tell you every pub from Land's End to John o' Groat's, with a particular aversion to Welshmen and Jews.

I recollect the shocked look of disgust on the face of a staid cleric entertaining a party of Wykhamites in Winchester's most respectable hotel, when Carpenter, who, with myself and one other, had dined and wined not wisely but well, launched out into some of his most scandalous anecdotes. The hush that fell in that room could have been cut with a knife !

In our present circumstances such a fellow was a godsend, and presently, having sampled his water-bottle, Maddocks, Snewin, O'Donnell and I sat round him, with other interested men from the Platoon crowding round, while he launched into a selection of stories that kept us rocking with laughter, careless to shells, which were bursting on the ridge, Boche shrapnel which now and again came close, and all else forgotten for the nonce.

" Coo," gasped Snewin, dabbing at his streaming eyes, " 'e'll make me ribs crack ! 'Ere, Corporal, an' what 'appened to the girl then ? " he queried as Carpenter with his rich rolling voice paused dramatically.

" Ah, laddie," he said sententiously wagging his finger at Snewin, " haven't you sufficient imagination to fill the blank. I'm afraid your eagerness to know was just like Mary's. She *would* look into everything ! "

Another roar of merriment ensued as we caught the allusion—and so the afternoon waned and night's shadows began to lengthen, and the Platoon, suddenly shifted from all gloom by Carpenter's powers of narrative and imagination, turned to the night's work with cheerful spirits and healthy outlook which a particularly heavy job of lugging rations over that devastated ground by Contalmaison, under a nasty shower of Boche shells that kept screeching and bursting round us as we trudged up and came back, failed to shake. As far as we were concerned each one of us took one of the new rookies in tow and taught him the elementary lore of safety in the midst of death, as far as we were able to.

II

Another sunny day dawned. Breakfast a cheerful meal—Maddocks is a darn good cook—and Carpenter started the morning chirpily. Arms inspection by Mr. Walker, who afterwards assembled the Platoon, and gave us the news. Progress is being made, but there is no doubt that the Boche resistance is stiffening. He tells us the French are still going on well, but Peronne is yet in Hun hands. Heavy fighting is taking place in Delville, Trones and High Wood. The Indian Cavalry we saw the other day, charged in Delville Wood, gained some ground, but was cut to ribbons. Our Division has been scrapping heavily. We shall be moving up to-night. It appears that in the dark last night while the 3rd Brigade were attacking below the Switch Line between Pozieres and Bazentin, the South Wales Borderers and the Gloucesters lost direction, fell foul of one another, and had a hell of a scrap before they found out their mistake.

" By heck ! " remarked O'Donnell. " What a bloody pity ! Bad enough to be done in by the blasted Huns. But funny bein' killed scrappin' your own blokes ! "

" Well, what would you expect ? " enquired Carpenter. " There were Welshmen there, and wherever you come across those blighters you are sure to land into trouble."

All the morning we were busy getting things ship-shape for the move. After our dinner the Orderly Sergeant made his appearance and ordered us to take our bivvies down. Our ground sheets were packed away, all the litter gathered up, and we cleaned up the hill-side, leaving it far tidier than we found it.

In our corps, and especially in our 2nd Battalion, this cleaning-up of all billets and halting-places was almost a fetish. Many a time have we had to occupy billets left in a terrible state by other units, but no one has ever been able to grumble at filthy billets when the Rifles have been before them !

Captain Sherlock and the Sergeant-Major came along, inspected our late camping-ground carefully, and presently we moved off by platoons down Sausage Valley in the late afternoon. In single file we moved, stumbled, twisted and turned about through the churned and broken ground, to eventually reach Scott's Redoubt and settle down in its dug-outs. The redoubt trenches were deep and well sand-bagged and had withstood the past fortnight's fighting pretty well. Deep dug-outs carefully boarded up, wire beds and all sorts of odd comforts testified to the skill and painstaking industry of the Boche. It looked as if he had meant to stay here for good. The dug-outs were a mass of litter, ragged uniforms, belts, flat caps and *pickelhaubes*, a wonderful hunting-ground for the souvenir hunter. We even discovered some German hairy packs, which they call *tornisters*, strapped with overcoats and boots— complete—as if their owners had left them at the last moment in the stress of combat and hasty retreat. The half of my section, including Carpenter, settled down in a dug-out, and we got ready to meet what might occur next. Sentries were put up here and there, and the usual trench routine commenced. We were in support and liable to go up forward at short notice.

Maddocks and Snewin scrounged wood, not a difficult matter here, as burnable debris was lying on all sides, while O'Donnell and I cleaned our abode properly. As night fell we " drummed up," had our meal and then, chaffing and smoking, we fell to yarning in the trench, the dug-out being too close and uncomfortable.

The bombardment was raging as usual, and the Boche reply was feeble and spasmodic, just a few clumps of shells now and then, that fell conveniently distant from us.

" Looks as if Fritz has his belly full and is suffering from a dose of indigestion," remarked O'Donnell. " His bloody fire is quite feeble."

" I expect with all the tons of stuff we are chucking over at the roads and dumps behind his lines he is finding it hard to get ammunition up," said Carpenter. " By all the gods, laddies," he added with a shudder, " I should not like to be trudging all loaded up on his lines of communication. It must be a proper horror ! "

" Aye," chimed in Maddocks with gusto. " Fritz is getting the same kind of medicine 'e used to dish out to us early last year, the swine ! It fair used ter put the wind up me at Richbourg and the 'ulluch road, with his bloody stuff bursting and roarin' day and night, and our artillery lyin' quiet becos they 'ad no bloody ammo ! It's a change ter belt the 'ide out of Kaiser's mob like this ! "

" By the way, Carpenter," I queried, " and what have you been up to during the last eighteen months ? You've been so cursed busy with your tomfoolery and yarns, I haven't had a chance to ask you ! "

" You may as well ask E——," he answered in his usual grandiloquent style. " It is like an Odyssey. I got into the 9th Battalion at first, mucked about round Ypres and got slightly hit on the knee in the daylight counter-attack at Hooge last July, when our old man, Colonel Chaplin, got done in. Then they sent me to convalesce at the casualty clearing station at Poperinghe, and discovered that I had trod the boards. Ah, laddie ! I got collared by the ' Fancies ' and spent some happy months amusing the troops, and once more amidst the whirl of wine, women and song ! But alas, last November I fell foul of a gilded popinjay of the Corps staff. This bloody son of Satan told me I was swinging the lead and leading the life of a disreputable rake—so lo, they bundled me off to a trench-mortar school and eventually back to the 14th Division trench-mortars ! But I had no mind to spend the winter in those rotten, watery trenches at Ypres, so a slight dose of frost-bite, and presto, I find myself in the 5th at Sheerness again ! My reign there was but fleeting, France was calling. At Havre they attached me to the Trench-Mortar School, gave me a stripe and made me a ' canary ' on the training ground. Fine place, Havre ! Plenty to drink, a variety of tongues and figures which appeal to my soul, and there I stayed until Haig, in his misguided mind, thought it fit to bash the Huns. And here we are, boys ! " he added whimsically with a grin.

" Begob, Carpenter, ye old scrounger ! " exclaimed O'Donnell. " You've had it pretty cushy. It's been roses, roses all the way for you all right. Can't understand how some of you fellows manage to get away with it like this ? I have been at it since March '15 and niver a chance of a scrounge ! "

" Ah, well, it requires tact and ' nous ' ! " replied Carpenter with a cunning smirk. " Then I am a good mixer. When I went in front of the M.O., with frost-bite, I discovered he was an American immersed in Shakespeare ! And, boy, I gave the best performance of my whole career in front of a very appreciative audience of one ! I declaimed the soliloquy of Henry the Fifth to him in such a manner as held him spell-bound. Then I damned Bacon for all I was worth, threw in some guff about the glories of the old towns of England—and by the time I had finished he said perhaps a winter in Blighty would do me good ! "

" Blimey ! " said Snewin with unfeigned admiration. " You blokes with the back-chat always click. Every time I try to swing it a bit they allus catches me out ! "

The night freshened and we sought the shelter of the dug-out.

III

Ting! Bang! Clang! Ting-ting-ting! The noise of shell-cases being banged furiously brought us out of sleep with a start. It was pitch dark. For a few moments we groped about in the dark, banging and crashing into each other.

"Ow!" I heard O'Donnell's yowling howl. "Mind me fingers, you clumsy lout!" Carpenter struck a match and soon a candle dispelled the immediate gloom. From the trench above the clanging had increased and spread over all the redoubt. Dull plops were sounding overhead and a blast of dust came floating down to us.

"Gas!" yelled Maddocks. "Get yer masks on. That's the gas alarm being sounded."

We fumbled for our respirators, clapped them on and sprang up the stairs and out in the open, rifle in hand. Men in gas-masks were manning the fire-step, crouching. The air was full of wisps of vapour settling down into a dense fog at the bottom of the trench and swirling about our feet and legs. Gas-shells in thousands were swishing down all over the place.

"Eh, laddies!" came Carpenter's muffled voice. "The Boche is staging a special performance, but it looks as if he is getting the bird!"

Mr. Walker, in gas-mask, came hurrying round, rousing men from dug-outs. The gas alarm clanged on, the sentries beating lustily on the shell-cases that hung here and there for this purpose. We strained our eyes over the parapets and towards the switch-line position between Pozieres and Martinpuich, where a heavy fight was roaring and crashing. Anyhow, the Boche, thanks to our sentries, had not caught us napping, and beyond the bother and discomfort of the gas-masks he is merely wasting ammunition, for nothing!

We stood-to for some time, fuming and angry that our sleep had been so rudely dispelled, the gas-shells dropping with unabated fury throughout the night. We began to sweat, the air in the gas-mask, impregnated with chemicals, was close, uncomfortable. I got a nasty headache and the nose-grip chafed me. However, it could not be helped. We could not remove the respirators and were forced to bear them the whole night through and, willy-nilly, make a vigil of it. Fires were lit here and there in the redoubt. We dodged about with bits of dampened blankets and Hun overcoats, beating and flapping them about in an endeavour to disperse the gas. O'Donnell was swearing and growling like a bear with a sore head. I stood on the fire-step, angry but resigned. Carpenter, after dodging about for a bit, looking after the Section, suddenly curled himself up on the *banquette*, rested his back against the traverse-side, and, gas-mask notwithstanding, went to sleep. And so the night passed, bleak and miserable. The stars paled, the sky lightened and suddenly the gas-shells stopped. Probably the Huns had plastered the whole area to interfere with the reliefs and ration parties.

"Whew!" croaked O'Donnell. "This bloody mask is givin' me the jim-jams. Another hour of it and off it comes, gas or no gas!"

"The perishin' shelling has stopped," sighed Maddocks with relief, "it'll be all right presently. Coo! I 'opes those bloody gunners gets their guts blown to 'ell, the blankety asterisks!"

Gradually it became light. More fires were lighted, a last vigorous flapping with our improvised fans, Carpenter woke up with an ejaculation and cried: "By the beard of the most holy Mohammed! I feel as if a thousand rotten eggs had been slung at me! Perish this damned mask!"

A welcome sight. Our Platoon Sergeant comes round the bay with his mask curled up on his head!

"All right, you men. You can take off your

respirators, but don't go into the dug-outs yet. They'll have gas in 'em still ! "

Oh, blessed relief ! I sling off the cumbersome respirator and inhale deeply of the fresh morning air, sticking my head upwards. There is still a sickish, sweet, unpleasant tang about. Our smarting eyes fill with tears, but what matters it ? After hours of confined and painful breathing in the folds of the mask even the most putrid French farmyard midden would have smelled sweet !

" The Lord be praised ! " exclaims O'Donnell. " I felt like bursting. Me throat's dry, me mouth is like a latrine. Come on, let's make some tea. Carpenter, old man," in wheedling tones, " how's your canteen ? Have you got a drop of the crathur, then ? "

" Aha ! " cries that cheerful rogue, shaking his water bottle. " There's life in the old dog yet ! But mind, you Irish mad-head, only a dram all the way round ! "

We all have a pull at his famous bottle gratefully, and to make things better the rum issue makes its appearance. With new vigour coursing in our veins the discomfort of the night is relegated to the limbo of forgotten things, and we bend our attention to the needs of the present amidst a babble of cheerful chaff and merriment.

Snewin and Maddocks chop up the wood, fires blaze, canteens boil and breakfast is on the board.

" Oh, hell ! " cries a disappointed voice in the next bay, and one of the new draft in our Section comes round with a woebegone expression on his face.

" What's up, laddie ? " enquires Carpenter quizzically. " Why all this thusness, when old Sol, in his chariot of fire, rides the heavens, chasing away all gloom and inundating earth with his beneficent glamour ? "

The man goggles at him, mouth wide open.

" Bother the bloody sun ! " he says crossly and

viciously. " We've lost all our blasted breakfast
cheese ! Those bloody, sneaking, perishin' rats !
I'd laid our cheese ready for frying and just turned
me eyes to the fire, when a big black rat nips acrost,
grabs the 'ole 'unk of asterisk cheese, and jumps over
the parapet with all our ruddy breakfast in 'is mouf.
I couldn't catch 'im, Corporal," he adds pathetically,
" and the blokes there are blamin' me for it
all ! "

" Ha ! Ha ! Ha ! " cackle Snewin and Maddocks.
" The blokes in the Animal Sercieties will give you
a bloomin' medal for feeding the 'ungry, perishin'
rats ! "

We all double up at the expression of chagrin,
futile anger and baffled hopelessness on the man's
face, and then O'Donnell :

" Do you really like cheese ? " he asks with
interest. " All right, me lad, you can have some ! "
And before the indignant Snewin can stop him
hands our morning's supply to the fellow, who
snatches it up, babbles his thanks and nips back into
his own bay.

" Well, you are a one ! " hoots Maddocks, glaring
at him. " Givin' our breakfast away. What the
'ell are we to eat now ? "

" Eggs, me boy, eggs ! " answers O'Donnell
grandly. " This is a mornin' for eggs and bacon,
not cheese ! " He snaps his gas-helmet on, goes
down in the dug-out and comes back with the eggs
he has carefully carried for the last few days.
Maddocks is completely pacified and we sit down to
a luscious breakfast as the early rays of the morning
sun strike the redoubt with golden shafts of light.

The night's vigil made us very sleepy after
breakfast, so by ones and twos we drifted about,
seeking odd corners in which to snatch a few hours'
sleep. Carpenter and I yarned a bit and presently
dropped off.

The Platoon Sergeant shook me up roughly at
about 10 a.m.

" Come on, wake up, you men ! " I heard his voice booming about. " Get a move on ! "

I opened my eyes and sat up. O'Donnell and Maddocks were also getting to their feet.

" What's up, Sergeant ? " I queried, fully awake now and blinking in the sunshine.

" One hour sentry," he answered. " The whole blooming Platoon's asleep in every odd corner they can get at. Not one man awake. If Mr. Walker or the O.C. come around they'd have a proper fit. You three men can take a turn for the next three hours ! "

" Have a heart, Sergeant ! " cried O'Donnell appealingly. " Old Fritz can't get down at us, you know."

" Why, I am letting you off easy," answered the non-com. " I am going to turn the rest of the Platoon to clear the gas from the dug-outs ! You can join in if you like," he added meaningly.

" Oh, that's all right, Sergeant," cut in O'Donnell hastily, " we'll keep a look out."

" Mind you do, and are awake when the officers come round, then ! " And the Sergeant clamped away to rouse the men.

" Might be worse ! " grumbled O'Donnell. " All we have to do is to keep our eyes open for the Skipper. Anyhow, two of us can go to sleep and the other keep cave. Come on, let's toss up for turns," fishing in his pockets for a coin.

I was lucky, got the third turn, so while Maddocks got to the fire-step and stood up, O'Donnell and I made ourselves comfortable in the corners, and the hot sunshine, the drone of the British bombardment and the balmy atmosphere overcame us and we were off into deep slumber again. O'Donnell woke me later, and still half asleep I got up to relieve him.

" We'll get some dinner, when this sentry spell is over," he said. " Carpenter's just been by swearing like a heathen. He's been in charge of some fatigue parties in the dug-outs and he was as hot and sweaty as hell," and with a chuckle, " his bottle is empty and he's drinkin' water ! " and with that he went to sleep.

It was hot ! Everything quiet round me, it was difficult to keep my eyes open. Those hours in gas-masks had tired all of us out. I kept gazing away at that eternal pall of smoke over the woods and ridges, unheeding the booming and drumming guns, closing my eyes and dozing on my feet, shaking myself into wakefulness with jerks and starts, confused dream shapes flitting before me. I kept thinking of Marriner, Rodwell, Oldham, the stress and tear of these last few days . . . gradually I started dozing off again, as the sun beat down on my steel helmet.

A slight noise suddenly jerked me into wakefulness. I turned round, startled, for one instant my scattered wits refused to function, then, with a stentorian yell of " Stand-to " that rang through the silent trench with a hoot like a horn of discord, I made one frantic grab for my rifle and fired a blind shot at the corner of the traverse, for my startled eyes had lit on a crawling, creeping form in grey crowned with a shining German *picklehaube*, slinking round on us !

" What the 'ell ! " howled Maddocks in a startled voice jumping to his feet.

" The Lord preserve me, I'm dreaming ! " yelped O'Donnell sliding quickly off the fire-step.

" Hey, stop, you bloody fool, you nearly killed me," came in indignant tones from the supposed " Boche." " I was only pulling your leg ! " And he came forward. His face had gone pasty and his eyes flickered. It was, I think Thompson was his name, one of the few surviving members of the British Guiana contingent attached to our Corps, a bit of a humorist in his way. He'd gone down a dug-out, found a Boche helmet and overcoat and had donned them to put the wind up the boys.

" Serve you ruddy well right," I cried wrathfully.
" What do you think you are playing at ? "

" What was that shot ? " enquired a voice. I
turned round, the Skipper and Mr. Walker, followed
by the Sergeant-Major and our Platoon Sergeant,
had come into our bay on hearing the bang of my
rifle. Thompson, to do him justice, explained.
For a moment I thought he was in the soup all right,
but the Skipper couldn't keep a serious face on it.
He laughed. His example was infectious, we all
joined in.

" You'd better be careful, Thompson," he admonished, " it was a foolish thing to do, especially so
near the front line. It might have caused a minor
panic ! " and they all moved off. Old Mac in passing
by winked and grinned at me and then said : " Ha,
my lad, they caught you sea lawyers napping that
time ! "

For the rest of the afternoon my chums pulled my
leg unmercifully, declaring that anyhow I'd had the
wind up so bad I could not shoot straight.

Carpenter was getting restless towards late
afternoon, muttering and moving about aimlessly.

" What's up with him, Don ? " I enquired.

" Don't you know ? His water-bottle's empty and
he is scheming ways and means to fill it again ! " he
answered grinning.

" No use, Carpenter," I told him. " This time
there's no hope. You'll have to do what Asquith
advises, ' Wait and see.' "

" Ah, laddie," he answered morosely, " you are
right. Patience is certainly a virtue, but the flesh is
weak, and I have a terrible yearning for the drops
of nectar that good old Bacchus dispenses ! And,"
he added with a sigh, " my hopes are nil, my powers
are vain ! "

" They are non-existent," said Don, " all the booze
has gone ! "

IV

As dusk fell the Platoon Sergeant appeared.

" Come on now, pack up and be ready to move ! "
he said briskly. " We are going up the line ! "

" That's done it," says Maddocks. " We're in for
more dirt, lads ! "

" Aw, come off it ! " interjects Snewin busily
hunting for lice. " What's come over yer ? Cuss
these bloody chats ! They've bin biting and playing
race-'orses up and down me legs and belly all
day ! " he added warmly, then : " Ah, got yer ! "
as he seized one and cracked it with grim satisfaction
between his two thumb-nails.

" Expect it will be the front line this time,"
remarked O'Donnell, putting the finishing touch
to his equipment. " The Batt. has not been in yet ! "

" It's all the same, laddies," Carpenter declaimed
sententiously. " It is all a checker board of nights
and days, whereon we are shifted and flung about as
the player wishes. We know not why and care a
damn sight less ! And that reminds me. . . . Once
when I was broke in Manchester . . . I wandered
the streets on a Sunday morning . . ." And he
plunged into one of his comical and ludicrous
narratives.

" My Gawd ! " cried Maddocks in horror. " Fancy
being broke and in Manchester *and* on a Sunday
morning. It'd give me the creeps. Must be as bad
as the Jew who went to Aberdeen selling whisky
to Scotsmen, and now is dead broke and can't raise
the fare to 'op it ! "

" Come on, No. 9, get a move on, and file out ! "
The order reached us, and we ambled on sheep-
like in the wake of our Platoon Sergeant, over the bags
and forward into the dimness lit by the glare of the
pounding bombardment and the flicker of the
star-shells.

We tramped on, stumbling over half-seen obstruc-
tions, swinging round shell-holes and moving ever

forward. After detours, stops and hurried spurts, with the ground on a slight slope before us, we came to a final halt, by a sketchy-looking, half-tumbled communication-trench.

A patter of rapid flowing talk from half-seen figures.

"Who the hell are you?" enquired Carpenter, edging out a bit.

"Guides from the 2nd Welsh to lead you up," answered a voice from amongst them.

"Hell!" growled he. "I don't know. The farther I try to dodge away from the Welsh, the more I run into them. Mind your gear, boys, they'll pinch the lot if you give 'em half a chance!"

A subdued chuckle greeted this repartee.

Machine-gun-fire can be heard quite close. We must be somewhere near the front line.

"Say, chum," I shake one of the Welsh, "where do we happen to be? Is the front line ahead?"

"Eh, mon," he answers in his sing-song voice, "this trench leads into the front line, but you've got to be careful, there's no wire out, and if you don't know it you'd as like as not walk in Fritz's trenches!"

Mr. Walker now came in front. We plunged into the shallow trench and made our way up, bumping and halting and growling and groping. We were moving up an incline. Now and then occasional shells crashed here and there, stuttering machine-guns rattled away in short bursts. Our guns seemed to have lifted their fire and slackened up a bit immediately in front of us, although southwards towards Delville Wood, Guillemont and beyond they were popping away with unabated vigour.

"Wonder if we have to go slap-bang over the top?" muttered O'Donnell in a whisper from behind me.

"Don't be such a Jonah, Don," I whispered, half turning round. "We're only relieving the front-line troops!"

At length we debouched into the firing-line. It looked a pretty nasty spot on top of a slight fold in the ground, a shallow trench about five feet deep, made up mostly of linked shell-holes with layers of hastily thrown up sand-bags. Very lights were going up steadily, throwing a greenish yellow glow around and revealing the dark crouching forms of the men we were relieving. We squeezed our way through, jostling the chattering Welshmen, eager to get out of it. No. 9 Platoon led on for some time, and finally we reached our ultimate position.

" Mon, this is a bad spot ! " whispered one of the garrison, hastily gathering their belongings from the trench. " Fritz is half round here, he has got snipers in the tree stumps over there," with a vague gesture, " and machine-guns playing over. There's dead ground in front here."

" How far is the blighter ? " asked Carpenter from a Welsh Corporal.

" Oh, about five hundred yards on one side and nigh on eight hundred on t'other," he replied while shepherding his men. " Mind how you move in daylight though ! An' the whole bloody place is swarming with stiffs, too ! " and he led his men out after wishing us good luck.

Presently the Welsh had gone and we began to take stock of our surroundings.

The night was dark and it was difficult to form any idea of things until daylight. Mr. Walker and the Platoon Sergeant came round, and the former gave Carpenter a general idea of the position. We were at a sharp angle of the position, the front line forming a right angle at this spot, our Section being the occupants of the actual bend with No. 10 Platoon farther down. On our right the German firing-line, the famous Switch running from Martinpuich to Pozieres, towered above us some five hundred yards off, our left dipped down the incline and the Hun position stood amongst scattered groups of tree-stumps some eight hundred yards away on the top of another rise. On this side the ground dipped sharply from our front line into a small valley which rose again in gradual folds to the Boche trenches.

" Oh, well," said O'Donnell. " Fritz is far enough anyhow, but sure there's hardly room to stand straight in dacently."

" And, Corporal," added Mr. Walker, " keep a sharp look out and get the men to deepen the trench as much as they can before daylight. If you light fires be careful of the smoke ! "

" Hell, Don," I remarked, looking up at the ring of Very lights rising and falling on two sides, it looks as if we were back on the Ypres Salient, doesn't it ? "

" Yes, begob, with smell and all complete ! " he assented. In fact the sharp tang of death and corruption was strongly noticeable here.

Snewin went on as first sentry, and we others began the task of making the trench more comfortable, digging into the chalk and dampish earth. We had no shovels, but fortunately plenty of German entrenching tools, far better than ours for sustained digging as they are really small shovels with straight handles, were lying on all sides.

" Christ ! " ejaculated Maddocks, working beside me. " This bloody trench is paved with dead men ! " His trench shovel had bitten deep in some poor human wreck crushed and buried on the trench floor, and a revolting miasma of foul odour enveloped us.

" Get some sand-bags quick, E——," he cried, coughing. " Let's shift this beggar out of it." Quickly and gaspingly we tugged at half-seen boots and legs, enveloped sand-bags round the grisly horror, and then, with the help of another of the new men of the Section, heaved the whole mass of corruption over the parados.

" Whew ! " gasped Maddocks. " I 'opes there ain't any more inside round 'ere. It gives me the bloomin' 'orrers 'avin' to tackle these bloody undertakin' jobs. I shan't get the taste out of me mouf fer days an' days ! "

With alternate bouts of digging, dozing and sentry duty we passed a comparatively quiet night, and when the dawning morn had put the stars and Very lights to flight we found that here and there we had deepened the trench by about eighteen inches to two feet and could move about in it under cover, except at the very apex of the bend. With the light we could see more of our immediate neighbourhood, but we became aware that Hun snipers and machine-guns would trouble us. In fact, the unpleasant drone and plop of bullets and sharp bursts of machine-gun-fire began with the first peep of daylight.

Mr. Walker came round at stand-to, rum was served out and in the growing light the whole field of action stood revealed.

A bare valley sloped down from us and rose again to the Huns, who were clinging to a few clumps of tree stumps, bushes and wreckage of parched, sered greenery forming the outlying approaches to Bazentin Wood. Our own trenches sloped down and then bent sharply through the wood, the Bazentin villages and beyond to Trones Wood.

But what a shambles stood revealed to our eyes ! Bodies of British and German soldiers formed practically a carpet from our parapet right across the valley and to the very edge of the Boche line. Dead men, shell-holes and bits of arms ! In the hollows and patches of dead ground over this eight hundred yards of terrain the slain, in all the horrible attitudes of sudden death, were lying in heaps, Briton and Hun intermingled, at peace at last ! To see these heaps of poor, mangled and rotting flesh, shapes which a few days previously had been healthy, vigorous men in the prime of life, full of laughter and the zest of youth, with ambitions, strength, vitality, now blackening and breaking up under the blazing heat of the July sun, made one think of the

utter futility and pity of it all. Would the authors
and causes of this wastage of fine human material be
here to see this result of their mad, childish and
criminal folly perhaps it might save a future holocaust of youth, thought I, goggling at this scene of
sublime horror with spell-bound gaze.

On our left the ground rose steeper and the
German entanglements loomed on the skyline on top
of the rise. This side was brown and bare of cover,
crossed by a road half-way up, all pitted with shell-
holes, and with a trail of death. Looking through
the periscope one could follow the phase of the last
attack by the line of British bodies leading up to the
switch trench. Here, Irishman and Midlander and
Welshman had been attacking ; hastily-dug bits of
trenches and heaped clumps of sand-bags criss-
crossed this Golgotha, and now and then a shell
droned and burst in amid this mass of dead, sending
up geysers of earth and smoke and shattering still
further these pitiful lines of broken humanity.

" Howly Saints av God ! " cried O'Donnell, who
was peering through a periscope as well. ' 'Tis
an open cemetery leading up to Kingdom of Hell !
May God rest their poor souls ! "

" Aye, laddies ! " remarked Carpenter quite
soberly for once. " The cheapest commodity on the
market, human flesh ! And the Shylocks and
hucksters of the world are selling it in wholesale
lots ! You, O'Donnell, with your poetic fancy and
Irish temperament, ought to write a tragic ode on it
that would rouse the world, and I should love to
declaim it and lash these dirty dealers in human
sorrow and tribulation with the whip of truth !
Gray was right. The path of glory leads but to the
grave, if and when you can even get this ! "

" I don't know, Carpenter," I put in, " that you
are exactly right. If this unholy slaughter leads to a
better state of things in the world the price will be
worth it ! Surely, all this pain, blood, agony and
sacrifice will not be in vain ! "

"Laddie, I'd like to think so," he replied whimsically, "but the flesh is weak, and man has a short memory. All this will be forgotten a few years hence, except by those of us who survive the furnace. To rouse mankind out of the selfishness it wallows in, like a hog in a mud-hole, it will require an army of golden-voiced singers and men of action. You'll have to bash sense into their thick heads, not just sloppy sentimentality! Anyhow, away with all this! We live and move, think and are hungry, what matters anything?" And with a gesture he struck an attitude and began to sing softly: "Vesti la giubba" from *Pagliacci*.

"Wot the 'ell is he yowlin' now?" asks Maddocks, cocking an eye on him curiously. "'E's the queerest N.C.O. I've met! It sounds all gibberish to me. Gawd Almighty! All you blinkin' blokes in this Section is fair barmy!"

Crash! Bang! came a shell out of nowhere. Tac-tic-tac! cluttered a machine-gun.

"Laugh, clown, laugh!" yelled Carpenter as Maddocks dived for the parapet.

"Ha! Ha! Ha!" cried O'Donnell, smacking Carpenter heartily. "Come on, laugh, you bloody tragedian!"

The morning gun-fire now started blazing and banging away. Pozieres and Martinpuich were enveloped in a shimmering cloud of brick dust and dun-coloured haze, but the German front lines were neglected by our gunners.

"Better get some breakfast going, boys!" I said to my chums. "I can do with a drop of tea!"

"Yea, laddie, let us look after the inner man," quoth Carpenter briskly. "Come on, Don, get the cans full. Have we any wood?"

"There's some bits down the trench there, Corporal," said Snewin. "Come on, Maddocks!" Both of them got their jack-knives out and prepared to go.

"Oh, blast the bloody tin 'elmet!" cursed

Maddocks and removed his head-piece, chucking on his soft peaked cap he fished out of the haversack. The wood was soon sliced and tea was presently bubbling. Only tiny whiffs of smoke soared up from our fire, but apparently they attracted the attention of the Huns, for as we sat down, eating cheese and biscuits and sipping our tea, a sniper somewhere began to plonk shots into our sand-bags overhead.

" Blast 'im ! " complained Maddocks crossly. " Why the 'ell can't they let us 'ave a bit of breakfast in peace ! 'Tain't fair, I says ! "

" Perhaps 'e smells the bloomin' tea, poor sod ! " said Snewin sympathetically. " And 'e's got a bit wild like ! "

" Leave him be ! " quoth Carpenter. " He'll soon get sick of it and pack up."

" You wait till I've finished ! " said Maddocks darkly. " I'll make him sick of spoilin' me mornin' grub, the bloody asterisk ! "

" Leave well alone, Maddocks," I counselled. " He is not doing any harm. Anyhow, it's too hot to bother ! "

But it is difficult to shift fixed ideas. Breakfast over, and we more or less settled down : O'Donnell scribbling, I reading my *Three Men in a Boat*, and Carpenter idly humming and day-dreaming. Maddocks rose, grabbed his rifle and turned to Snewin : " Come on, old cock, grab a periscope and we'll stir this bloody 'Un ! " he cried, and, accompanied by his pal, disappeared into the angle of the trench.

Jerome K. Jerome's drollness amused me and now and again I chuckled. It was a fine, sunny morning and comparatively quiet. I lost all consciousness of my surroundings, and the book gripped all my attention. Suddenly shots, a cry and a heavy fall, jerk me back into reality.

" What the hell's that, O'Donnell ? " I say, startled. Carpenter has disappeared round the bay at a run and his voice floats back to us : " E——, Don, come here, quick ! "

We dash round and pull up short. Carpenter is bending over Maddocks, who is twitching and crying feebly. Snewin is flat on his back in the trench, his helmet fallen off, a bluish hole in between his eyes, which are open and stare blankly at the sky. His shattered periscope flung in a corner. He's dead !

" Come on, E——, help me hold Maddocks ! " yells Carpenter suddenly. I run forward and kneel by him. Maddocks is struggling and kicking fiercely. Blood is pouring down his face. His eyes are open and glare wildly, and he is mouthing blasphemies and incoherences.

" He's hit in the head," cries Carpenter, exerting his strength to hold him. " I think the poor lad's gone dotty. Lie still, boy ! " he adds, essaying to hold him down. " Quick, slap a bandage on him and pass the word down, Don."

" Lemme alone—you asterisk—— ! " yells poor Maddocks. " Ow ! Me 'ead ! It's a bloody train ! Lemme catch it ! " While Carpenter holds his hands and kneels on him, squirming to dodge his kicking feet, puffing and struggling, I grab his head and slap iodine and bandage on. The bullet has hit him just above the temple and then ploughed its way through the top of his skull. Poor blighter won't last long ! But meanwhile the shock and the hurt to his brain has sent him completely mad. We are no longer dealing with our chum, but with a crazy, pain-laden beast who does not understand or realize anything except that he lives in a world of pain and agony.

He tries to bite at me, but somehow the bandage is fixed, and just as I pin it he breaks loose and, yelling crazily, jumps on top of the parapet. A splatter of machine-gun-fire greets his appearance. Bullets whizz, whang and smack all about on our sand-bags, sending up spurts of earth. We grab the poor lad by the legs and heave him bodily in the trench, sit on him and keep him down by sheer weight and force. O'Donnell, the Platoon Sergeant and Mr. Walker run in with a stretcher-bearer.

" He's gone mad ! " I cry.

The stretcher-bearer gets some morphia tablets out, and after a fearful struggle, in which we have to hold poor Maddocks by the throat and force his mouth open, we compel him to swallow it. His struggles grow feebler.

Mr. Walker looks on with pity and a troubled face. " How did it happen, Corporal ? " he asks as Carpenter, his face streaming with sweat, rises.

" They tried to find where the sniper was, sir ! " he replies ruefully. " But he got them first ! "

Another burst of machine-gun-fire strikes the bags.

" Come on, men, get the poor lad out," says Mr. Walker. " This spot is too unhealthy ! "

Maddocks now is moaning softly and kicking feebly. The morphia has overpowered him and his vitality is getting low. We pick him up, I by the head and the stretcher-bearer by the feet, and stagger round to Platoon headquarters, from whence he can be taken away by stretcher. Other men lift poor Snewin up and cart him out as well.

Later, we return to our post. Two more of our pals have gone the way of all flesh, suddenly without warning ! We pass the remainder of the day in subdued mood. Even old Carpenter refrains from joking !

CHAPTER NINE

I

THE sudden demise of Maddocks and Snewin weighed on us all day. Two more useful, good, dependable lads gone! Again our Section became short-handed. O'Donnell remained moody all day, and neither my efforts nor Carpenter's witticisms served to drag him from that melancholic phase the Irish, like all Celt and Slavic races, fall into from time to time. The afternoon wore on hot and sultry. The guns and their crews even seemed to feel the oppressive quality of the heat, and had slackened down considerably. Some of our planes were rising and dipping in the sky followed and spattered about by the fleecy clouds of the anti-aircraft shells. A great rattle of machine-gun and rifle-fire from the direction of Trones Wood, on the other side of Bazentin Wood and an occasional burst in our direction from the Huns facing us. In that torrid heat the smell of dead bodies tainted the atmosphere. Just above us on the parapet a group of German dead were lying heaped up, swollen and festering with clouds of fat, blowsy flies buzzing all over them. Big, hefty-looking fellows of the 77th and 184th Infantry, by their shoulder straps. For some time Carpenter and I stood looking at these pitiful heaps of dead youth through our periscopes. All youngsters, hardly a bearded face amongst them. More bodies in odd corners of the trench itself, in between the sand-bags, trampled in the muck and mud of the floor, on the parados. There had been heavy scrapping here. This shallow ditch had changed hands two or three times during the last four days, and there had been no time to remove the fallen.

" What a terrible whiff ! " said Carpenter to me. " Laddie, the more one sees of this bloody butchery, the more one wonders why the gods permit man to exist at all ! " and he shook his head sadly. " Unthinking animals, that's all we are, just mere brutes ! "

Captain Sherlock came down with the Sergeant-Major at evening stand-to.

" Sergeant-Major," he said, after having had a good look round, " to-morrow morning we'll have to cover some of these bodies up, somehow, the place is like a charnel-house."

He had a few kindly words for us, and gave us some smokes, before moving off into No. 10 Platoon.

Night fell, and with it a heavy blast of gun-fire which hit the German front line in a roaring tornado of bursting projectiles, flattening and destroying all in its way.

The battle blazed away on our right, but our own frontage remained quiet. We went on with the job of improving our trench and covering up as many relics of humanity as we could, in our immediate neighbourhood. O'Donnell began to shake out of his moodiness, and Carpenter resumed his limericks and stories. Life is a curious thing in war. Men whom you like and with whom you may have been in close, intimate touch for months suddenly get struck down and die. You feel sorry for them, for a fleeting instant you realize their poignant loss, but presently vain regrets are cast aside and one plunges back into the activities of the moment. New people take their place and life goes on. It is no matter of callousness or indifference, but the exigencies of war demand all one's energies, and though one may regret the parting of particular pals deeply, this game of life and death makes such imperative demands that cannot be ignored, and so our sensibilities become dulled and all our feelings are submerged in this bottomless pit into which youth in its countless numbers is plunging to oblivion.

Another lovely summer dawn ! What will this day bring forth, I wonder, as I gaze at the lighting sky and glance across the valley from my sentry post ? The trench is jumping into activity again, the men getting ready for the morning stand-to.

" Awake, for morning in the bowl of night hath

cast the stone that puts the stars to flight ! " cries
Carpenter, yawning and shaking O'Donnell.
" How's that for a good bit of poetry, laddie ? "
he asks cheerfully.

" It is to be expected that ye'd know Omar, you
boozy blighter ! " retorts O'Donnell rising. " I've
no time for the philosophy of negation. If it's
poetry ye want, give me Byron, or those that sing
of the birds, the sky and the sea ! "

" Why, what's wrong with old Khayyám ? "
retorts Carpenter hotly. " At least he understood
mankind and must have been a nice tolerant old
chap, with whom one could have spent an interesting
hour ! "

" Aye, Carpenter, that may be, but like yourself
he was only a specialist in wine and pubs ! " answered
O'Donnell contemptuously. " He'd nothing to
say about the subtleties of life ! "

" Come on you two ! " I broke in. " This is a
front-line trench, not a debating society ! Get some
tea going, Don ! "

Mr. Walker came down for the stand-to and
remained by us for some time, scanning the valley
carefully, then :

" Corporal," he said to Carpenter, " we shall have
an unpleasant job to do this morning. We must
get out in front and bury some of these bodies.
The smell is absolutely awful. I'll see what Captain
Sherlock thinks about it ! " and he moved off down
the trench.

" Hell," said O'Donnell, " this is a nice bloody
job ! What will Fritz do to us if we get out in
daylight in front of the trench ? "

" He might be glad of the job," remarked
Carpenter. " He's also got a nose, you know ! "

" Yes, but a damn nasty habit with bloody fire-
arms, too ! " I chimed in.

The morning deepened and we waited for this
burial job in front of the line with considerable
trepidation. An unpleasant task at all times, it

became doubly so with the prospect of being fired upon as well.

Captain Sherlock and the Sergeant-Major came along and had a careful look.

" There's a lot of dead ground here, Sergeant-Major," said the Skipper, pointing in front of our position, " and very likely the Boche won't fire when they see we are burying dead ! Send a small party out first ! " and turning round, " you, E—— and O'Donnell, leave your equipment behind, find a couple of shovels, and get over into that dip there," pointing to a spot some fifty yards in front, a sort of hollow heaped with bodies. " If the Boche sees what you do, and leaves you alone, other parties can go out."

I took off my equipment with great misgivings, and with O'Donnell went in quest of shovels.

" By God, E—— ! " muttered the latter. " 'Tis the most unpleasant and windy job I've ever tackled How d'ye feel ? "

" Pretty shaky," I replied with a wry grin, " it isn't exactly a picnic we are on."

We came back with the shovels and carefully got ready to make a dash for it.

" Now, men," warned the Captain, " make straight for the hollow, don't hesitate ! "

With beating heart and a feeling of nervousness I bowed my head and plunged over the parapet much as a swimmer taking a header into deep water, running and dodging down the incline hell for leather. I could hear O'Donnell panting and gasping beside me.

A spatter of machine-gun-fire greeted our appearance, but suddenly stopped. We reached the hollow. Behind us the ground gradually sloped to our trench, before us it still fell downward into a valley and then rose in undulating folds to the German trench. On our right the valley twisted round and then ended with another steep ascent to the switch line. Bare brown hill-sides criss-crossed with the wreckage of shallow trenches, heaps of sand-bags, covered with shell-holes, with the bare stumps and a confused mass of bushes on our front and left and carpeted with the slain, and a few yellow patches of dried grass. And over all this ground the carcases of men lay in confused abundance. In groups, heaps, twos and threes and insolated. On the bare earth, in the shell-holes, half buried beneath sand-bags, crouching, kneeling, on their backs or with head buried in the ground, Briton and Teuton, with a litter of equipment, empty cases, rifles. Some of the dead in gas-masks.

We ran desperately and flung ourselves down in the hollow, flopping on the dead pantingly, regardless of everything but the need of cover.

" The howly Virgin save us ! " panted O'Donnell with his roving eyes questing around anxiously. " What an awful spot we've landed in. I wonder what the bloody Huns will do now ? "

I wriggled and half rose with a shudder from the still form I had fallen on.

The Boche machine-gun after that first burst of fire had stopped. From farther off the pounding of the artillery and the burst of shells come to us in waves, but here nothing stirred except the slight breeze blowing up the valley. The sky was blue and shimmering with heat. An awful odour of death and decay rose all about us, striking as with a physical blow, overpowering, suffocating.

" Let's get to it, Don," I cried hurriedly. " They can't get at us, we are in dead ground. Let's shift some of these poor blighters and cover them up quick before we start getting sick ? "

We moved. The pitiful group lying here were British, belonging to the Welsh Regiment. One second-lieutenant, tall and powerfully built, lay sprawled flat, his blackening features marred by an awful wound about the mouth. Lying half across him a private, his back all shattered. Two others, half crouching, head in ground and backs arched, nearby. Must have been caught by a slam of shrapnel. We grasped them gingerly, half turning them together, and then we began to dig furiously, covering these poor remains with a thin layer of earth. No time to remove equipment or anything else. Just working to conceal under the kindly earth the fell work of their fellow-humans.

A scrambling noise above us, sound of voices, then a hail from the Hun line. We paused. Carpenter, standing up right above us, yelled, " It's all right, the Boche has understood. They have a party working on their parapet at the same job ! "

" Thank the Lord for small mercies," I muttered.

A few other men came down, and for the next two hours we worked quickly and without pause in this horrible charnel house of death, corruption and foul odour. We were sick with it all. Without regard to friend or foe we just put these poor shattered remains of men in the nearest shell-hole we could, and covered them up from the attack of sun, flies and rats, heaping as much soil as we could dig quickly, over them. It would be idle to describe the condition or hurts of these poor victims of men's folly, and political senselessness. The task was grisly, horrible, Men of all ages lay here in all attitudes of sudden death. Callow youths in their teens, and mature men of forty. Briton and German alike fallen in the course of duty. Equally brave and pitiful, struck down like mown grass.

" Ah, laddies ! " muttered Carpenter, busily digging near us. " This is a side of war the papers don't say much about ! "

Gradually we cleared our slope, working back towards our line.

Glancing across I glimpsed some grey figures busily engaged over yonder at the same task, and a few standing still, looking over their trench. A Hun looked up and waved at us. O'Donnell waved back.

" Come on, let's bunk ! " I said anxiously. " You

never can tell how long this game can go on. Somebody may fire a shot and then it's all up ! "

Eventually we paused. We certainly had managed to hide a lot of these poor lads under, and our immediate neighbourhood was clearer.

" Come on, boys," advised Carpenter, " back we go ! " Saying which he led the way back and we ran and scrambled in.

" Whew ! " cried O'Donnell, wiping his perspiring face with a dirty-looking handkerchief. " I feel as sick as a dog ! " And he rushed round the bay towards the latrine.

I hastily drank some water and peeped over the top. The men were coming back in twos and threes. The Huns had also paused and were getting back into their line. The temporary truce to bury the slain was over !

II

O'Donnell reappeared—pale and wan—and sat down heavily on the fire-step near me. For some time we remained silent. The hubbub and clangour of the guns became plainer and plainer, they had recommenced their battering at the German lines. The Boche replied at odd intervals and isolated crumps began to burst here and there in our front system.

It was now just after eleven and a very hot oppressive day too ! The sky, cloudless and very bluey, hazy with heat. A hot searing sun beating down on us.

" My God, it is hot ! " gasped O'Donnell. " It's like a bally furnace. What with the damn burial party and all I feel worn out ! "

" Nonsense, laddie," exclaimed Carpenter with a twinkle in his eye. " Be thankful for such a fine morning ! "

We started chatting idly while cleaning our rifles, and attending to all those little personal services that, rain or shine, must be seen to. Suddenly a drone started up in the sky. Aeroplane of some sort. We looked upwards, straining our eyes and craning our necks. Out of the blue a dazzling white speck appeared, growing momentarily larger every minute.

"Eh, boys! It's a Boche!" cried out O'Donnell suddenly. "Look at the crosses on its wings." The droning increased as the plane sped rapidly towards the British lines.

"I suppose the beggar is scouting," O'Donnell continued, gazing up at the enemy bird-man. "I hope he doesn't drop any ruddy bombs or comes down and starts machine-gunning us! Do you remember the mad Major doing that to the Germans at Ypres last autumn, E—— ?"

"I never saw him, but have heard quite a lot about that!" I replied, still looking up.

Suddenly more droning in the sky and all of a sudden a dazzling white plane seemed to hurtle out of the sky and drop on the Boche, while at the same time the sound of a burst of machine-gun-fire came to us faintly from the sky.

"It's one of ours, laddie!" cried Carpenter excitedly. "There's an air fight on!"

The trench woke to life, men gazing upwards at this new spectacle.

The second plane had fallen on the first like a plummet, and all in one instant it seems the two machines were twisting, dodging and spitting fire at each other like a couple of tom-cats.

The German, after firing a short burst, was circling with engines roaring and smoking, apparently trying to get away, while our fellow above him was following his twists and turns, skilfully firing short bursts whenever he thought he'd get a bull.

The trench was now all astir with fellows watching this exciting spectacle. Anti-aircraft gunners had ceased from firing and the two antagonists, like knights of old, were tilting at each other in a clear arena.

Tilting and swaying, dipping and rising, engines

bursting into sudden drumming roars, the two planes twisted and manœuvred round each other, gradually edging closer to our line.

We watched intently, excited. This battle in the sky was a wonderful thing to see. I had seen any number of enemy planes come over at odd times, dropping bombs and machine-gunning troops. I had even witnessed the spectacle of a Zepp raid over London earlier in the year; but this was the first time I looked on an air combat at close quarters, and the sight enthralled me. I could, to a degree, imagine the feelings of the antagonists. It was a question of skill and nerve and the ability to seize the momentary opportunity! A different and better way to fight than that we had to endure in the mud, mess and confusion of the ground, battered at by unseen forces, running up against murderous machine-guns; and when we did get to close quarters, having to scrap in a confused, animal-like manner, with earth, wood and much cascading round us, bombs and shells bursting and our senses blunted, tattered and distraught. Whereas, there above, the man was able to concentrate on his job, free from all handicaps, and had to match his individual personality against his opponent. It may have strained one's nerves, but it was a man's fight against another man, not a contest with soulless machines!

"I say, E——," gabbled O'Donnell jerkily, grabbing my arm and shaking me in his excitement. "Look! They are getting lower. Our fellow is above him, by God!"

The trench was seething with suppressed emotion. Carpenter was craning his scraggy neck and drumming nervously with his fingers on the trench wall and whistling softly every time the planes let rip a tap-tap-tapping burst.

The machines had come down much lower, and as they turned and twisted in circles we caught sight of a flurry of black crosses and red-white-blue discs.

Captain Sherlock was farther up the trench, looking through his field-glasses, old Mac was near him.

Suddenly, after a confused twirling and a loud roaring sound of engines, the Boche plane seemed to dive earthwards, while our fellow flew above and close behind it, pouring a hail of bullets into the unlucky Hun.

A triumphant yell rippled along the trench, some men in their excitement flung their steel helmets in the air. The two battling planes were only some hundred feet up above us, the Hun still striving desperately to break away towards his lines. Wisps of smoky vapour were rising from his machine, his engine was roaring and blasting away spasmodically, filling the sky with the noise. The whirr of crazily-spinning propellers sounded like the buzz of thousands of bees. " Hooroo ! " yelled O'Donnell, capering like a madman. " Let him have it ! "

Suddenly Carpenter seemed to jump out of his concentrated stupor. With an inarticulate cry he ran to the end of the bay, where a Lewis gun, with ready drum, stood leaning. With a quick motion he slapped its two struts on the sand-bags, took a quick sight, and poured a stream of rattling slugs slap-full into the belly of the Hun machine hustling and roaring overhead.

The plane staggered, seemed to stop for an instant, a cloud of black, thick smoke poured out, and then, with a sickening lurch, the unfortunate flyer turned and hurtled earthwards, rapidly to smash with a crashing, rending crash, tail upwards, in no-man's-land, half-way up the ridge. A huge explosion, clouds of smoke and red, angry flames shot upwards and wrapped the machine in a pall of destruction. The British plane shot upwards, circled round for an instant, and then, as the Hun Archie batteries began to slam at it furiously, spattering the sky with their fleecy clouds and bursting shells, its engine roared out and he dived away, and presently his dazzling surface became a little mote and disappeared in the blue, vainly pursued by the groups of bursting shells.

A huge cheer rose up from our fellows. O'Donnell slapped Carpenter heartily on the back with :

" That's the stuff to give 'em ! Jolly good shot, me boy ! "

" I bet our fellow will curse you like hell," I said grinning. " You've deprived him of a bloody air victory ! "

" Well, I couldn't help it," said Carpenter apologetically. " I saw that blasted Lewis gun in the corner, and it suddenly came over me to let go at the bally Boche ! "

" Jolly good work, Corporal," said Captain Sherlock, coming up. " I will certainly mention it."

The plane blazed furiously for a few minutes and then collapsed in ruin. The unfortunate man, or men, in it must have been consumed in that funeral pyre.

" I hope the poor blighters were dead," I said with a shudder, " before they hit the ground. It must be awful to die pinned down in such a blaze as that."

I had hardly spoken when a furious blast of high-explosive shells hit our parapets and began to crash and plop all around us. The Boche artillery, stung into reprisal by the destruction of their plane, had started retaliating. We crouched behind our flimsy defences while the fury of their bombardment raged and roared, crashing in traverses, showering us with debris and sending earth gouting up in geysers and sand-bags flying. A rattle of machine-gun-fire added itself to the din, and a quiet morning was transformed into a blasting roar of sounds and death that beat at us without pause. Whistles shrilled out. We squeezed ourselves flat against the heaving, quivering trenches, half blinded with smoke and dirt.

Our guns now chimed in and the afternoon became a seething horror of continual concussions that beat at us, dazing and numbing our senses and perceptions. There were no dug-outs here where we might at least have escaped into comparative safety. We had to remain crouching where we stood, gritting our teeth and controlling our shrinking, trembling bodies as best as we could. One felt oneself completely alone under this storm of fire, cut off and divorced from the companions around, self-preservation uppermost in one's mind, all faculties concentrated on the problem as to how best to escape the hovering, menacing annihilation that threatened on all sides. Feeble cries of " Stretcher-bearers ! " rose here and there from the twisted and wrecked trench-line.

It seemed centuries before the bombardment abated and finally ceased. We remained tense and strained for some time, until, at length, tired and dazed, we looked up fearfully into each other's face.

" Good lord ! " gasped Carpenter. " Laddies, I feel as if I hadn't got any bones left."

O'Donnell got to his feet silently, an expression of fearful wonder, such as I had never seen before on him, imprinted on his mobile and expressive features. One of the new men who had been crouching near us was moaning and shaking.

" What's the matter, chum ? " I whispered hoarsely. " Are you hit ? "

" No—no ! " he whispered shakily. " But, oh, my Gawd ! This is awful ! It's just about shook all the guts out of me ! "

" Grip hold of yourself, it's all over ! " Carpenter told him roughly. " Don't make a bloody fool of yourself ! "

We gazed around at our trench, lost in wonder that we were still alive. In parts it had been flattened out, broken down, heaped into lumps and hummocks. Fearsome bits of human remains that had lain buried had been churned up anew and flung all about the place. The dead bloated face and upper portion of a Boche, still identifiable by the rags of grey, faded and mould-stained uniform still clinging to it in strips, lay right before us. A disgusting sight !

Men were digging away here and there trying to restore some means of communication, for here and there the flattened trench was riven open and movement in daylight would have been fatal.

Mr. Walker's voice came to us from the next bay. Between him and us lay a confused heap of sand-bags and rubble.

" Are you men all right in there ? " he yelled out anxiously.

" Yes, sir ! " replied Carpenter. " We are just going to shift this lot, sir, and try to get a bit of cover up."

" Try to get in touch with No. 10 Platoon if you can," he answered. " The communication-trench is blocked."

" Go on, E——," said Carpenter, " get down and find out, while we dig out a bit ! "

I moved farther down, creeping and crawling carefully over the exposed spots. Now and again machine-guns spattered out and their bullets whizzed by over me unpleasantly. The trench line was all in the same condition for a considerable length, but I managed to get into No. 10 all right and ran into the Platoon Sergeant, Brooksbank, busily superintending digging operations. They had been pretty lucky, only a couple of men wounded slightly. I told the Sergeant about the communication-trench.

" Yes, I know," he said. " We are trying to dig down to it from here. It's not so bad, might have been a bloody lot worse ! "

" They've made a mess of our blasted trench all right, curse them ! " I said, and after exchanging a few more words, began to creep, dodge and run back to my own corner.

III

The boys had been working hard and the bay looked more shipshape, and it was now possible to get at the rest of the Platoon under reasonable cover. O'Donnell was busy chopping wood, and Carpenter was filling two canteens from the water-bottles.

" Yes," I said coming up, " we can do with a drop of tea. It'll wash all the muck from our throats."

" All the same, laddies," Carpenter remarked wistfully, as he carefully slid the two billies by the handles on to a bayonet he stuck in the trench side, and heaped the wood shavings under, " I wish we had something stronger than tea to remove the sour taste we have. I feel like the morning after the night before ! "

" That's right," chimed in O'Donnell with emphasis, " I'd like to get hold of the bloody Kaiser in one hand and some of the Brass Hats in the other and bash their blasted heads together until they saw some sense and stopped this large-scale butchery."

" Why, what the hell has come over you, Don ? " I queried in amazement. " I've never heard you talk like this before ; I thought you liked a bit of a scrap ! "

" By the powers and so I do ! But this is gettin' past a man-to-man affair. The blood and the toil and these everlasting shells smashing and tearing at everything are gettin' me down, E——! " he answered vehemently.

" Forget it, Don, and have some tea," cried Carpenter cheerfully. " As for me, I have given up puzzling over this bloody affair. I mean to jog on, have my bit of fun and enjoy life while I can, because you know what old Omar Khayyám in his sound philosophy says about it, Don ? "

" And what did that ould pub crawlin' toper know about it ? " answered O'Donnell up in arms at once. " All he could blather about was wine, wine, wine ! "

" You wrong the old gentleman," Carpenter said

warmly. " Listen," and he declaimed with fine
verve and dramatic effect :

> " When you and I behind the Veil are past,
> Oh, but the long, long time the world shall last,
> Which of our Coming and Departure heeds
> As the sea's self should heed a pebble cast."

" Oh, very true ! " snorted O'Donnell. " But
that's the policy of despair, me bhoy ! "

" Despair, my foot ! " rejoined Carpenter. " I
don't know why I came. I don't know where or
when I'm going. I like the flesh-pots of Egypt, and
while I'm here I'm going to enjoy myself as much
as I can ! "

" I don't blame you, Carpenter," I chipped in.
" It's the only way to look at things. Come on,
let's eat ! " and we fell-to to a cold meal of bully
and biscuit washed down with tea.

" I'm going to lie down and get a bit of sleep,"
said O'Donnell as we finished our meal. " We're
bound to be chasin' about all night. Give me a
shout when it gets dusk ! " and he curled himself
up and was asleep in a few minutes.

" I hear the Black Watch is relieving us to-night,"
remarked Carpenter. " The Platoon Sergeant told
me."

" That's funny," I said amazedly, " we've only
been in two days. What's the game do you think,
Carpenter ? "

" Well, if you ask me, we are going out so that we
may be flung at our friends yonder ! " he rejoined.
" I only hope that I find means of replenishing my
bally cellar ! It's positively horrible to stay here
hour after hour with nothing to drink ! "

We sat down on the fire-step and chatted idly of
this and that for some time. Old Carpenter, a born
gossiper on every and any topic, was interesting to
talk to and the time passed pleasantly enough. After
the *strafe* the afternoon had been calm and even,
and now, as the sun began its downward dip in the

west, the pounding artillery began its monotonous song again and began to fall on the Boche trenches with all its usual vigour. The noise did not disturb any of us. It was so commonplace that O'Donnell never even stirred and his slumbers continued uninterrupted.

Carpenter and I were in the middle of a heated discussion when, without warning, the Boche batteries flung another dose of stuff straight into our trenches. " As I was saying, E——," had begun Carpenter complacently, " Opera is all very well. . . . Look out," he shrieked suddenly, jumping up in his alarm. " My God, they're started again."

A swishing rush and an awful b-l-a-am ! Our trench rocked and swayed suddenly, a shower of sand-bags came sliding and tumbling all round us. I made a headlong dive for the trench wall as a shell burst on the rim of our parapet and scattered its pieces all about. Smoke and dust eddied round. I heard a terrible cry and a gasp, then all sound ceased for me except the awful crump, crash of shells falling like a very deluge of fire.

For about twenty minutes this mad serenade went on and then suddenly stopped, leaving the air aquiver, dust settling down, and the trench garrison shaken and bewildered. I cautiously looked up, a gap appeared in the parapet just before me and all the sand-bags were lying scattered in the trench. The metallic tac-tac-tac of a machine-gun rang out and a drone of bullets spattered on to the parados. Carpenter rose with me.

We look past the gap to the corner. Some sand-bags had been flung about by the force of the exploding bursts. O'Donnell was still lying there, sundry sand-bags across his legs and covered in chalky white dust. A splotch of blood was forming and widening on the front of his tunic. Heedless of the gap I ran across with Carpenter panting behind. O'Donnell's arms were beating about helplessly.

" Don, what's up ? " I cried, as I reached him,

while Carpenter, more practical than I, started to fling the sand-bags from off his legs.

O'Donnell's pain-laden eyes opened, a smile appeard on his wan, pale face. "Ow! E——!" he gasped painfully. "I'm hit badly in the chest. Holy Mother of God, how it burns. Water!" He sucked eagerly at my bottle. Carpenter ripped his tunic open and "Good God" he gasped. I looked. Poor old Don's chest was a mass of raw cavities of flesh spouting blood all over the place. He jerked his head weakly, coughed and brought up a rush of blood.

The Platoon Sergeant appeared at this minute. "What's the matter? Who is hit?"

"O'Donnell, Sergeant!" I replied, then: "Stretcher-bearers," I yelled frantically.

"E——! E——!" cried O'Donnell in a feeble voice.

I bent over him sadly.

"I'm going! Just like the others!" he whispered. "Take . . . my note-book . . . everything. Ah!"

A paroxysm of pain shook him. He coughed, frothed and suddenly lay quiet, with heaving chest and pitiful eyes.

Carpenter and the Platoon Sergeant were bandaging him, while I knelt by, talking and trying to comfort him. Again he shook, gripped my hand with convulsive fingers, strove to speak, rolled his eyes wildly, and suddenly went limp as the stretcher-bearers arrived.

The Sergeant shook his head. "He's gone or going," he said. "Poor blighter, his chest is like a sieve."

He lay still. His eyes were glaring and the familiar pallor of death was fast spreading over his features. I choked back a sob as we helped place him in the stretcher.

Poor gallant O'Donnell was gone!

In the stress of the moment I could scarce realize the loss. It had been so sudden and unexpected that

I could not grasp the fact that O'Donnell, who a little while ago had been so cheerful and vital, had now taken his last road, his great spirit just snuffed out like a candle. It was unbelievable. I remained there stunned and stupified, holding poor old Don's blood-stained note-book in my hands, staring into vacancy.

"Buck up, E——!" said Carpenter kindly. "We've lost a good pal and splendid chap, but we have to carry on just the same!"

"Yes, I know," I replied despondently. "But you don't realize what this means to me. I am the last of the Section in just twenty days! They've all gone one after the other. Look at Rodwell and O'Donnell, Carpenter. Fine lads, splendid pals, with wonderful character and gifts—lost to the world in this man-trap!" and I raved with futile rage.

"Come, come," comforted Carpenter. "I know it's hard to lose one's pals like this. But all the repining won't help. It's up to us to survive and see that they did not fall in vain. That's the best we can do!"

"You are right, Carpenter," I rejoined with a sigh, "but it's a pretty nasty thing to be bearing constantly!" and with that we set to and cleared the trench again. I handed Don's papers and note-book to Mr. Walker, and came back sitting silently on the fire-step while night fell, stars came out, Very lights soared and the British artillery went on with its bombardment. And so I remained for many hours, Carpenter beside me, communing with my thoughts and thinking of my lost pals, all gone to feed this unnatural Moloch.

At length we heard a clatter of accoutrements and a subdued whispering of voices. The reliefs were at hand. Gathering our belongings, we stood up as some Jocks entered the bay. The Black Watch, belonging to the 1st Brigade. Low-voiced instructions, the Jocks growling at the state of the front

line, a few parting words, and we quitted this ill-
omened line. The Platoon, like a long undulating
snake, swayed and crept across trench-lines and
holes, dipped and rose up, and, without any incident
to speak of, we made our slow way back to Scott's
Redoubt, crawled in the dug-outs and went to sleep,
too tired to bother about anything else.

Up fairly early. The dug-out is close and stuffy
and it is preferable to breathe the air up above than
swelter and frowst down here. I go up the stairs.
Carpenter is already astir and busy reorganizing the
remains of the Section, getting rations and generally
making himself useful. I am rather apathetic and
downcast. O'Donnell's death has been the last
straw. All my pals are gone. Existence here is
going to be pretty drab, there's only Carpenter now
with whom I can share common thoughts. I
miss O'Donnell's cheeriness, Rodwell's impassioned
arguments, Oldham's unobtrusive efficiency and
Marriner's broad humour and funny rascalities.
The fellows left in the Section are callow youths,
unseasoned and raw, and it will take months to lick
them into shape and discover what they are made of.
The spirit of comradeship and confidence has gone
for the nonce ! What a terrible pity ! I feel all the
poorer and wretched, and I am conscious that
O'Donnell's and Rodwell's loss is a waste of
talent that would have been of worth after this
bloody struggle is over. Britain's future leaders in
all walks of life are falling over these battle-fields
day after day. Who will fill the gap of this lost
generation ?

Thus musing I step out in the open. Another
clear day. Certainly this month is being very com-
plaisant to the god of war. It has been pretty dry
so far, only two or three days' rain the last three
weeks.

" Hallo, E—— ! " Carpenter greets me. " How
are you feeling, lad ? Come on, dig into some
grub ! "

" Ta, old scout, I need it ! " I answer emphatically. " I feel pretty rotten ! "

" I know, I know, laddie ! " he answers sympathetically. " Take it easy. Do as I do. Just follow Fate, which does too fast pursue, as Dryden once remarked ! " and he bustled about cheerfully. His whimsical chatter cheered me up and we fell-to.

" By the way, E——," he remarked presently, " the Australians have come up and they are lying over yonder," and he pointed in the direction of La Boiselle and Mash Valley. " Presently, laddie, you and I will gather some Hun souvenirs, and descend upon them. Mayhap they will have the wherewithal to fill our empty bottles with something that cheers. Thus," he added with one of his threatrical gestures, " in the words of the immortal Horace, rendered into vulgar English, we shall join both profit and delight in one ! "

" All right, you old scrounger," I answered, laughing in spite of myself. " I'll come. But can we leave the Redoubt just as we like ? "

" 'Tis a trifle ! " he answered lightly. " A word to the Sergeant and 'tis done ! "

" All right, Carpenter, you see the Sergeant and I'll scrape together some souvenirs," I replied.

There was no lack of these latter. Scott's Redoubt had plenty of Boche gear lying about. I soon got together a few bits of brass eagles, shoulder-straps— we had quite a collection of these—Infantry, Guards, and red-and-yellow artillery ones, soft caps, etc. ; and presently moved off with Carpenter, who had managed to square the Sergeant somehow.

" These Australians are new to France," said that whimsical individual. " They are bound to have some booze lying about, and they'll want souvenirs."

We crossed the ground, slowly picking our way through the half-obliterated trench-lines, up hill and down dale, past the bare, tortured ground of what had been La Boiselle. Scarce a brick remained of it, and the site could only be traced by a signpost, freshly put up, and the half-destroyed tracks that had once been its roads. Down in Mash Valley the Australians were in bivouac.

Fine-looking men, tall, lean, bronzed and keen, busy settling down. We made our way down their transport lines and Carpenter began his quest after juice.

Very soon we were amongst a crowd of them and exchanging badinage and jests. Carpenter was in his element. Surrounded by these sons of the Antipodes he started in with his yarns and jokes and soon had the company in a roar.

Our souvenirs were disposed of quickly. Money we didn't want, and somehow or another four mysterious bottles of *vin rouge* and a small amount of cognac materialized.

" Come on, you lads ! " said a Colonial in a hearty voice. " You'd better have some tucker with us ! " and led us to where a cook was busy frying steak and onions.

" Ha ! " said Carpenter, sniffing appreciatively. " You fellows know how to live all right ! "

And we sit down to a hearty spread. We were invited to take a hand at a game of euchre, but as this was quite new to us we refrained, and presently, leaving the hospitable Australian lines, we made our way back to our dug-outs in Scott's Redoubt, Carpenter carefully camouflaging his liquid spoils in a sand-bag.

" There's just enough for us," he said apologetically, " and a little tot for the Sergeant. If we go back bottle in hand we'll never reach our bally dug-out ! "

The Sergeant was highly delighted with our gift and we spent the rest of the afternoon in comparative comfort. Our water-bottles full of *vin rouge* and a little over for present needs.

" By gosh, Carpenter ! " I said admiringly. " I believe you'd sniff booze a hundred miles away ! "

" I'm like the water diviners ! " he said comically.

" When any alcoholic mixture is within a certain distance my nose twitches and I find it. Ah, laddie, it's a great gift ! "

Later in the afternoon Mr. Walker assembled the Platoon and told us that we were going up to dig an advance trench.

" Hallo ! " I murmured to Carpenter standing near. " We are going to be for it again ! "

As shadows began to fall, and the guns resumed their ululating chorus, we drew picks and shovels and moved down by Platoons. The whole Company was on the move. Captain Sherlock took the lead and in files we moved forward towards the switch line on the top of the ridge.

Past the heap of bricks that marked Contalmaison, skirting the ruined cemetery, stumbling and falling amongst the debris and shell-holes. Darkness deepened and the familiar Very lights shot up, shed their momentary lustre and went out, making the landscape darker than before. Crossing trench-lines full of men, eventually we got into the front line and halted for a bit.

The front was unnaturally quiet here. Only the rare tapping of a Boche machine-gun traversing was to be heard and an occasional shell shrieking away overhead.

We rested against the trench-side waiting for the order to go over.

Eventually Mr. Walker gave the command in a low voice and we crawled across the top and inched forward into no-man's-land. The ridge and the switch trench on its summit loomed ahead, rising gradually before us and outlined against the sky.

We had to move carefully, here, amongst a welter of shell-holes and corpses which were lying about profusely.

Presently we crossed a road, moved onwards for about fifty yards or so and halted. We lay prone on the ground, stretched in a long line at one-yard intervals. Occasional bursts of fire buzzed above our heads as the Hun machine-guns fired a few rounds. It was a fine night, but clouds were drifting and blowing over above, obscuring the stars.

The signal at length was given and we began to dig in the soft earth. We got down to the work and, as silently as we could, we bit into the ground. An hour's hard work and we were down a foot or so and an irregular trench-line came into being as if by magic. Now and again our picks stuck into horrible, soft and soggy bundles, and then we had to halt, remove these tragic relics of men and find them fresh resting-places.

" Cripes," whispered a Cockney voice in shaky accents, " it's a bloomin' open-air asterisk cemetery we are working in ! "

And in the intense darkness, momentarily dissipated by the pale gleam of Very lights, which forced us to stand still, the work went on. When more bodies were disturbed in our digging that very apt couplet crossed my mind : " No lights, but rather darkness visible, served only to discover sights of woe."

Presently, when the trench was two feet down, the order came down for a rest, and we sat, hot and sweaty, in the half-dug trench, while Mr. Walker and Captain Sherlock went up and down noting the progress we had made.

" Ah, my lad ! " whispered Carpenter to me. " This is dry work, reminding me when I played grave-digger in *Hamlet* in front of a very unappreciative audience of blasted Welshmen in Cardiff ! " And he unstrapped his bottle and took a long swig at its contents. " By the gods ! " he sighed with content. " That is better. A draught of wine and lo, the shadows scatter and content invades the soul ! "

" Wot is the matter with 'im ? " whispered someone on my farther side. " That bloke seems to be off 'is rocker 'arf the time. Blimey, 'e talks like a bloody parson ! "

I chuckled silently. Carpenter's antics were a source of wonder to many fellows in the Platoon. Nobody ever knew whether he was serious or jesting.

" Looks as if we are going to occupy this confounded trench in a night or two," I said to him, " and the fun will fly, I bet ! "

" What matter, laddie ? " he replied. " If we do not fight here we shall somewhere else, sooner or later, so what boots the ground, provided Fate be kind ? "

" I wish I could look at things in your careless, detached way ! " I said with feeling. " But I can't help thinking of what's gone before and what may lie ahead ! "

" Detached manner ? " he replied with unwonted fervour. " If you but knew how my flesh quails at the thought of battle you would pity me. But one must strive to make light of things, else courage goes ! "

I was about to retort when the Boche suddenly opened up, and for a quarter of an hour or more lashed and flailed at our front line behind us with a shower of shells. We crouched low in our half-built trench watching his display of wanton fury. It died down at length and we went on with our digging.

With occasional spells of rest we went on with our work. The Boche apparently had no inkling that we were constructing an assault trench under his very nose, for he never disturbed us.

Captain Sherlock came along again and gave us a word of warning.

" Don't scatter the earth too wide men, otherwise in the morning the Hun will spot this trench and wreck it, although," he added grimly, " our guns will keep his nose down to-morrow ! " and he strode off.

" Come on, Carpenter," I cried, as I glimpsed him having another pull at his bottle, " don't kill

Bacchus. Come and pick this out and let's make a good job of it ! "

" Patience, laddie, the night is young yet ! " he replied tolerantly and putting his bottle away, got the pick going and we got to work with a will.

CHAPTER TEN

I

QUIETLY and stealthily we went on with our digging, whispering to each other occasionally. At times our picks and shovels clinked faintly when they struck stones or lumps of chalk. At length the sky began to lighten and show signs of the coming dawn, the Very lights began to pale—we felt sleepy and full of that lassitude that seems to overtake man in the early hours. Our trench was complete—a shallow ditch running like a fresh gash along the line—just a three-feet-deep ditch sufficient to hold the attacking wave of men— no more.

Captain Sherlock came striding along its rim, outlined in the dark background, looked down on us still labouring manfully, exchanged a few muttered words with Mr. Walker and then :

" It will do now, men ! " he said. " Get out quietly and fall in, in file ! "

" Thank the powers for that ! " muttered Carpenter with relief, as he gave me a hand up and we scrambled out of the trench. " It is time for good boys to be in bed ! "

We moved off quickly, eager to get back to our dug-outs and have a sleep, stumbling over the bumps and shell-holes, cursing when on account of the murk we bumped into unsuspected obstacles, pausing when Very lights flared up, disturbing rats busy over their horrid feasts on the pitiful dead, mute, pathetic victims of the recent fighting. The rats dodged about squeaking alarmedly, to pause farther off, reluctant to leave their feeding-ground, watching us with gleaming red eyes.

We regained our front line and dropped in, thankful that the enemy was unaware of our night's activities. The Huns were very quiet in this hour preceding dawn, their line on the rise wrapped in silent gloom, only visible in the intervals when the Very lights soared up, burst and bathed the landscape in momentary brightness. Only an isolated shot now and again came from the switch line, and at times the sharp staccato rattle of some machine-gun idly traversing, more as evidence that the enemy was awake and alert, than with the idea of inflicting damage. Its bullets whizzed harmlessly high over our heads.

As we made our way down the communication-trench our guns broke out into activity, and away over Pozieres, Martinpuich, the edges of High Wood and beyond, their flashing bouts incarnadined the sky, and the switch line stood silhouetted darkly against a glowing rosy background. Our gun-fire had resumed its customary activity and was systematically engaged in pounding the enemy positions to pieces.

Shivering in the keen dawn breeze we hurried on with hardly a glance at our surroundings, up and down beyond Contalmaison and finally, without further hold-ups, we entered Scott's Redoubt and groped our way to our dug-outs in the feeble early light. Old Mac somehow had contrived to get some dixies of tea for us and we gratefully drank the warm liquid before scrambling down into our holes and seeking sleep.

" I'm dog tired, Carpenter ! " I muttered as I flung off my equipment and nestled in a corner on a heap of Boche overcoats and other emergency coverings.

" Yes, we've done a good night's work," he yawned and we turned over and sank into slumber while another summer's day sprang into being in the world above.

It seemed as if I had only been asleep five minutes when I was awakened by a rough shake. I sat up, dazedly collecting my wits, and muttered grumblingly:

" What the hell's up now ; can't you let a fellow have a bit of sleep ? "

" Come on, E——, show a leg. It's gone eleven and you are wanted up above ! "

Fully roused now, I got up slowly and flung my

equipment on hastily. The droning din of the artillery bombardment came to my ears muffled. I became conscious of my surroundings. In the semi-darkness of the dug-out lit spasmodically by a guttering candle end which threw flickering shadows, half revealing and half concealing the oddments littering it, I descried Carpenter's form standing on the lower step.

" Who in thunder wants me ? " I growled. " I thought after the night's work they'd have left us alone for a spell. I feel washed out and as limp as a rag."

" The Platoon Sergeant is asking for you," proceeded Carpenter. " I don't know what he wants. Anyhow, have a swig of this first ! " and he handed me a mug. I gulped the contents down. The mixed draught of *vin rouge* and rum caught my breath, but soon sent a grateful glow through me and shook me up. My head cleared.

" Ta, old Scout ! " I gasped gratefully as I grabbed my rifle and made my way up the steps. " You've saved my life ! "

" Nothing like a tot when you feel blue ! " he answered cheerfully.

I ran up and emerged into the sunlight.

A fine, warm day, redolent with the glamour and glare of mid-July, greeted me. The redoubt trench was crowded with the men busy cleaning their arms, shaving, munching their food, or sitting down chatting and chaffing in little groups. The gun-fire had increased and was blazing away along the whole line of German positions on the sector. The ridge from Pozieres to Martinpuich was a heaving ocean of spouting earth and a hazy cloud of reddish brick dust, interspersed by the flashes of bursting crumps and huge columns of black smoke. An arresting spectacle in the glare of the midday sun.

" Are you looking for me, Sergeant ? " I queried, turning to our Platoon boss, who was standing near the dug-out entrance.

" Yes, E——," he replied, looking up, as I spoke, from his note-book, in which he was busily jotting down something. " You are wanted in Company headquarters at once ! So get down there as quick as you can ! "

" Right ho, Sergeant. I wonder what they want me for now ! " I answered, slinging my rifle and turning my steps towards the Company-office dug-out without further ado. I keep on glancing aloft as I move down. The Boche is again flinging his blasted shrapnel about and it is bursting high in the air, here, there and everywhere, with long, dark drifting tails of smoke. He is particularly concentrating on the approaches to Contalmaison, over the welter of broken tree trunks and confused litter that was once Mametz Wood and above all the small woods and coppices of the sector.

Company headquarters seem pretty busy. All the officers of the Company are there, with signallers, stretcher-bearers and other odd men squatting in the trench by it busy packing up their gear. An air of expectancy and feverish activity is noticeable. I look for the Sergeant-Major and report to him.

" Oh, here you are, E——! " says old Mac. " Come inside, the Skipper wants you ! " And he leads me in while I speculate on what possibly can be the matter as I follow him in.

Captain Sherlock, seated at the table, is having a confab with the officers ; maps litter the ammunition boxes serving as the impromptu board.

" Rifleman E——, sir ! " says the Sergeant-Major. I step forward, halt and salute.

" Oh, yes. Thanks, Sergeant-Major ! I want you to act as my runner, E——," the Skipper tells me, turning in my direction. " You had better find a place somewhere by the entrance ! "

" Very good, sir ! " I reply, click my heels, salute and quit the dug-out. Old Mac is standing outside busy with some N.C.O.s. I find a place amongst the signallers,

" What's coming off, chum ? " I enquire from the Signal Corporal. " Everybody seems to be on their toes all of a sudden."

" Don't you know ? " he replies, eyeing me curiously. " The Batt. is goin' over the top to-night. We are in the second wave behind ' A ' Company. The whole bloody line is attacking, Australians, us, a London Territorial Division, and I don't know how many more ! It's going to be a proper do all right ! "

" Hell ! " I ejaculate disgustedly. " And I am going to do runner in all this ! Chances of survival lowered by fifty per cent at least ! "

I sit down and pull my *Three Men in a Boat* out and lose myself in the comicalities of Jerome's book for a while, the sunshine falling in the trench in patches. Everybody is busy round me. The C.Q.M. and the Sergeant-Major are issuing out bombs, sand-bags and all sorts of odds and ends. Orderly Corporals, the Orderly Sergeant, N.C.O.s, Lewis gunners keep coming and going. The buzzer is sounding continually. Signallers are coiling up 'phone wire and messing about with their instruments. The stretcher-bearers are equally at work. At length a dixy of stew and some tea come up. I share in with the Company headquarters people and tuck in. I'm a bit hungry, and God knows when I shall get another hot dinner. After it I have a snooze, propped up against the side of the dug-out. The afternoon wears on.

" Runner ! " yells a voice. I jump up. The Skipper has come to the dug-out entrance. I run forward.

" Take this chit to Battalion headquarters and give it to the Adjutant," he orders, handing me a folded field-service form.

I grab my rifle, sling it, and move down towards Battalion headquarters, some four hundred yards behind the redoubt. The artillery fire is increasing on both sides. Our gunners are firing rapidly and the shells are swooshing through the air at a prodigious rate. The Boche is replying strongly with shrapnel, high explosive and tear gas. The air vibrates with the shock of explosions and a thin vapouring pall hangs up in the sky, dulling the sunshine.

The weather is hot and hard and the ground dry. Shell-holes everywhere, with no trace of water in them.

I hear the drone of a plane's motor up above me. A machine of ours is sailing serenely through the blue and now and again, as the sun's rays catch it, it gleams like a molten silvery jewel. All at once the sky all round it is speckled by small, spreading, vapourish clouds, spurting red flashes. The Boche anti-aircraft gunners have spotted it and are plastering the sky all round it with their shells. Twisting and looping, dipping and rising, it seems to dodge from the spreading white puffs of the anti-aircraft shells as if by a miracle, treating the sweating Boche gunners with amused contempt. A few minutes more and the plane zooms and then dashes off like a streak and gradually becomes a sparkling speck on the horizon, with Archie still pursuing him doggedly, but in vain! An airman's life must be a fine, exciting adventure filled with incident and interest. Very risky, yes, but still the individual has a big element of control over his fate and can take a tilt at his opponent in the spirit of the knight of old. And as a compensating measure the flyer is free from the mud, blood and drudgery of the ground-bound infantryman. If stricken, then death is swiftly merciful. How I envy the fellow! His work done, he can land in some quiet Picardy backwater, away from the turmoil of the front, free from lice and discomfort!

II

Musing thus I hurried on my way and reached Battalion headquarters. The Colonel and Adjutant are sitting at the office table, maps before them, doubtless preparing for the night's work. A clerk is busy tap-tapping on the portable typewriter. As I salute and hand over my chit I glance at the C.O. A stout fellow, " Beecham," as he is affectionately known in the Battalion. In his forties, greying at the temples, lean and brown, with short, clipped moustache. Every inch a soldier, keen as mustard, and always in evidence in moments of stress. His D.S.O. and South African ribbons stitched on the breast of his tunic are a little faded and the worse for wear. He is in deep conversation with the Adjutant as I enter and the latter seems to be remonstrating with him.

" But, sir ! " I hear him say deprecatingly, " there is no need for you to go right up with the attack to-night ! The Company officers will be able to direct operations ! "

" You know very well, Moore," answers the C.O. in emphatic tones, " where a Colonel of the Rifles should be on such occasions. Hallo, here's a runner. Well ? " and he turns towards me. I salute and hold out the chit. The Adjutant takes, reads it, and passes it to the C.O.

" Very good, runner ! " says the latter to me. " And how is the going up there ? "

" Fairly quiet as yet, sir, only slight shelling ! " I answer.

He scribbles a reply quickly, and : " Take this back to Captain Sherlock," as he hands the message over, " and before you start back look into the Mess over there and tell the Sergeant I sent you ! " with a jocular smile.

I salute, go out and go across to the Mess Sergeant.

" And what the blazes do you want here ? " says that individual. " You blokes are always hangin' about here like bees round a honey-pot ! "

" The C.O. sent me across. I am ' C ' Coy's runner ! " I answer.

" By the Lord Harry ! " he replies, pouring some whisky in a pannikin. " The old man fair spoils you blinkin' messengers ! " he growls. " Come on, drink up quick, I'm busy ! "

" Ta, Sergeant," I answered, gratefully drinking up this token of the C.O.'s thoughtfulness. " Here's luck to the Old Man ! "

The whisky served as a good antidote to my fatigue and I quickly made tracks for Scott's Redoubt and Captain Sherlock. The afternoon was passing and things were beginning to get lively. The gun-fire is increasing in intensity and is falling in ever-growing fury on the Boche positions. On their own side the Huns are by no means taking it lying down and are doing a lot of counter-battery work. A con-tinuous stream of crackling shrapnel is bursting over all our approaches to the front line. Doses of high explosive are falling along our entrenchments and wreaking further havoc in the coppices and woods, from which all greenery is fast disppearing, leaving a desert of broken, blackened trees and shell-hole-pitted glades. Another week of this and Mametz, High Wood and Delville Woods will have disap-peared as completely as La Boiselle, and only a few stumps and riven roots will mark their site.

The rubble heap that was once Contalmaison lies desolate under the hot July sun, now and then shells burst in it, sending up clouds of red brick-dust, smashing still further its broken brickwork and shattering some tottering wall that has managed to survive thus far.

I reach Company headquarters and again squat amongst the signallers after delivering my note. Everything is orderly confusion now. Our Company is going to support " A " and will form the second wave of the attack to-night. Everybody is in a high state of tension and I have a busy time running to and fro to the platoons with last-minute instruc-tions. We shall be moving up at 8 p.m., and as soon as it gets dusk " A " Company will move up into the assault trench we dug last night while we take over the front line from them.

At about 5 p.m. there came a period of quiet in my duties and I took advantage of it and paid a flying visit to my dug-out, and get some grub together. Carpenter was there busily packing up and swearing like a trooper.

" What's the matter with you, has your philosophy failed you ? " I enquired on entering.

" Philosophy ? One needs to be a sanctified apostle here," he answers heatedly. " The remainder of this cursed section are all raw men, or boys I should say, and God help me when we get up yonder ! "

" Oh, they'll be all right once the show starts ! " I told him optimistically.

" It may be so, but I haven't a man who can use a Lewis or sling a bomb properly ! All they can do is to form fours, confound them ! No matter though, it may turn out all right, but I shall be like a shepherd's dog chivvying sheep all night ! "

" You look after yourself, Carpenter ! " I said seriously. " It's going to be a nasty job, by the look of it ! "

" Yes, laddie ! " making a wry face, " the Gods of chance will decide as to the dishing of the lucky numbers. Come, drink, and as my Khayyám says : ' Fill the cup that clears to-day of past regrets and future fears ! ' " and with a laugh he poured out some of the last of the *vin rouge* into a mug and we drunk a silent toast. I gathered some grub, parted with him and returned to my nook by Company headquarters.

The Boche shelling has increased suddenly. A heavy barrage is falling on the left where the Australians are concentrating. They are not neglecting us either here. Now and again shells burst unpleasantly close. Just as I am wrapping up some food and filling my haversack ready for the morning, a flight of heavies crashes farther along plump into the trench amongst No. 10 Platoon. A cloud of dust blows down, cries and the familiar " stretcher-bearers ! " I jump up, Captain Sherlock comes to the door.

" Find out what's happened, runner ! " he orders.

I dash up the trench and bump into a white-faced corporal.

" Poor blighters ! " he cries. " What a bloody mess ! "

I came forward. A shell has dropped plump into the bay into a group of men and burst, wrecking the whole place and blowing four men to bits. The stretcher-bearers are working at a gruesome task. They are gathering arms, legs and blobs of flesh from amongst the debris and shoving them into sandbags anyhow. I view the scene with sickened feelings and bulging eyes. Inured as I am to sights of death and blood, I feel like retching as I gaze around. One would hardly imagine what a mess four men blown to pieces can make. Entrails and blood spattered and splashed everywhere, a blackened trunk minus head and arms and with the upper part of a leg only is lying on the top of the half-wrecked parados. A ghastly relic ! Busily the stretcher-bearers get on with their work. A couple of men with frightened eyes and white faces are looking on and sucking their breath nervously. And all the time the din of the artillery is increasing, and black, dirty trails of smoke spring up in the sky above us as shrapnel shells burst and their contents come spattering and popping all round. I hastily retire and report to the O.C.

" A great pity ! " he mutters sadly. " More men gone and the Company under strength ! " He sighs and re-enters the dug-out, while I methodically finish the task of packing my rations away in the haversack, and then adjust my equipment more comfortably. I also roll up and tie a couple of empty sandbags on my ammunition straps, the usual procedure when attacking, to enable men to make head-cover or strengthen a wrecked position by filling their sandbags.

III

It is now close on 8 p.m. Our artillery has increased its raging, tearing blast of fire, the Boche's guns are slakening down.

Captain Sherlock, wrapped up in a burberry, steel-helmeted, and carrying stick and revolver, comes out. The Sergeant-Major, two signallers and myself follow him. Orders are passed down and the platoons quit Scott's Redoubt.

No. 9, led by Mr. Walker, passes below us and commences to scramble into the open in double file.

Carpenter comes by, helmet at the back of his head, neck open, and a careless grin on his lips. Taking things for granted, nothing seems to shake the equanimity of his faun-like nature. Life to him is just a stage play and he likes a principal role !

" Cheerio, Carp ! " I cry, and wave my hand. " Keep your pecker up and a steady hand ! "

He looks up and with a dramatic gesture. " The gods preserve us, laddie ! We shall meet at Philippi ! " he cries, and leads on. . . . This is the last glimpse I have of him as behind Mr. Walker he marches on up the incline, the sky flecked by bursting shrapnel and dusk rapidly falling. I have seen his name since in the casualty list. He sleeps somewhere about that ridge leading up to Martin-puich, another name in that great tale of dead. And his restless spirit undoubtedly wanders in that Elysium where the gods feast and laugh at puny man ! Carpenter was a misfit in this humdrum modern world. His outlook belonged to the robuster age of the Elizabethans ; he would have been more at home quaffing ale with Kit Marlowe and other fascinating rapscallions in some roaring, boisterous tavern in the Cheap, where his wit would have been thoroughly understood and appreciated, than to be flung on the boards of provincial theatres declaiming before stolid bucolic crowds, deaf to the subtle appeal of majestic poetic fancy.

Forward we move in the deepening dusk over the rubble and mess of the battle-field with the artillery swishing and roaring overhead and flecking the ridge with gusts of flashing flames.

In the front line at last, crowded with " A " Company's men, our fellows merge and talk in eager, excited undertones. The Skipper speaks earnestly with " A's " commander, a tall, slim, dark boy of my own age. He hands over and passes the word down to his men to get ready to move.

The Boche fire has slackened down. Darkness is falling and the Very lights are springing up here and there. It is a close, muggy evening, the stars are gleaming in the dark night sky, not a stir or breath of air.

Suddenly our gun-fire breaks out into an awful burst, falling on the ridge like a very avalanche of destruction. Huge flames intermingled with clouds of earth and smoke spring up, throwing glowing sheets of red and yellow light to the heavens.

Under cover of this devastating deluge of hammering chaos, " A" Company's men gradually creep out to the assault trench in small groups. Presently they have all gone and we stand in the front line tense and expectant. Our little group with Captain Sherlock is wedged in with number 11 Platoon.

" Strewth, " says a man near me, " an' this is a Saturday night ! Wot price the New Cut now, eh, chum ? " with a huge grin.

Time creeps on slowly. A tornado of shells falls and blankets all the German line. They are swishing over so thickly that we can't even hear the burst of the explosions. Just a continual roar, like crashing surf breaking on reefs. An unbroken ululating noise throbbing and beating in our ears, making our senses reel. The ground is trembling with its vibration.

The men are shaking with excitement. Their eyes eager, sparkling with the thrill that action brings to the soul of man. Civilization's veneer drops off like a worn-out coat and man reverts to his original role of ruthless hunter, eager for the grapple with his quarry. The whole gamut of emotions that overtake men at such moments pervades us.

9 p.m.! "'C' Company!" yells the Skipper suddenly. His whistle shrills. The Sergeant-Major, the signallers and I spring up behind him.

A terrific roar of sound, faint shrill cries and cheers, another inferno of bursting, leaping flames falls on the ridge and under this covering barrage "A" Company has sprung out of the assault trench and is moving up in a long straggly line towards the enemy. Pheep! Pheep! go the Platoon Commander's whistles to the right and left of us. The men tense, cheer, and scramble up into the open at a loping run, holding their bayoneted rifles high. The darkness is split by flashes from the explosion of shells, a reddish glare bubbles and boils beyond the ridge as the barrage creeps forward. Very lights are soaring up in thousands.

"Come on, the Rifles!" "Give the bloody 'Uns 'ell!" yell voices. Groups are breaking out into songs, cries and roars, as we move forward towards the assembly trench and beyond into that red-lit hell of fighting, struggling men.

Whew! Whew! Whew! shriek the shells overhead. Tac-tac-tac-tac-tac! Machine-gun bullets swish over, round and before us, plopping and spurting into the ground. Men, caught by that deadly swathe, stagger and fall here and there. We cross the assembly trench at a run and surge beyond it, stumbling over shell-holes and debris.

A scattered trail of dead and wailing wounded shows that "A" has not got forward unscathed.

Some men in front of me begin to fire raggedly, and old Mac jumps forward furiously.

"Stop that bloody firing, you lot of asterisk bastards!" he yells, running into them. "You are firing into your own men ahead!"

The firing stops. We pant and struggle onward

up the slope to where "A" Company is trying to
break through into the Boche position.

A chalk-plastered panting man comes towards us,
looming through the gloom, and yelling : "O.C.
'C' Company! O.C. 'C' Company!"

"Here," cries Captain Sherlock, pressing forward.

"Hurry up forward, please!" yells back the man.
"'A' Company is held up in the wire and is being
shot to bits! The Skipper says will you reinforce
him!"

"All right, man, come on." Another blast on his
whistle and our Commander leads us forward at a
quicker pace. The machine-gun bursts become
thicker and their fire sweeps over our ranks. Shells
are bursting here and there. We are now scrambling
through broken wire and tripping and tumbling over
holes. A little ahead we can see shadowy figures
plunging down into the trench on the ridge. Our
line heaves over and we are tearing through the
broken entanglements littered with still forms and
twitching figures.

Tac-tac-tac! Tac-tac-tac! Another murderous
burst of fire falls upon us. I duck low and a strand
of wire slaps me in the face. I hear a short quick
gasp near me, a body pitches forward and slumps at
my feet. I peer fearfully at it for an instant. It is
the Sergeant-Major! Poor, kindly, gallant old Mac
has been snuffed out suddenly! No time to pause,
I tear myself free and catch up with the Skipper as
our Company jumps in the trench pell-mell in a
welter of bomb explosions, bursting shells and blasts
of machine-gun-fire.

I fall headlong on a soft yielding something.

"Ow, careful! Oh, Christ! Oh, God!" groans
a distraught, feeble voice from underneath. I
scramble to my feet quickly. Beneath me in the
half-light I see young Corporal Woodward of "A"
Company. Pale-faced, sweat-streaked, his features
working.

"Get me out of here," he gasps at me wildly. "I

am hit in the groin, my leg is broken! Oh, be careful," his voice rises to a shrill shriek. " Get me out ! Where are the stretcher-bearers ? Oh, they will all trample on me ! "

I am sorry for the lad, but I cannot stop even to dress him. The battle is going on all round me and my place is by the Skipper's side. I dodge sideways and down into the trench.

A confused mass of frenzied men digging at the parados for dear life. Lewis guns popping away on top. Sounds of bombs from the flanks. A few dead Germans trampled underneath, one still alive half-fallen in a corner, gasping and groaning his life away.

Captain Sherlock, revolver in hand, urging the men to dig. I approach him at a run just as ominous messages reach him.

" No. 9 Platoon has got in further down. Mr. Walker has been killed," comes one. Poor old Walker. Wonder how Carpenter has got on ?

" A " Company's officers have all disappeared. Their Skipper is dead. Very few N.C.O.s left. A proper mess. The survivors are confused and inclined to be panicky, surging hither and thither aimlessly until Captain Sherlock and our fellows get in amongst them and steady them into some semblance of order. The Boche now begins to shell this trench heavily and a pall of dust, smoke and acrid fumes catch at our throats, blind us, and knock out all our remaining senses, while the awful tac-tac of machine-guns and bomb explosions seems to come from every side.

" E——, verbal message to Battalion head-quarters," cries the Skipper at me. " Get down there as quickly as you can. Ask the C.O. whether I shall consolidate this line or attack the next trench. Hurry back with the answer ! Sergeant, get the men to dig harder," he yells at an N.C.O. " Line the parapets, splash the next line with rapid fire and Lewis guns ! "

I scramble up and away as the Company opens fire. Head low and gasping and panting I break into a shambling run with machine-gun bullets, shell-bursts and all sorts of things crashing and falling about me. The sky is a great red glare. I keep on tripping over dead and wounded, falling into shell-holes full of groaning men, my throat parched, eyes smarting, in the general direction of the Battalion Command. Scattered parties of men loom up through the murk, making their way forward carefully, and I keep on yelling : " Battalion headquarters ! Battalion headquarters ! "

Eventually I locate old Bircham, the Adjutant, and the M.O. with some stretcher-bearers and signallers, in a shell-hole half-way back to our front line.

The C.O., steel-helmeted, is about to jump up as I reach him and gasp out my message.

" All right, runner," he cries, " we are going up. Lead the way ! "

I turn round and at a dog-trot take the lead, the others close behind me. The Germans are belting the whole front of attack heavily with all they have got. High explosive, shrapnel, and gusts of machine-gun-fire. Our guns are replying and his whole back areas are under a terrible bombardment. Far away to left and right the firing is more intense. We are compelled to take cover in shell-holes at slight intervals, as the machine-guns sweep over us. These are full with our poor battered and wounded fellows, and a chorus of groans and gasps and cries for stretcher-bearers rises from all over the field and can be heard even through the roar of the battle.

" Come on, Moore ! " cuts in the Colonel. " We must get to this front line quickly ! " He gets up and is preparing to dash forward, when a frightful gust of machine-gun-fire comes at us and sends us to earth again. The poor Colonel, however, is not quick enough. He stands still for one instant, seems to hesitate and then sags forward and slumps. We catch him just in time and lower him to earth.

"Go on, Moore," he gasps, "I'm all in—go forward to the Battalion!"

The M.O. and the stretcher-bearers get to him. "All right, men, don't fuss! I shall be all right." He tries hard to master his pain. His face has gone pale. He coughs and splutters. We stand hesitant while they rip his tunic open. He is saturated in blood.

"Gosh!" whispers one of the stretcher-bearers, "all over the chest!"

The Adjutant remains indecisive for a moment. Bircham looks up and gasps painfully.

"Don't stop. . . . Hurry . . . clear the situation . . . it's all in your hands now!"

"Very good, sir! Good-bye and good luck, come on, runner!" he answers, and as we move on ahead, the poor old Colonel is placed on a stretcher and the bearers stagger off with their dying burden. Gallant old Bircham! A lump rises in my throat. The Battalion has lost its beloved leader and the country a brilliant soldier!

Painfully we move ahead, and at length we reach the line. The Adjutant has a short talk with Captain Sherlock. The trench has been consolidated and parties have been pushed forward in the communication-trenches. Our guns are battering away at the Boche reserve and support trenches down the slope. Furious sounds of combat come from the flanks.

The Adjutant dashes off somewhere. Our Skipper looks round at the men and suddenly the order comes down to attack the Boche second line. The Lewis guns open a sharp covering barrage, and with a short, sharp yell the men dash over with Captain Sherlock leading on. We run fast and furiously, jumping over obstacles. Blam, comes a shell! Men fall and melt away and we are pushing on. Rifle-fire breaks out from the German line. We are getting near, it is a matter of seconds when a terrific machine-gun-fire comes at us from front and flanks. The straggly line of men caught full tilt staggers drunkenly. Men crash to earth, dead and dying, knocked over like nine-pins. We are forced to halt and lie down while Very lights go up in all directions and a veritable tornado of bullets buzzes, rings and spurts everywhere. T—ing, rings my steel helmet. I feel a shock as if a heavy weight has struck me on the head. My senses reel. Gingerly I feel the top of my steel helmet and my groping fingers encounter a jagged line riven through its top. I shiver. Without the helmet I would be a corpse now!

A few men are lying near me, and after a few minutes' pause, panting and exhausted, a whisper reaches me. " Pass the word along to retire to the trench."

I creep away to the left a little, crawl over a dead body and pass the word on. The Boche is throwing hand-grenades over and they burst with a sickening smash. The whole ground is being swept with gusts of fire. I begin to creep back. I hear painful gasps and catch sight of a figure painfully creeping on hands and knees. God Almighty! It's Captain Sherlock! I inch rapidly towards him and overtake him.

" Are you all right, sir ? " I cry. He turns towards me.

" I am hit somewhere in the body," he answers haltingly. Crash! Crash! Shells burst near us, covering us with dust. Their fragments drone and plop with vicious swishes.

" Come on, sir, it isn't far now," I cry, and am turning to give the Skipper a hand when there comes another terrible burst of fire, splurging and pattering all about; the Skipper gives a convulsive jerk upward. He is nearly upright for a moment and then without even a single cry, crashes to the ground and lays still. I pause, appalled. The good old

Skipper has gone! He is winging away with the great company that is passing out to-night! My God . . . we are being cut to ribbons. Useless to linger here in the open under this terrific dose of death. I gather myself together, spring up, and careless of consequences I leg it as fast as I can, and with a last rush I regain the trench where, amidst a confusion of tumbled sand-bags, bodies sprawling about, gusts of smoke, flares, explosions, the remains of " A " and " C " Companies, with a leavening of men from " D," are furiously digging and getting the trench into some state of defence, under the direction of a second lieutenant. My role as runner ended, I revert to my status of rifle-man and join in the work with a will. The bodies of dead men, both ours and the foe's, are lying about everywhere. The Huns must have left this trench in a hell of a hurry. Their packs, overcoats, arms, and piles of stick bombs are scattered on all sides. There is a confused hurly-burly going on. It is pitch dark except for Very lights and explosion flashes. We are getting in each other's way, cursing and blaspheming. We go on for some time. At length the Adjutant reappears and turns to the nearest officer in sight.

" The Royal Sussex and the 10th Gloucesters have failed on both flanks. The attack is a wash out," he jerks out sharply, " we will have to retire back. Captain Fison will take charge of the withdrawal. Get ready for the move. Meantime, send some men down the communication-trench to keep the Boche off! " and with that he disappears.

The subaltern turns round : " You, and you, and you, get down the trench and help the bombers. Hold on till the order is sent down to you."

I get going with three other men, unknown to me, and we creep down the communication-trench, half-blown down, treading dead Boches underfoot. Sharp, dull thuds of exploding bombs further down. The bombers are busy keeping Fritz at arm's length. We turn a corner. A dim shape, white-faced, is crawling slowly towards us on his belly just like a great slug.

" Ow, my guts ! " he groans, coming forward slowly. " Let me by, I am shot to pieces ! "

We scramble over somehow while he makes his painful way onward. We debouch into a deeper stretch of trench, a block farther down, and some shadowy figures crouched behind it. An officer is busy lobbing grenades over. I deliver my message : " All right, men," he answers, " get behind us and pass your grenades over. The Huns are farther down the trench ! "

We do as ordered, and crouch down ready for anything. A few minutes, and a terrific bombardment crashes down on the Boches. Very lights go soaring up in all directions in bunches, just like a Crystal Palace display of fireworks. The Germans further down in the trench cease bombing, and scuttle away to seek cover probably.

The bombardment lasts for a few minutes only— a quiet hush succeeds the uproar. Only the staccato rattle of machine-guns comes to our ears. A little breeze springs up, while we wait tensely. Minutes pass, nothing happens. At length the officer turns to me and says :

" Strange that no order has come down. Go up into the front line with another man and find out what is happening."

" Very good, sir ! Come on, chum ! " and I move off. We get over the ground quickly. A hush has fallen on the battle-front. For some reason I have an uneasy feeling. The man behind me stumbles and makes an awful clutter. " Can't you move quietly," I snap at him crossly. " There's no need to make a noise ! "

We debouch into the front line. There is a sub-dued murmur of voices. I take a step and halt transfixed. The trench is full of Germans !

I turn like a flash, push the man behind, and

whisper fiercely : " Get back ! The bloody place is swarming with Huns ! "

" Oh, my gawd ! " he replies dumbfounded. " Where are our blokes ? "

" They must have retired and forgotten all about us ! "

We beat a hasty retreat to our party.

" The Huns are in the front line, sir ! " I tell the Sub. " The Battalion must have retired."

Consternation appears on all faces. There are nine of us including the officer, and we appear to be cut off.

The men mutter uneasily. The Sub. turns round to us and says :

" There are only two things we can do. Stop here and fight it out, or get over the top and try to get back to our lines. What is it going to be ? "

" Let's try and get back, sir ! " chorus the men anxiously in whispers.

I look at them and my heart wilts. They are all raw youngster, men of the last draft. The subaltern is also one of the new arrivals, unknown to me until now. How I wish that I had O'Donnell and Rodwell with me and the old reckless gang ! In their company this fix would have been just a spicy adventure, but with these inexperienced lads a ghastly and nerve-wrecking ordeal.

" All right, men, crawl over the trench top in single file behind me," ordered the officer. " A half left turn and a spot of luck should bring us to our lines."

IV

Very quietly we scrambled out of the trench and crawling along we began our journey, casting wary glances all about us. We advance slowly and carefully, stopping stock-still every time that a flare goes up. The noise of battle has died down here although by Pozieres it continues with unabated fury. The

Australians are attacking in that direction. Here, only occasional shells are falling and an occasional rattle of machine-gun-fire. The night is fine and dark and it is certainly helping us. We crawl and crawl, and gradually our sense of direction forsakes us. We presently reach a partly dug, badly battered and empty trench extending left and right and running right across our frontage.

We slither in and clamber up on its further side. The officer whispers back : " Keep going, lads ! I think we are over the main Switch Line ! "

I have my doubts, but nevertheless pass his words down.

Groans and feeble cries come from the shell-holes about us. Flares are constantly shooting up from all the points of the compass. Shell-holes and fragments of all kinds litter the place. Perhaps after all the officer is right, think I.

We advance onwards still carefully crawling on our hands and knees. Another trench line looms up ahead of us. Occasional rifle-shots are being fired from it in our general direction. I put a spurt on and draw level with the subaltern.

" I believe this is our fire trench," he says, turning to me. " Now, you men," he continues as he halts and the others come creeping up, " I think we've reached our destination. Some of you stand up and shout that we are British. Some sentry might get the wind up and fire into us, otherwise."

" Careful, sir," I warn him in an urgent voice. " Better make sure first that it is our line ! " But I am too late. Some of the fellows who are in a very nervous and strained condition, and are eager to get in and get the suspense over, have sprung to their feet at his order. " Stop your bloody firing there," yells one, " we are the Rifles ! "

The firing stops abruptly, there is a momentary hush, then hell seems to break loose. Bunches of flares go rocketing up into the sky, burst and shed an unearthly glare that dazzles us momentarily.

Machine-guns, rifles, bombs and what not blaze and come at us from all directions.

" Die Englander ! Die Englander ! " The shout goes rippling down the trench line and dim figures rise lining the parapet. We have bumped into another trenchful of Germans, and that unlucky shout has brought them buzzing round our ears like swarms of angry, maddened bees.

" Oh, Christ ! The bloody Boche ! " howls a voice in dazed, shocked tones. I fling myself down and begin to slither away, my heart pounding like a hammer in my breast. There is a sharp clatter as the Boche machine-guns sweep like a scythe over the ground. Cries and choked groans come to me. Our little party, caught by that terrific sweep of fire, has been practically wiped out. I dash into a shell-hole, sweating with fear, and lie doggo. The firing stops, everything calms down. The Huns doubtless are watching carefully, not sure of what there may be out here. Scattered rifle-shots ring out and more flares go up.

I am so near the trench and so acute have my perceptions become that I can hear the tinkle of the empty cartridge cases as they are ejected from the rifles and fall on the trench floor, and the gruff mutter of Teutonic voices. A noise near me makes me turn quickly, fingers on trigger and bayonet ready.

" All right, chum," whispers a scared voice in uncertain accents, " there are three of us left here." The survivors of our unfortunate party slide into the shell-hole carefully.

" We can't stop here," I whisper to them when they are all in. " It will be just sheer suicide directly it gets light. We'd better crawl away farther out, lie to in some shell-hole and find out where we are in daylight. We can wait until nightfall then and we can have another shot at getting away. Or perhaps our fellows will attack again and get us out of this mess."

"All right, chum," says one of them, "lead us out!" Carefully and very warily we got out and once again we started moving about in the dark. In this corner of the battle-field, with trenches meandering all over the place, and in the dark, it was very confusing. The Very lights were shooting up from all directions in a seeming ring all round us. We slithered and crawled for some time until again we approached another trench. Grown wary through our late experience, we decided to go to cover in a biggish shell-hole and wait for daylight. We settled down and I got the men to dig some sort of cover. Counted out the grenades—two apiece I found—and began our patient wait.

Dawn rushed to replace night. Objects began to appear clearer. A stillness seemed to have fallen here. Only the rumble of the guns, coming to us as a sullen rattle, could be heard. Birds began to cheep-cheep. This was a Sunday morning dawn.

Daylight increased and with it I got a shock that sent cold shivers down my back and filled me with sick apprehension. The trench in front was also held by the Germans and what was worse, by some means or other, they had spotted us.

"Tomm-ee!" came a voice from the trench. "Hands up!" Followed by the crack-tan-pun of rifle-shots and the ping of their bullets.

"My Gawd, it's all up!" cried one of the men in a shaking voice and cracking nervous whisper near me. "The bastards have spotted us!"

"Shut up you bloody fool, keep quiet!" I answered roughly. "Lie still, you fellows. If it's all up we'll take some of the swine with us if they come out. They'll never bother to take us alive. They'll do us in like a lot of lousy rats!"

We lay tense, silent and shaken. In that awful agonising moment, certain that death was about to swoop, my past life seemed to spread itself before me like a picture. School-days, fun, frolic, half-forgotten scenes. I thought of the calm greens and quiet fields of England bathed in the sunny calm of a summer Sunday morning. The chiming of church bells, the carefree labourer wending his way to some cosy village inn, arrayed in his Sunday best, shady pools and secluded streams with anglers on their banks patiently waiting for the fish to rise. Birds chirping and flitting through the trees, sweet-smelling Kentish lanes, wind-swept downs, the green hillocks of Oxfordshire with their quaint villages, all that savoured of life in the ideal. While here was sweat and agony waiting for fate to strike. My poor lost pals fallen in their prime. Chaotic thoughts flitted through my mind. This waiting for the inevitable was well-nigh unendurable. One counted the slow drag of time moving to blank futurity.

And at intervals that cursed voice from the trench broke through the stillness with its honeyed invitation, immediately followed by rifle-shots. Daylight was fast approaching. Much more of this terrible wait would have driven me to some rash course. We fidgeted with dry mouths and wary eyes. The others, new to war, were feeling this strain perhaps more than I. Their wan, drawn faces and fearful eyes registered sheer horror. I felt as a rabbit must feel when the snake hovers over him and is about to strike. A sudden fit of futile rage shook me like a fever—" By God," I spat out savagely, " I'll make these blasted Huns pay dear for my carcase ! " and I gripped my bayoneted rifle convulsively. I do not know where my fit of anger might have led me, for all at once the world seemed to burst asunder in a terrific roar of sound. A fiery hot flame seemed to lick and lash at my neck. A buzzing roaring noise beat in my ears. I felt bewildered, confused. Through the haze and flashing spots dancing before my eyes I made out some distorted grotesque figures bobbing up and down all round, and the flashing glint of bayonets. I staggered drunkenly to my feet, appalled. Sharp guttural cries. I looked around confusedly and saw one of my fellows stagger up with his hands held high. I became aware that a party of Germans must have slipped out of their trench, crept up and pelted us with grenades !

V

Threatening faces closed round me and gestured and mouthed incoherences. I moved forward hesitatingly to be instantly surrounded, hustled and pushed forward towards the Hun trench. I went dazed and all at sea, my mind a seething mass of emotions, my neck burning like the very devil, and still grasping my rifle proceeded to clamber in when, with a snarl, a gigantic German thrust a pistol in my face and yelled : " Die waffen runter ! schnell ! " Luckily for myself I knew enough German to understand. Down went my rifle, and quickly I dumped my equipment.

Another red-faced, whiskered, dirty-looking Boche waved a stick grenade threateningly at me and rasped out something unintelligible to me, but unmistakable. The fellow with the pistol, however, who seemed some type of N.C.O. of sorts, waved him away, and he retired rumbling to himself.

I began to gather my wits. The sun was rising and his first shafts were bathing the scene in light. We appeared to be in some sort of a hastily dug trench at the edge of a slope, the ground gradually dropping behind towards a mass of broken brick-work and a wrecked miniature railway-track. An attempt at a communication-trench was discernible behind, but it was only knee-high. A group of dusty-looking young German soldiers hustled us to a clearing behind the trench where some dead Germans were stretched out covered with overcoats and ground-sheets.

To my surprise these fellows were rather friendly and grinned and gestured at us. My neck was paining me considerably, and blood was dripping on my tunic. I must have caught a few bomb splinters when the grenades burst upon us in the shell-hole. I sat down, got my field-dressing out, dabbed the iodine on, it stung like hades, and wrapped my neck in bandages, one of our chaps helping me. The others were practically undamaged. Presently a couple of Germans with fixed bayonets waved us on down the hill and on to a dug-out entrance. We stepped in. It was full of men, flies, and foul, stale odours. On the whole, except for lowering looks here and there, the occupants were decent enough and looked on us with amicable curiosity. I began to recover my equanimity and tried to make the best of a bad job.

Now that daylight had come the British artillery recommenced its systematic bombardment and it was an uncomfortable feeling to be under the fire of one's own guns. The Germans did not like it a bit and appeared to be scared. Brick-dust, gouts of earth, bags, and all kinds of nondescript debris rose and fell and clattered about. The walls of the dug-out, sunk into the side of the hill, quivered and shook. I had no idea our fire was so fierce. Crash—smash ! a shell bursts on the dug-out top—there's a fall of earth, dust eddies in. The Germans scramble about and swear heartily.

" Ha ! " cries one, shaking his fist at us. " Dieser verfluchter artillerie ! Immer bombardieren. Ach die Englander sind schwinehunden ! "

The ground shook and the dug-out rocked. We were motioned farther in and then led down a broad flight of steps.

" Eh ! " said one of our fellows nervously, " what are they going to do with us now ? Are they going to do us in, below ? "

" Nonsense," I replied reassuringly, " all that's over. They have captured us now, and they don't seem too bad ! "

Down we went some forty feet. Passed a corridor lined with timber and filled with double-decker beds, finally being shepherded into a small room all boarded up. A tall, broad young officer was sitting at a table sipping coffee, while a kneeling orderly was lacing up his field-boots.

The room was lit by electric light, and there was a single bed, mirror, chair and table in it. I noticed a packet of Player's cigarettes on the table and wondered how they'd got there. A pretty smug safe retreat below ground. We were lined up in front of him and he looked us over.

" Does anyone speak German ? " he queried slowly.

" Very little," I replied in that language, " but I speak French."

" Then," he began in that tongue, looking at me very straight, " why did you attack last night, eh ? "

" I cannot tell you, I am not on the Staff ! "

" Ah, well," he replied languidly, " you will be questioned later. I am too tired. Are you wounded badly ? "

" Oh, no, only slightly by bomb splinters."

" You will be attended farther down the line. I am now going to have you taken to Beaulancourt, behind the line, and on the way down you can have a taste of your own guns ! " he added bitterly. " Nah lose ! "

We quitted his den and made our way upstairs. I noticed on regaining the main dug-out on the surface that most of the soldiers were Hanoverians. Across the cuffs on their tunic they bore a blue stripe about an inch thick on which was written " Gibraltar." What an irony of fate ! British soldiers falling into the hands of men belonging to what was once a Regiment in British service, who had taken part in the siege of Gibraltar and still carried that battle honour proudly. This fact may have accounted for their friendliness. We came out in the open while there was a lull in the shelling. A German led the way, we followed in single file with another Boche bringing up the rear, At a loping run to dodge the exploding shells, for it would have been indeed thick had we been struck by our own artillery, we made for the heap of debris and tottering walls that represented the village. This must have been Martinpuich. A long, steep street leading downhill towards a main road. A terrible scene of desolation and destruction bore witness to the effectiveness of our ordnance. Dead men, looking like heaps of rags, were scattered here and there, some of them horribly mangled and torn, minus legs, arms and other parts of the body. Wrecked transport limbers and a line of slain and horribly swollen horses along the whole length of the village street. It looked as if on some recent night our gunners must have dropped their pills on some rationing convoy. Broken walls, heaps of bricks, smashed furniture and household articles lay strewn everywhere, pathetic *lares et penates* of French villagers, and now only fit for fuel purposes !

Hopping, skipping and jumping, dodging obstacles and .obstructions, partly constructed trenches, camouflaged battery positions, and being jeered at by occasional Huns, some of them scowling horribly, we gained the main road, and tramped along it in glorious sunshine, while behind us the British artillery thundered on. We were moving towards an unknown future—our fate in alien hands—with captivity before us God knew for how long. Gone were the days of careless laughter, every ambition we might have had stifled, ours only to wait with patience while others carried on our task on those blood-soaked battle-fields, where our best and our finest were dying. The gods of chance had played us a scurvy trick and the Harvest was being garnered.

The soldier is a man of action, and as such he is generally silent. There are times, however, when he has to break through this reticence of his and speak out.

This random narrative is concluded on the 21st Anniversary of the events it chronicles. Looking at the faded scraps of letters and hasty impressions written under fire, memory bridges over the gulf of the years, the scenes unfold themselves once more as if etched upon a canvas. The years have not been kindly to us. Our Captains and Chiefs have departed ; their going prematurely hastened by the floods of splattering poison ink lesser minds and envious hearts have flung at them. These flingers of garbage live on and wax fat though their years be many. We, the survivors of the ordeal, linger in a new age, bewildered. In the eyes of a generation that knew us not our struggles are dim and faded— just another legend !

Rodwell's trenchant words seem to find an echo in the tale of contemporary events. The cry of our dead seems to come to us as a clarion call to action. They did their work, but those who so eagerly took over the reins when the soldier's job was done, and erected chicanery to the place of truth, failed us— and in these muddlesome days of peace and economic strife they have lost us what we gained in war— dignity—respect—unity ! Their political somersaults are fast edging us towards a new holocaust of youth to make of it another financial holiday.

And yet. . . . On the fruitful leas of Picardy, by Flemish hop-field, Italian peak, Macedonian plain, wherever our far-flung battle-line stood, the corn and the fruits, the trees and the flowers, flourish and bloom anew, the birds pipe the sound of laughter, the lowing of cattle, the busy rattle and whirr of harvester and winnower ring out again through the golden days of high summer.

Below that soil, enriched with the blood of Britain's

youth, our friends lie, Marriner and Rodwell, O'Donnell and Carpenter, Walker and Sherlock, gallant Bircham, sleeping eternally in the midst of that glorious throng of our vanished legions—their strife over, their duty done. In the words of that young bard who found rest amongst them, they have turned those foreign fields into hallowed corners that are for ever England!

In the quiet watches of the night, the shades of our departed comrades seem to rally round us anew, beckoning us onward to the road we should tread.

Can we rise to the occasion and recapture our erstwhile spirit and march on shoulder to shoulder —peer and worker, poet and peasant, rich man and beggar man, in our olden spirit of comradeship, and fulfill the reality of the England we fought for? So that when we stand on a bleak November morn silent before the symbol of Britain's sacrifice, we may forget the spectacle-loving throng that crowds around seeking the lure of pageantry, and we may proudly lift our hearts in full communion with the hovering spirits of our departed pals and truly say: "Brothers, the work is accomplished!" Thus will they rest. This the monument that will remove all the mockery and the ill-concealed sneer that a careless and cynical posterity has attached to the soldier's dictum:

"DULCE ET DECORUM EST PRO PATRIA MORI."

INDEX

251

www.ingramcontent.com/pod-product-compliance
Lightning Source LLC
Chambersburg PA
CBHW030406100426
42812CB00028B/2853/J